W9-BTD-260

The Dictionary of Marketing

RONA OSTROW
Associate Professor/Librarian
Baruch College, City University of New York

SWEETMAN R. SMITH
Assistant Professor/Business Reference Librarian
Fashion Institute of Technology, State University of New York

FAIRCHILD PUBLICATIONS
NEW YORK

Fairchild Book Division wishes to thank Ron Cohen, City Editor
of *Women's Wear Daily,* who served as consultant, for his assistance,
expertise and invaluable suggestions on this *Dictionary.*

Standard Book Number: 87005-573-9

Library of Congress Catalog Card Number: 87-82654

Printed in the United States of America

To
JEANE and MORTY GOLDBERG,
STEVEN and CINE OSTROW
and
LAURIE SMITH

Publisher's Note

Publishing a *Dictionary of Marketing* is a presumptuous act on the face of it. Any ten specialists on marketing will give you at least 11 definitions of what it should cover.

And in the dynamic atmosphere of the marketplace, *marketing* concepts will change weekly, if not sooner.

Given all of these reasons to cease and desist, our intrepid authors, Profs. Ostrow and Smith, having completed the first dictionary in a proposed trilogy—*The Dictionary of Retailing*—faced up to the challenge with enthusiasm and the librarian's talent for research, detail, and accuracy.

Since the authors established a good working relationship with Ron Cohen (a *Women's Wear Daily* editor) while he acted as consultant on *The Dictionary of Retailing,* he remained a consultant on this project as well. Several staff editors assisted along the way, including Dara Wertheimer and Sonja C. Yelenovic. Joe Miranda, a senior editor, who worked on the retailing dictionary, served as "mother hen" for younger colleagues.

This publishing odyssey has been marked by a few glitches, including the disappearance of conspicuous chunks of the manuscript, but the team remained unflinching, if weary.

And now the deed is done. Early response has been encouraging. Marketing is a vital aspect of the American, even the world, scene. Profs. Ostrow and Smith are taking a modest writing "sabbatical." Then on to *The Dictionary of Advertising* to complete the trilogy.

E.B. Gold, Manager
Fairchild Books

Preface

Marketing is an activity concerned with the supply and demand for goods, services, and ideas in the society at large. It is an academic discipline as well as a practical business endeavor and, as such, has developed a complex, unique language. This dictionary is a comprehensive, nontechnical review of that language including terms marketers frequently encounter in direct marketing, marketing research, international marketing, advertising, salesmanship, wholesaling, and retailing. We have included, in addition, the principal marketing trade associations and a number of illustrative charts and graphs.

Words and phrases have been assembled from glossaries, word lists, dictionaries, text books, periodicals, newspapers, and various other sources. On the rare occasions when we could find no consensus on the meaning of a word we have exercised our judgment and chosen the one which we regard as most accurate. When we have included more than one meaning for a word we have done so because we found the word used in more than one way. Synonyms are indicated by "see" cross references, e.g., "MARKET AGGREGATION see undifferentiated marketing." We have occasionally italicized words within a definition to indicate that additional useful information will be found under that term.

A & P MIX The manner in which funds are allocated to support a firm's advertising and sales promotion efforts.

A LA CARTE AGENCY An advertising agency which charges its clients on a per job basis for the specific services it provides them.

ABANDONMENT STAGE The final stage in the life cycle of a product. The product may have been successful and saturated the market, or it may have failed to find a market at all—either way, the producer no longer finds it profitable and discontinues its manufacture.

ABC ANALYSIS A technique used to identify those items in a firm's inventory which provide it with the highest sales. The technique is used for planning and control purposes. Items are listed by sales volume and classified into three categories: A) those that account for the largest percent of sales and must be stocked at all times; B) those that account for medium levels of sales; and C) those that account for the lowest level of sales. Lower levels of stock may be maintained for the B and C categories.

ABOVE THE MARKET PRICING See *pricing above the market*

ABOVE THE MARKET STRATEGY See *pricing above the market*

ABSENCE OF DEMAND A demonstrated lack of interest in a product or service so that a considerable segment of the market either feels no need for the product or service or is unwilling to pay the price asked by the seller. See also *demand*.

ABSOLUTE ADVANTAGE A trade theory model used to demonstrate the advantages of national specialization and subsequent trade. The position of a nation in international marketing is greatly enhanced if it is the sole

1

producer of a product or can produce the product more cheaply and efficiently than any other nation. If, instead of producing all products within its own borders the nation produces only those goods for which it has an advantage and trades with another country having the advantage in another product, both trading partners will benefit. See also *comparative advantage*.

ABSOLUTE COST ADVANTAGE See *absolute advantage*

ABSOLUTE PRODUCT FAILURE The failure of a product to recoup in the marketplace the investment made in its development, production, and marketing.

ABSOLUTE SALE An agreement between a buyer and a seller in which both parties agree that there will be no conditions or restrictions affecting the sales transaction.

ABSOLUTE THRESHOLDS The point at which sensory stimuli first become discernible. This is important to marketers seeking to discover means of differentiating their product in the marketplace as well as those seeking to create effective advertising messages. The basic premise is that people no longer consciously sense stimuli above or below certain limits. See also *just noticeable difference*.

ABSORBED FREIGHT COST See *freight absorption*

ABSORPTION OF FREIGHT See *freight absorption*

ACADEMY OF MARKETING SCIENCE (AMS) An association of marketing faculty and practitioners working to promote marketing education. AMS is also concerned with the standards of the field, and addresses itself to the economic, ethical, and social aspects of marketing. The association supports research and the exchange of information between its members and between the industrial nations and developing countries. Among the association's publications are its membership roster, the *Journal of the Academy of Marketing Science (JAMS)*, a quarterly *Newsletter*, an annual index of *JAMS*, and its annual proceedings: *Developments in Marketing Science*. It also publishes books and monograph series.

ACCELERATED DEVELOPMENT STAGE See *retail life cycle*

ACCELERATION PRINCIPLE See *accelerator principle*

ACCELERATOR EFFECT See *accelerator principle*

ACCELERATOR PRINCIPLE Describes the effect an increase or decrease in derived demand (demand at the consumer level) may be expected to have on the production sector. For example, a relatively small decrease in demand for housing at the consumer level may be expected to have an increasingly profound effect at various levels of the production/distribution system. Building supply houses, manufacturers of plumbing fixtures and pipe, and copper and iron producers, etc. will experience a substantial decrease in demand for their products. The small decrease on the consumer level triggers larger decreases at the production level—thus the application of the term accelerator.

ACCENT In fashion merchandising, an accent is the particular point of emphasis used by the designer to give the style a point of view.

ACCEPTANCE (1) A written promise to pay, as in a promissory note. (2) Favorable reception of a product, brand, or line of products by the consuming public.

ACCEPTANCE SAMPLING In quality control, the use of statistical sampling to determine the quality of produced goods and materials. A representative number of items is checked from each lot. The results are used to determine the acceptability of the entire lot. Acceptance sampling is part of a manufacturing firm's inspection process. See also *quality control.*

ACCEPTANCE STAGE See *fashion cycle*

ACCESSIBLE SITE A site for a retail establishment that may easily be reached by customers and employees. The driving time and/or distance to the site is short and the store's parking area is easy to enter and leave.

ACCESSORIES See *accessory equipment*

ACCESSORY EQUIPMENT Products, usually movable, having a lower cost and shorter life span than installed equipment and which are not incorporated into the finished manufactured product (e.g., tools and office equipment). Although accessory equipment is often charged to the capital budget, it may be treated as an expense item in some organizations.

ACCIDENTAL EXPORTING See *casual exporting*

ACCOUNT In marketing, an account is generally taken to mean a customer with whom the marketer does business.

ACCOUNT EXECUTIVE In advertising, an executive who serves as a liaison between an advertiser and its advertising agency, and who coordinates all aspects of the agency's work on behalf of its client. The account executive oversees and directs the planning, research, copywriting, artwork, media selection, ad production, sales promotion, public relations, and accounting functions of the advertising agency.

ACCOUNT OPENER In bank marketing, an account opener is a gift or premium given to a depositor by the bank as an incentive to open a new account or add to an existing account.

ACCOUNT SUPERVISOR See *account executive*

ACCOUNTING The American Institute of Certified Public Accountants (AICPA) Committee on Terminology has defined accounting as: "the art of recording, classifying, and summarizing in a significant manner and in terms of money, transactions and events which are in part at least, of a financial character, and interpreting the results thereof."

ACCUMULATING See *assembling*

ACCUMULATING BULK See *assembling*

ACCUMULATION See *assembling*

ACCUMULATION PROCESS See *assembling*

ACG See *address coding guide*

ACHIEVED PENETRATION A measure of the number of persons in a potential target market who are actually the purchasers of a product or service.

ACHIEVEMENT NEED See *trio of needs*

ACQUIRED NEEDS See *secondary needs*

ACQUISITION BUDGET Funds to be used in acquiring customers through sales promotion activities and advertising.

ACQUISITION COST Any of the expenses associated with obtaining inventory through either manufacturing or buying the product. For the

3

manufacturer, all the costs associated with beginning production are considered acquisition costs (raw materials, new plants or equipment, etc.). For retailers and wholesalers, acquisition costs are the expenses for record keeping and handling the paperwork for each order, thus influencing the *reorder point (ROP)* and the *economic order quantity (EOQ)*.

ACTION PROGRAM In a marketing plan, those specific steps which are calculated to achieve the plan's objectives.

ACTIVE See *active buyer* and *active subscriber*

ACTIVE BUYER In direct marketing, any customer whose last purchase was made within the last 12 months. Also called actives and active customers.

ACTIVE CUSTOMER See *active buyer*

ACTIVE EXPORTING Activities of firms which vigorously seek export business.

ACTIVE MEMBER In direct marketing, particularly in such operations as book and record clubs, any member who is currently fulfilling the original commitment or who has already fulfilled that commitment and has made additional purchases in the last 12 months. The member has either paid a fee (on a 6-month, annual, or lifetime basis, etc.) for the right to receive information about and/or actually purchase items, or has committed himself/herself to make a minimum number of purchases during a particular period of time by virtue of goods and/or services already received.

ACTIVE SUBSCRIBER A customer who has committed himself/herself to receive regular delivery of magazines,

books, stamps, or other goods and/or services for a period of time currently in effect.

ACTIVITIES, INTERESTS, AND OPINIONS INVENTORY See *AIO inventory*

AD See *advertising*

AD SPECIALTIES See *advertising specialties*

ADAPTATION The ability of both individuals and organizations to respond to the surrounding environment, including both opportunities and threats.

ADAPTIVE BEHAVIOR THEORY A theory of evolutionary change in which firms most capable of adapting to changing conditions in the marketplace are seen as having the best chance of survival.

ADAPTIVE-CONTROL MODEL A method used by some firms to set the advertising budget and to measure the sales effect of advertising expenditures. The model assumes that the advertising sales-response function changes through time due to changing competitive activity, advertising copy, product design, and economic climate.

In order to be successful, the advertising budget should remain flexible and periodically be re-evaluated to allow for the changing marketing environment.

ADD-ON SERVICE A service provided by the Direct Marketing Association, which allows customers to request that their names be added to specific mailing lists.

ADDITIONAL MARKUP An increase in the original retail price of goods, commonly due to an error in original marking or because the value of the merchandise has increased.

4

ADDITIONS In direct marketing, names of either individuals or organizations newly added to a mailing list.

ADDRESS CODING GUIDE A guide used by direct marketers, which contains the actual or potential beginning and ending house numbers, block groups and/or district numbers, zip codes, and other geographic codes for all city delivery service streets in the U.S.

ADDRESS CORRECTION REQUESTED A message printed in the upper left-hand corner of the address portion of a piece of mail which authorizes the U.S. Postal Service to provide the known new address of a person no longer at the address appearing on the mailing. The Postal Service charges a fee to direct marketers requesting this service.

ADJUSTMENT 1) The settlement of a customer's complaint to the satisfaction of both the customer and the marketer when differences arise regarding price, quality of goods, etc. The adjustment may entail the resolution of differences or a refund. 2) In the management of retail charge accounts, the correction of such errors as overcharging, improper recording of purchases, or incorrect dating. 3) A lowering of price, as in the case of damaged or soiled goods, to promote their sale.

ADJUSTMENT ALLOWANCE Compensation made to a customer to settle a claim or complaint. See also *adjustment.*

ADMA See *Association of Direct Marketing Agencies (ADMA)*

ADMINISTERED CHANNEL See *administered vertical marketing system*

ADMINISTERED CHANNEL SYSTEM See *administered vertical marketing system*

ADMINISTERED DISTRIBUTION SYSTEM See *administered vertical marketing system*

ADMINISTERED MARKETING NETWORK See *administered vertical marketing system*

ADMINISTERED PRICES See *administered pricing*

ADMINISTERED PRICING Prices which are set by the seller rather than by competitive market forces and are designed to meet the seller's objectives (such as return on investment). Prices may be set, or administered, by the manufacturer or other marketing channel members. The seller may hold this set price steady over a period of time, but unless the firm sells directly to the ultimate consumer, other channel members may make the set price difficult to hold. For example, wholesalers selling to discount outlets will tend to bring down the price set by the manufacturer. Most firms do administer prices; all firms engaged in monopolistic competition do. Also called business-controlled pricing.

ADMINISTERED VERTICAL MARKETING SYSTEM A system in which the channel members, while retaining much of their autonomy, are informally coordinated in their marketing activities by the dominant member of the channel. Dominance is achieved through the exercise of political or economic power rather than through outright ownership. See also *corporate vertical marketing system* and *contractual vertical marketing system.*

ADMINISTERED VMS See *administered vertical marketing system*

ADMINISTRATION See *management*

ADOPTION See *adoption process*

ADOPTION CURVE A distribution curve which graphically represents the diffusion of an innovation as various groups adopt new products. The curve illustrates the number of adopters who have purchased a new product or service during each time period beginning with the launch date. It takes the shape of a normal statistical distribution in that a small number of people adopt the innovation when it first becomes available and this rate of adoption increases until 50% of the potential users have tried it. After this point has been reached, the number of individuals adopting the product within each time period decreases until there are no potential adopters who have not yet tried the innovation. An alternative method of representing the same process is the diffusion curve, an S-shaped curve which results from plotting the cumulative number of adopters against time. See also *diffusion process*.

ADOPTION CURVE (CUMULATIVE) See *adoption curve*

ADOPTION PROCESS 1) A decision-making activity entered into by consumers when they are confronted by new products or services. It entails a number of stages: awareness, interest, evaluation, trial, and finally, if the product is purchased, adoption. Post adoption confirmation, i.e., the decision to purchase the product or service on a regular basis in the future, is sometimes treated as a part of the process. Also known as the buying decision-making process and the consumer's decision process. 2) In fashion merchandising, the adoption process is the diffusion of styles and trends from their point of origin; e.g., from a particular social class, to other classes or segments of society. See also *diffusion process*.

ADOPTION PROCESS

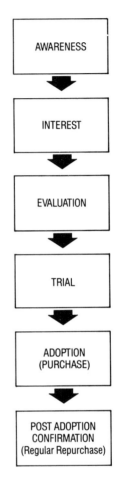

ADOPTION PROCESS SEGMENTATION VARIABLES The stages that each consumer must pass through in the process of becoming a regular user of a product or service. These stages include awareness, interest, evaluation, trial, and adoption. For a new or unconventional product or service (such as home banking by computer) these stages offer a key to segmentation.

ADVANCE DATING The practice of setting a specific future date, after shipment and after the invoice date, when the terms of sale become applicable. For example, under the terms "2/10, net 30 as of March 1," a 2% discount will be made for payment within 10 days and the net payment period will be calculated from March 1, regardless of the shipping and/or invoice dates. Advance dating is sometimes used to allow for transportation of merchandise and sometimes to encourage orders in advance of the normal buying season. See also *seasonal dating.*

ADVANCED SALES TRAINING Ongoing or continuing training for sales personnel, sometimes intended as a refresher course, but more often providing more sophisticated and problem-oriented sales techniques. Advanced sales training is much more concerned with strategies and skills in consultive selling, system selling, and sales negotiation than in sales force indoctrination training. See also *sales training.*

ADVANCED TRAINING See *advanced sales training*

ADVANTAGE See *comparative advantage, absolute advantage,* and *competitive advantage*

ADVERTISEMENT See *advertising*

ADVERTISEMENT MANAGER See *advertising sales manager*

ADVERTISER An individual, firm, or other organization that originates or sponsors an advertisement or advertising campaign. The advertiser, whether the client of an advertising agency or the producer of in-house advertising, may be a political candidate, a manufacturer, a retail organization, a wholesaler, an association, or public service organization, etc.

ADVERTISING The paid nonpersonal communication of a message intended to sell or promote a product, service, person, idea, or issue. The sponsor of the message is almost always identified. The media employed to transmit advertising include newspapers, magazines, television, radio, direct mail, etc. The goal of advertising, which may be regarded as a marketing tool, is to persuade, remind, or inform the target audience. There are, basically, only two types of advertising: institutional or corporate advertising, and product or brand advertising. Both are a part of the promotion process, which, in turn, forms the marketing communication system. See also *institutional advertising* and *product advertising.*

ADVERTISING AGENCY An independent organization equipped to provide all phases of advertising for its clients. The agency prepares and places advertisements, and may perform related research and promotional activities. In a full-line agency these services are paid primarily by commissions from the media that carry the advertising (a percentage of the dollar value of the media they purchase for a client). For example, if an agency purchases $100,000 worth of space in a particular magazine, the magazine bills the agency for $85,000 and the agency bills the client for the full $100,000, keeping the difference to cover costs and profits. The agency typically consists of a group of experts on various phases of advertising. Most large advertising agencies have at least four departments: 1) research—which collects data on customers; 2) creative—which prepares and produces copy and art; 3) media—which selects the vehicles for the ads and buys the time and/or space; and 4) account management—which serves as a liaison between the client and the agency. Agencies often specialize in the type of goods they handle (such as consumer goods, industrial goods, international business, services, etc.). See also *a la carte agency* and *boutique agency,* which are specialized types of advertising agencies that provide other than full service.

ADVERTISING ALLOWANCE A sum of money paid by a manufacturer or producer to a reseller (usually a retailer) to compensate the reseller for the cost of locally advertising the producer's product. Such advertising is most generally aimed at the ultimate consumer and is developed at the local level in support of a particular product, line, or brand. Also known as coop money. See also *cooperative advertising* and *promotional allowance.*

ADVERTISING AND PROMOTION MIX See *A & P mix*

ADVERTISING APPEAL The central theme, motif, or idea of an advertisement which tells the potential consumer what the advertised product or service offers and why it should be purchased.

ADVERTISING APPROPRIATION The total amount of money allocated for an organization's advertising program during a specific time period. The appropriation may be based on a percentage of past or projected sales, calculated according to the cost of the task at hand, or a combination of the two.

ADVERTISING BY NONPROFIT ORGANIZATIONS See *noncommercial advertising*

ADVERTISING CAMPAIGN A planned advertising effort which extends over a period of time and which is designed to promote a particular product or service. The advertising campaign involves setting objectives, determining an advertising budget, positioning the product, deciding on a message, selecting the ap-

propriate media, and measuring the campaign's effectiveness.

ADVERTISING GOALS Those specific purposes which underlie an advertisement or advertising campaign. Most advertising has as its goal the stimulation (within a particular time frame) of some specific and immediate activity on the part of the consumer. See also *advertising objectives.*

ADVERTISING MANAGER In business organizations, the employee responsible for supervising the development of advertising for the firm. Also reviews and approves ads which are ready to be placed in the media. See also *advertising sales manager.*

ADVERTISING MEDIA All of the channels employed by advertisers to reach their audiences and convey their sales messages. Advertising media include print media (such as newspapers and magazines), broadcast media (radio and television), outdoor (such as billboards), transit (such as car cards and posters in stations), and point-of-purchase displays.

ADVERTISING MEDIUM See *advertising media*

ADVERTISING MESSAGE The creative component of an advertisement or advertising campaign. The function of the message is to carry out the advertising objectives of the product or service. The message depends for its success on its ability to engage the attention and interest of the largest possible audience and to motivate that audience to act in a particular way.

ADVERTISING OBJECTIVES The communication and sales objectives assigned to advertising, which flow from prior decisions regarding the product's target market, target position, and marketing mix. Advertising objectives may inform, persuade, or remind. If they inform, they may tell about a new product or service, suggest new uses for the product, correct false impressions about the product or service, announce price changes, build the company's image, or reduce consumer fears. If intended to persuade, the advertising objectives may be to build brand preference, to encourage brand switching, or to simply persuade the customer to purchase the product or service. Finally, if its advertising is intended to remind, the objectives may be to inform the customers as to where the product or service may be purchased and to remind them that it may be needed at a later date. See also *advertising goals.*

ADVERTISING PLATFORM The main issues or selling points an advertiser wishes to include in an advertising campaign.

ADVERTISING RECALL See *aided recall* and *unaided recall*

ADVERTISING RESPONSE FUNCTION See *response function*

ADVERTISING SALES MANAGER The employee of a media organization (newspaper, magazine, television network, etc.) responsible for selling advertising space or time to prospective advertisers. In the broadcast media more commonly called a sales manager. See also *advertising manager.*

ADVERTISING SALES-RESPONSE AND DECAY MODEL A model used to measure the response of sales to advertising in an effort to determine the most appropriate advertising budget. The model was developed by M.L. Vidale and H.B. Wolfe and postulates that the change in the rate of sales at a particular time (t) is a function of four factors: 1) the advertising budget, 2) the sales response constant,

3) the saturation level of sales, and 4) the sales-decay constant. Vidale and Wolfe developed the following formula to determine the optimum advertising expenditure of any given firm:

$$\frac{dS}{dt} = rA \quad \frac{M - S}{M} - S$$

where:

S = rate of sales at time t

$\dfrac{dS}{dt}$ = change in the rate of sales at time t

A = rate of advertising expenditure at time t

r = sales-response constant (defined as the sales generated per advertising dollar when $S = 0$)

M = saturation level of sales

d = sales-decay constant (defined as the fraction of sales per time unit when $A = 0$)

In essence, the equation states that the rate of sales will be higher, the higher the advertising expenditure, the higher the untapped sales potential, and the lower the decay constant. The model may also be used to estimate the profit consequences of alternative advertising budget strategies. See also *advertising sales response curve.*

ADVERTISING SALES-RESPONSE CURVE The graphic representation of the relationship between advertising expenditures on the horizontal axis and the results in sales on the vertical axis. The usual assumption is that sales will increase as advertising expenditures increase.

ADVERTISING SPECIALTIES Items of little value (pencils, key rings, ash trays, etc.) which carry the name of the firm or product, its picture, logo, etc., and which are used as giveaways. The objective of such advertising is to create goodwill.

ADVERTISING TARGET See *audience*

ADVERTISING THEME That recognizable portion of the advertising message which carries over into several different advertisements for the same product. The theme provides continuity.

ADVISOR PROJECT A five year study conducted by Professor Gary L. Lilien of M.I.T. in the 1970s in which he examined the methods by which industrial marketers set their advertising budgets and in which he attempted to evaluate those methods. The project took part in two phases known as ADVISOR 1 and ADVISOR 2. In ADVISOR 1, Lilien and his associates sought to develop marketing expenditure norms for industrial marketers. The study found that industrial marketers tended to first determine total marketing expenditures as a percentage of sales (the M/S ratio) and then determine the amount to spend on advertising as a percentage of the marketing budget (the A/M ratio). When the ratios are multiplied, they give the advertising-to-sales ratio (A/S). ADVISOR 2 was designed to extend and verify the results of ADVISOR 1, and to determine the most effective level of spending by industrial marketers and the best split of the spending between advertising and personal selling. The study led to the building of several models for setting marketing and advertising budgets for industrial marketers.

ADVOCACY ADVERTISING Advertising whose objective is to support a particular belief or course of action on the part of its audience. It is designed to induce or discourage certain specific forms of activity with regard to controversial subjects. See also *cause marketing* and *cause-related marketing*.

ADVOCATE CHANNEL A personal communication channel consisting of company salespeople contracting buyers in the target market.

AFDT See *Air Freight Decision Tool (AFDT)*

AFFECTIVE COMPONENT In attitude research, particularly in the tripartite view or structural approach, the affective component is the individual's overall feelings of like or dislike about a service, product, or similar object. It is the emotional component of attitude formation. See also *attitude*.

AFFILIATION NEED See *trio of needs*

AFFILIATIVE GROUP Any reference group such as the family, church, school, etc. to which an individual actually belongs.

AFFIRMATIVE DISCLOSURE A procedure adopted by the Federal Trade Commission in its attempt to regulate advertising. The procedure stipulates that if the information contained in an advertisement is considered insufficient by the commission, it may require a company to disclose some of the limitations of its product or service within its subsequent advertising. This is done so that the consumer may judge the product's (or service's) negative as well as positive attributes.

AFTERMARKET The aggregate demand for parts and service which follows the sale of a product such as an automobile or computer.

AGENT In a broad business sense an agent is one who acts as an intermediary between two parties for the purpose of facilitating trade. For more restricted uses of the term see also *agent middleman, manufacturer's agent,* and *selling agent*.

10

AGENT INTERMEDIARY See *agent middleman*

AGENT MIDDLEMAN A wholesaling middleman (sometimes called an agent wholesaler or simply an agent) who, acting as a market intermediary, performs a number of wholesaling functions without taking title to the goods he sells and frequently without taking physical possession of the goods. The agent middleman is highly specialized and has an extensive knowledge of the market in which he operates. His principal function is to render assistance in the passing of title to goods from one party to another. Included under the term agent middleman are selling agent, manufacturer's agent, broker, commission merchant, and auction company.

AGENT WHOLESALER See *agent middleman*

AGGREGATE MONETARY DEMAND The total planned expenditure (within an economy) by consumers, firms, government, and foreigners on goods and services which are produced within that economy. Indirect taxes and import components are deducted before calculating the aggregate monetary demand.

AGGREGATION See *undifferentiated marketing*

AGGRESSIVE DEMARKETING RESPONSE TO SHORTAGES An approach to actual or anticipated shortages of the raw materials required for production. When companies feel they cannot produce enough goods to meet their customers' needs, they may take any or all of the following steps: raise prices sharply; cut product quality and new-product development; eliminate weaker customers; reduce customer services; allocate supplies to customers according to their ability to pay; cut marketing budgets for re-search, advertising, and sales calls; and drop low-profit items in their product lines. Aggressive demarketing in this fashion, however, may have unwanted negative consequences, especially losing the good will of many customers. See also *demarketing*.

AGRIBUSINESS The business functions related to agriculture. Agribusiness includes farming as well as the processing of food and other agricultural products, the manufacture of farm equipment, and the production of ancillary farm goods such as fertilizers.

AIDA See *AIDA model*

AIDA MODEL AIDA is an acronym for attention, interest, desire, and action; which represent the desirable qualities found in an advertising or personal selling message; i.e., it should get attention, arouse interest, create desire, and precipitate action. The concept was first propounded by E.K. Strong in 1924.

AIDED RECALL A method of testing a consumer's ability to remember an advertisement and hence, a means of determining the ad's effectiveness. Subjects are asked to identify advertisements they have recently seen or heard and are given hints or clues in the form of lists of products, brands, or company names in an effort to stimulate the memory.

AIDED RECALL TEST See *aided recall*

AIO INVENTORY In psychographic research, a method used to determine consumers' activities, interests, and opinions (AIO) by means of a life-style measurement survey.

AIR FREIGHT The use of airplanes for transporting goods. Because air freight rates are more expensive than truck or freight rates, this mode of shipping is usually reserved for situations in which speed is essential and/or distant markets must be reached. It is a particularly effective means of shipping perishables (such as fresh fish or flowers) and high-value, low-bulk items (such as jewelry). The cost of air freight may also be justified when it leads to decreases in inventory levels, the number of warehouses required, and packaging costs. See also *air freight decision tool (AFDT)*.

AIR FREIGHT DECISION TOOL (AFDT) A computer model designed to help shippers determine when to use air freight as the preferred mode of transportation.

AIR TRANSPORTATION See *air freight*

AIRTRUCK A coordinated mode of shipping goods which involves the combined use of air freight and truck freight. Its ease of use is made possible through containerization.

ALIEN CORPORATION The classification assigned by state governments to a corporation doing business within the boundaries of that state but chartered by a foreign government.

ALL THE TRAFFIC WILL BEAR See *profit maximization objective*.

ALL-YOU-CAN-AFFORD TECHNIQUE A method of developing a promotional budget in which all non-promotional marketing expenses are budgeted first and remaining funds allocated to promotional purposes.

ALLOCATING SKILLS The skills used by marketing managers to budget time, money, and personnel for the firm's functions, policies, or programs. Marketing managers use these skills to achieve effective implementation of the firm's marketing strategy. For example, an effective

marketing manager must be able to decide how much money to spend on trade shows, how to distribute sales personnel to various geographic regions, etc. See also *monitoring skills, organizing skills,* and *interacting skills.*

ALLOCATION The process by which large, homogeneous inventories are broken down into smaller lots as the goods get closer to the final market. Allocation may involve several levels of middlemen, each handling increasingly smaller quantities. Retailers complete the process by selling individual items to the individual consumer. Allocation helps to alleviate the discrepancy of quantity. Also called bulk-breaking, sorting out, and dispersion.

ALLOCATION

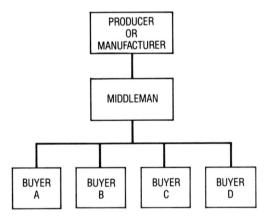

ALLOCATION PROCESS See *allocation*

ALLOWANCE A reduction from list or invoice price made by a manufacturer, wholesaler, or retailer in return for the performance of certain services or activities on the part of the customer or to compensate the customer for some other reason. For example, advertising and promotional allowances compensate wholesalers and retailers for the expenses incurred in promoting a product locally. Cost allowances compensate the customer for such problems as goods delivered late or damaged. Trade-in allowances compensate the customer for old equipment turned in when new equipment is purchased. See also *discount,* a similar form of price reduction and specific forms of allowance such as *cost allowance, trade-in allowance, promotional allowance, advertising allowance,* and *trade discount.*

ALPHAMERIC See *alphanumeric*

ALPHANUMERIC A contraction of the words "alphabetic" and "numeric." The term applies to any code or coding system that provides for letters, numbers, and special symbols (such as punctuation marks). These codes are often machine-processable and may enable the user to use a computer for such functions as inventory control. Sometimes called alphameric.

AMA See *American Marketing Association (AMA)*

AMBIANCE The pervading mood, tone, or atmosphere which characterizes a business establishment or other facility. In its marketing context, ambiance commonly refers to store environments. See also *atmospherics.*

AMERICAN MAILORDER ASSOCIATION (AMOA) An association of individuals and firms involved in mailorder marketing. The association serves a primarily informational function, reviewing books and products, issuing fraud warnings, and advising legislators. AMOA has its headquarters in Santa Cruz, California.

AMERICAN MARKETING ASSOCIATION (AMA) The AMA is the major professional organization for marketers. Its membership consists of marketing executives, market researchers, sales managers, promotion managers, advertising specialists, educators, and related individuals and organizations. The association supports marketing education by promoting research, sponsoring seminars and conferences, and organizing marketing clubs on campuses. The AMA publishes the quarterly *Journal of Marketing,* its proceedings, and a variety of books and pamphlets. AMA headquarters are in Chicago, Illinois.

AMERICAN TELEMARKETING ASSOCIATION (ATA) An association of telephone marketing businesses and related firms, based in Glenview, Illinois. The association seeks to promote the use of telephone sales and to improve the industry's public image. ATA publishes a quarterly newsletter and an annual *Membership Roster.* It also provides a speakers bureau, seminars, library, and educational standards for university courses.

AMOA See *American Mailorder Association (AMOA)*

AMS See *Academy of Marketing Science (AMS)*

AMS See *Analytical Marketing System (AMS)*

ANALYSIS OF CAUSAL RELATIONSHIPS See *causal research*

ANALYTICAL MARKETING SYSTEM (AMS) One of four subsystems of a company's marketing information system (MIS), which consists of a statistical bank and a model bank for analyzing marketing data and problems. The statistical bank is essentially a collection of statistical procedures or routines which may be used to extract meaningful information from data. These procedures include routines for calculating averages, measuring dispersion, and cross-tabulation of the data. The researcher may also use the multivariate statistical techniques contained in the statistical bank to uncover relationships in the data. These include multiple regression analysis, discriminate analysis, factor analysis, and cluster analysis. The model bank on the other hand, is a collection of models used by marketers to make marketing decisions. The bank includes models for new product sales forecasting, site selection, sales-call planning, media mix, and marketing mix budgeting. The models may be descriptive, verbal, graphic, or mathematical. See also *marketing information system (MIS)* and *model.*

ANALYTICAL PRICING See *marginal analysis*

ANNUAL MARKETING PLAN See *marketing plan*

ANTI-DUMPING TARIFF A tax levied against imported goods which are being dumped (sold at prices below those in the home market) on the domestic market. See also *countervailing duty.*

ANTIMERGER ACT (1950) See *Celler-Kefauver Antimerger Act (1950)*

APPEAL See *advertising appeal*

APPLIED BEHAVIORAL ANALYSIS See *behavioral engineering*

APPROACH The first few minutes of the contact between a salesperson and a potential customer. Approach is the stage in the sales presentation which is designed to gain and hold the prospect's attention. It includes the following three steps: 1) salesperson introduces himself/herself to the prospect; 2) salesperson "sells" himself/herself, the product, and the company to the prospect; 3) salesperson gets and holds the prospect's attention and interest. During the approach, the salesperson draws out the prospect to determine his/her needs. This information will later be used to convince the prospect of the advantages of the salesperson's product or service. There are many different approaches, including the benefit approach (which emphasizes the benefit to the prospect of doing business with the salesperson), the curiosity approach (in which the salesperson bases his/her presentation on the prospect's curiosity and interest), the dramatic approach (an eye-opening show or demonstration which often involves the prospect), and the factual approach (which uses an interesting fact about the product or service to capture the prospect's attention). See also the names of specific approaches.

ARBITRARY ALLOCATION See *arbitrary approach*

ARBITRARY APPROACH A method for allocating a firm's promotional budget in which the amount spent on promotion for a particular time period is the result of deriving an executive decision rather than from scientific analysis. Also known as arbitrary allocation.

ARBITRATION In negotiations, the process by which both parties to a dispute agree to submit the dispute to a third party for a binding decision.

AREA CLUSTER SAMPLE See *area sampling*

AREA SAMPLE See *area sampling*

AREA SAMPLING A method of probability sampling in which the stratified sample is made on the basis of geography rather than by demographics or other population characteristics. Geographic areas (such as city blocks) serve as the segments or primary units. The researcher divides the population first by mutually exclusive geographic areas and then draws a sample of the groups to interview. This method of obtaining a random sample is most useful when population lists are unavailable. See also *sampling, probability sampling, and random sampling.*

ARM'S LENGTH POLICY A practice in transfer pricing in which the home or parent company charges foreign subsidiaries the same price it charges firms who are not part of the organization.

ART In advertising, art is the illustration appearing in an advertisement (photographs, drawings, charts, graphs, etc.) as well as the layout of the visual components of the ad.

ARTICLES OF PARTNERSHIP A legal document that covers all items agreed upon by the partners in a business and which each partner has signed.

ARTIFICIAL TRADING AREA That geographic area specified by a firm as the territory in which it will conduct its business.

ARTWORK See *art*

ASCH PHENOMENON Named after a study conducted by S. E. Asch (published 1958) in which he demonstrated the influence groups have upon individual choice making. He found that if individuals can determine the expectations of the group to which they belong, they tend to adhere to those expectations in making purchase decisions.

ASKING PRICE See *price*

ASPIRATIONAL GROUP Any group to which an individual would like to belong (such as a little leaguer wishing to become a professional baseball player). For marketing, the implication is that the desire to emulate the chosen group influences consumer buying decisions. The little leaguer will want to eat the "breakfast of champions," the medical student will aspire to a Mercedes, the secretary seeking promotion to a management position will "dress for success," etc.

ASPIRATORY GROUP See *aspirational group*

ASSEMBLER See *assembling*

ASSEMBLING The process of developing an inventory of homogeneous products, such as agricultural produce, from the small lots of a number of small producers so that they may be handled economically further along the marketing channel. Goods so accumulated may be shipped and sold in larger lots and thus benefit from such factors as lower shipped rates (in carload or truckload quantities). Goods are brought to collection points by the individual small producers and collected by an agent middleman known as an assembler. Assemblers seldom take title to the goods they handle. Also called accumulating or concentration.

ASSEMBLY See *assembling*

ASSET The Financial Accounting Standards Board (FASB) has defined an asset as a "probable future economic benefit obtained or controlled by a particular enterprise as a result of past transaction" (1979). Simply stated, an asset is any item owned (such as cash, receivables, inventory, equipment, land, buildings, and good will) whether tangible or intangible.

ASSET CONVERSION A means of internally financing a firm's projects by liquidating one form of asset to employ elsewhere within the firm or repay a liability.

15

ASSET TURNOVER See *asset turnover ratio*

ASSET TURNOVER RATIO An indicator of the efficiency of a firm's investment in assets and a means of examining the company's operations over a period of time. It is calculated by dividing the company's net sales for the accounting period by its average total assets during the same period.

$$\text{Asset turnover} = \frac{\text{Net sales during the period}}{\text{Average assets during the period}}$$

ASSIGNED MAILING DATE In direct marketing, the date on which a list user must mail a particular purchased list, by virtue of a prior agreement between the list owner and the user. The user may not mail that list on any other date except with the specific authorization of the list owner.

ASSOCIATION ADVERTISING A form of horizontal cooperative advertising performed by trade associations (such as the Florida Citrus Growers Association) to promote primary demand for a class of products (such as Florida oranges). See also *cooperative advertising.*

ASSOCIATION ADVERTISING FORMAT A type of advertisment that conveys its message by establishing a relationship between an event, an activity, or an image and the product being promoted. For example, an ad using this format would seek to transfer the excitement generated by skydiving to a product such as beer. Distinct from association advertising which is a form of horizontal cooperative advertising.

ASSOCIATION OF DIRECT MARKETING AGENCIES (ADMA) A professional organization of firms engaged in multi-media direct marketing. ADMA sponsors seminars and workshops. Its headquarters are in Brookline, Massachusetts.

ASSORTING The process of developing a heterogeneous inventory of products for the convenience of customers. This function is usually performed by wholesalers or retailers in order to supply an assortment of products such as hardware, drugs, grocery items, etc. The convenience factor may motivate sellers to stock related items not directly associated with their principal line of goods. For example, a lawn mower dealer may sell grass seed and other related gardening items.

ASSORTING PROCESS See *assorting*

ASSORTMENT 1) A mix of similar and/or complementary products designed to provide benefits to a specific market. 2) In retailing, the range of choice within a particular classification of goods, such as style, color, size, and price.

ASSORTMENT BREADTH See *product width*

ASSORTMENT DEPTH See *product depth*

ASSORTMENT WIDTH See *product width*

AT THE MARKET PRICING See *pricing at the market*

ATA See *American Telemarketing Association (ATA)*

ATMOSPHERE See *atmospherics*

ATMOSPHERICS The environmental factors consciously designed to create a certain mood, develop a particular image, and/or stimulate sales. These factors include layout, architecture, color scheme, and other sensory stimuli. In retail stores, atmospherics are used to develop an image, draw customers, and increase the probability that customers will make purchases. In other environments, such as banks and offices, atmospherics may be used to inspire confidence. In sum, atmospherics are a form of nonpersonal communication. See also *ambiance*.

ATOMISTIC COMPETITION A condition in the marketplace in which there are so many competitors that no one seller can influence the price of the product or commodity they all make or produce. This condition exists in farm commodity production and in the women's ready-to-wear industry.

ATTITUDE A person's knowledge and positive or negative cognitive evaluations about an object such as a product or service. Attitudes are learned, enduring, and made up of three components: 1) knowledge; 2) affect; and 3) action tendency. Knowledge, the cognitive component of attitude, is usually expressed as a belief. For example, "I believe whole grain breads are nutritionally superior to white bread." The consumer's overall feeling toward the product is called affect, or the affective component. For example, "I prefer whole grain bread to white bread." The action tendency, or behavioral component is the consumer's readiness to act on his/her beliefs and feelings. For example, "I will buy whole grain bread on my next shopping trip." The more favorable a consumer's attitude to a product, the more likely he/she is to use and purchase the product or service. Marketers are, therefore, interested in changing negative attitudes as well as reinforcing the positive attitudes of satisfied customers. The enduring aspect of attitude enables the consumer to behave in a fairly consistent way toward similar objects without having

to interpret and react to every object in a fresh way.

ATTITUDE SCALE A measurement tool used to determine the intensity of a subject's feelings toward a product or other object. Subjects respond to a series of adjectives, phrases, or sentences about the product by checking whether they "strongly agree, agree, have no opinion, disagree, or strongly disagree" with each statement. Researchers then tally the answers to get an indication of the strength of consumer opinions.

ATTRIBUTE MAPPING In new product planning, a statistical means of analyzing a market in an effort to find openings for new products. Existing products are positioned on a chart called an attribute space with each position being determined by the product's characteristics. Open spaces indicate gaps into which new products may be introduced. Also known as market position analysis.

AUCTION COMPANY An agent middleman selling by the auction method; i.e., customers may examine the product before engaging in competitive bidding for its purchase. Commonly employed in the sale of agricultural products, such as fruit, tobacco, livestock, etc. The auction company receives a commission from the seller of the merchandise based on the final sales price. Also known as auction houses.

AUCTION HOUSE See *auction company*

AUDIENCE 1) The total number of individuals reached by an advertisement or other promotion. For example, the number of viewers seeing a particular television commercial or seeing a particular print advertisement in a magazine or newspaper.

2) The target group at which a promotional message is aimed. For example, marketers may gear their advertisements to appeal to a particular segment of the population, such as "yuppies." Also called target audience. See also *receiver.*

AUDIENCE COMP See *audience profile*

AUDIENCE COMPOSITE See *audience profile*

AUDIENCE COMPOSITION See *audience profile*

AUDIENCE PROFILE The characteristics of the audience reached by an advertising medium (print or broadcast) or a particular station, newspaper, or magazine, etc. It includes both demographic and psychographic characteristics. Generally presented as a percentage figure which may be compared to the population as a whole. Also known as audience comp, audience composite, and audience composition.

AUDIENCE SHARE The percentage of the total listening or viewing audience, i.e., those with their sets actually turned on, which are tuned to a particular program at a specific time.

AUDIENCE STUDY Survey research aimed at learning who the audience is for an advertising medium and how it reacts to the advertising message.

AUDIT An examination of a firm's accounting records and the evidence in support of its correctness. The audit may be internal or external. The internal audit is performed in-house by employees of the firm. It involves a review of the firm's business records, reports, financial statements, etc. to verify their accuracy and conformity to the organization's policies. The external audit, on the other hand, is conducted by a certified public accountant or other auditor employed by an independent outside accounting firm. The purpose of the external audit is to verify the record's compliance with generally accepted accounting principles (GAAP). The annual reports of publicly held firms contain the external auditor's evaluation of the firm's accounting techniques and the accuracy of its financial documentation. See also *marketing audit.*

AUDIT (MARKETING) See *marketing audit*

AUGMENTED PRODUCT The core product together with its attendant benefits and services.

AUTHORITY The power or right to give orders or commands, take actions, make decisions, and to expect obedience. See also *market division of authority.*

AUTHORIZED DEALER A dealer who has a contractual agreement (similar to a franchise) to sell the products of a particular manufacturer. The authorized dealer generally has the rights to the distribution of these products within a particular trading area.

AUTOMATED WAREHOUSE A warehouse which is controlled by a central computer and which utilizes sophisticated electronic materials handling systems. Automated warehouses require far fewer employees than traditional warehouses, thus reducing labor costs. They tend to be single-storied structures. The computer reads orders and directs equipment such as lift trucks and electric hoists to gather the goods. The computer then moves the goods to the loading docks and issues invoices. Automated warehouses are gradually replacing older, less efficient, multi-storied warehouses. They tend to have a lower incidence of employee injuries, pilferage, and breakage. Inventory control is also improved.

AUTOMATIC MERCHANDISING See *automatic vending*

AUTOMATIC ORDERING See *automatic reorder*

AUTOMATIC REORDER An inventory system in which supplies of staple merchandise are monitored and replenished only when they have been reduced to a predetermined minimum. At that minimum point a reorder procedure is activated.

AUTOMATIC SELLING See *automatic vending*

AUTOMATIC STABILIZERS Those aspects of government participation in the marketplace (through both expenditures and taxation) which serve to counteract trends in economic activity without necessitating policy changes. Unemployment benefits, for example, prevent incomes from falling as fast as they normally would in a recession, thus helping to stabilize the economy.

AUTOMATIC VENDING A form of non-store, non-personal retailing of goods and services through coin operated, self-service machines. Merchandise most commonly sold by this method includes cigarettes, candy, soft drinks, and hot beverages. Services provided by automatic vending machines include telephone calls via pay phones and banking services via automatic tellers.

AUTOMATION Any system or method in which many of the procedures are automatically performed or controlled by computers, robots, and other self-operating machinery (such as the use of industrial robots in modern automobile manufacturing plants).

AUTOMOBILE INFORMATION DISCLOSURE ACT (1958) Federal consumer legislation which prohibited automobile dealers from inflating the factory prices of new cars.

AUXILIARY DIMENSIONS OF A PRODUCT Features of a product, other than the product itself, which add to the product's attractiveness, usefulness, and consumer appeal. For example, packaging, warranties, repair services, and brand names are all examples of auxiliary dimensions of a product which may influence the consumer to select it over other products or other brands of the same product.

AVAILABLE MARKET The available market for a product or service consists of all the potential customers who can afford the product or service, who have access to it, and who have exhibited an interest in using or owning it.

AVERAGE COST The total cost of doing business divided by the quantity of goods either produced or sold. See also *cost, cost-plus pricing, average fixed cost,* and *average variable cost.*

AVERAGE COST PRICING See *cost-plus pricing*

AVERAGE FIXED COST The total fixed cost divided by the quantity of goods produced. A fixed cost is one that remains constant regardless of changes in sales volume. See also *average cost* and *average variable cost.*

AVERAGE INVENTORY OF AN ITEM See *average stock*

AVERAGE REVENUE The total revenue (income generated by sales, etc.) divided by the quantity of goods required to produce that revenue. The average revenue line is the demand curve facing the firm. See also *revenue.*

19

AVERAGE REVENUE LINE See *average revenue*

AVERAGE STOCK The amount which represents the midpoint between the highest and lowest inventory levels for a given period. The average stock is calculated by adding each month's opening stock figure plus the closing stock figure for the last month. The sum is then divided by the number of months being considered. For example: Average stock (January–December) = (Opening stock of each + December closing stock) ÷ 13.

AVERAGE VARIABLE COST The total variable cost divided by the quantity of goods produced. A variable cost is one that changes as sales volume changes (for example, delivery costs). See also *average cost, average fixed cost,* and *variable cost.*

AVOIDING COMPETITION See *status quo pricing*

AWARENESS The initial stage in the consumer adoption process during which the buyer becomes aware of the product but has gathered little information about it.

AWARENESS (OF NEEDS) See *need awareness*

BACK HAUL Reshipping freight over the route it has just completed. This may occur when shipping goods to a customer located between the warehouse and the plant.

BACK HAUL ALLOWANCE A price reduction given to customers who pick up their own merchandise at the manufacturer's or distributor's warehouse, thus saving the seller the cost of delivery.

BACK ORDER An order, or part of an order, to be shipped at a later date.

BACKHAUL ALLOWANCE See *back haul allowance*

BACKHAULING See *back haul*

BACKWARD CHANNEL A marketing channel running backward from the consumer to the middleman and, on occasion, back to the manufacturer or producer. The recycling of aluminum cans, the return of empty soft drink bottles, and the collection of waste materials are examples of backward channel activities. Also referred to as reverse distribution.

BACKWARD INTEGRATION Efforts on the part of a firm to buy or gain control of its supplier companies. For example, a large retail organization may own its own manufacturing facilities and operate its own distribution system.

BACKWARD INVENTION A product planning strategy in international marketing in which firms doing business in developing countries modify (and sometimes simplify) their products so that they may be more appealing in the domestic market. For example, water pumps ordinarily powered by electricity may be modified so that they are compatible with local power sources.

BACKWARD MARKET SEGMENTA-TION A means of identifying segments of a population on the basis of some kind of common behavior; e.g., the use of particular products or services or the viewing of particular television programs. The underlying assumption is that groups exhibiting common behavior will also share attitudes and beliefs and will react homogeneously to marketing programs.

BAIT AND SWITCH ADVERTISING See *bait and switch merchandising*

BAIT AND SWITCH MERCHANDISING The promotion of a product (the bait) at a very low price for the purpose of luring customers into a store. The retailer, who has no intention of selling the bait, attempts to sell the customer a more expensive item (the switch).

BAIT AND SWITCH PRICING See *bait and switch merchandising*

BAIT PRICING See *bait and switch merchandising*

BALANCE OF PAYMENTS In international trade, the balance of payments is the sum of all transactions between a country and its trading partners. Such transactions include merchandise trade, travel, income on investments, military expenditures, foreign aid, and flow of capital funds.

BALANCE OF TRADE The relationship between the values of a country's imports and its exports. A trade deficit exists when imports exceed exports. A trade surplus exists when exports exceed imports. See also *balance of payments*.

BALANCE SHEET A classified financial statement showing a firm's assets, liabilities, and net worth (i.e., owner's or stockholder's equity) at a particular moment in time.

BALANCED PRODUCT PORTFOLIO The mix of old and new products maintained by a manufacturer.

BALANCED STOCK In retailing, a balanced stock is an assortment of merchandise with sufficient breadth and depth to meet the demand of target customers while maintaining a reasonable investment in inventory. Also called model stock or ideal stock.

BALANCED TENANCY In shopping center planning, a condition in which the mix of stores is appropriate to the needs of the population of the surrounding area. Balanced tenancy is contingent on the center having a basic identity of its own.

BANDED PACK Related items offered at retail, which are held together by a tape or plastic film strip and are sold as a unit. For example, a can of shaving cream and a razor sold together in this manner constitute a banded pack. Also called a factory pack.

BANDED PREMIUM See *on-pack premium*

BANK MARKETING ASSOCIATION (BMA) A Chicago based association of public relations and marketing executives employed by banks and other financial institutions. BMA serves a considerable educational function, provides a placement service, and maintains an information center. It publishes *Bank Marketing Journal* (monthly), *Community Bank Marketing Newsletter* (monthly), *IC News* (bimonthly), an annual *Membership Directory*, and its *Proceedings* (irregular).

BANKRUPTCY The state or condition of being unable to pay one's debts. The debtor may be an individual or corporation and the bankruptcy proceeding may be voluntary (initiated by the debtor) or involuntary (intiated by creditors).

BANTAM STORE See *convenience store*

BARTER The direct exchange of goods or services between the parties involved in a commercial transaction without money being employed. In international marketing barter is regarded as a type of countertrade.

BASE PERIOD In economic and business research, a base period is a year or span of years used as a reference point and to which current data is compared.

BASE-POINT PRICING See *basing-point pricing*

BASE PRICE See *list price*

BASE YEAR See *base period*

BASIC LIST PRICE See *list price*

BASING POINT See *basing-point pricing*

BASING-POINT PRICING A pricing strategy in which the cost of goods has two components: (1) their cost at the point of production plus (2) the cost of transporting them from a designated center (the basing point), which may be different from the point of manufacture. Basing-point pricing allows the producer to charge all customers in the same area identical transportation costs regardless of the actual distance the goods are shipped.

BASING-POINT SYSTEM See *basing-point pricing*

BATTLE OF THE BRANDS The competitive struggle at the retail level between national brands on the one hand and middleman and retailer brands on the other. More recently, generic or "no-name" products have joined the competition.

BCG GROWTH-SHARE MATRIX See *Boston Consulting Group Matrix*

BEHAVIORAL ENGINEERING A part of learning theory which holds

that people behave in direct relation to what they believe will be the consequences of their acts. Behavioral engineering has been applied in limited forms in marketing, having more uses in personnel management. Also known as behavioral technology, applied behavioral analysis, and Skinnerian psychology.

BEHAVIORAL TECHNOLOGY See *behavioral engineering*

BEHAVIORISM In an advertising context, an application of the stimulus-response theory of learning in which a stimulus (an advertising message) is repeated often enough to produce the desired response (the purchase of a product or service).

BELIEF A thought or understanding held by a person about a thing or occurrence.

BELLY-TO-BELLY SELLING See *personal selling*

BELOW-THE-MARKET PRICING See *pricing below the market*

BELOW-THE-MARKET STRATEGY See *pricing below the market*

BENEFIT APPROACH A technique used by salespersons in the first few minutes of contact with a prospect. The salesperson attempts to focus the prospect's thoughts directly on the benefit to be derived from the good or service being sold. The benefit should be concrete and specific, such as a monetary savings. See also *approach*.

BENEFIT-COST ANALYSIS See *cost-benefit analysis*

BENEFIT MARKET SEGMENTATION A market segmentation technique which attempts to identify the benefits consumers seek in a product or class of products and divide the consumer market accordingly. For example, in the market for women's shoes, customers may seek comfort, high fashion, durability, practicality, versatility, etc. Market researchers have found, in general, that consumers usually want a combination of benefits, but stress one or more when making a purchase decision. Benefit market segmentation is also useful in uncovering opportunities for new products.

BENEFIT SEGMENTATION See *benefit market segmentation*

BENEFIT STRUCTURE ANALYSIS See *conjoint measurement*

BENEFITS CONCEPT See *bundle of benefits concept*

BENEFITS/FEATURES AP-PROACH TO SELLING See *benefit approach*

BIAS See *interviewer bias*

BID (1) An offer to buy, as in a public auction. (2) An offer to perform a task or supply goods made by a vendor at a price which he feels will be competitive and acceptable to the buyer. See also *sealed bid* and *open bid.*

BID BUYING See *bid*

BID PRICING See *bid, sealed bid,* and *open bid*

BIDDING See *bid*

BIG-EARLY, LITTLE-LATE METH-OD A method of developing media advertising schedules in which the beginning of the campaign is regarded as most significant and thus allocated the largest amount of money.

BIRDYBACK A coordinated transportation arrangement in which both air and ground modes of transportation are used. For example, goods would be shipped partly by airplane and partly by truck.

BLACK BOX A term used by marketing researchers to describe the con-

sumer's mind and to indicate that what goes on inside that mind is largely hidden from the researcher's view.

BLACK MARKET Trade in products, commodities, currencies, etc. which is in violation of the law; e.g., tax laws, regulations governing rates of exchange, price ceilings, etc.

BLANKET BRAND See *family brand*

BLANKET BRANDING See *family brand*

BLANKET ORDER A pre-season order placed with a vendor to be delivered in a number of later shipments. Quantities and styles may be specified, but detailed instructions regarding color, size, etc. may be included in subsequent orders.

BLUE LAWS State and local laws which prohibit retail stores from operating on Sundays or which restrict the Sunday sale of certain products; e.g., beer and liquor. Although this practice is usually defended on religious grounds, its effect is to reduce time competition between large and small retailers.

BMA See *Bank Marketing Association (BMA)*

BOILER ROOM A facility from which telephone salespeople make solicitations.

BONA FIDE SALE A transaction in which the seller acts in good faith regarding the terms of the sale.

BONDED WAREHOUSE A form of public warehouse which stores imported goods or other goods on which a tax must be paid prior to the release of the products for sale (such as cigarettes and alcoholic beverages). See also *public warehouse.*

BONUS PACK A promotional package in which the customer is offered more than the regular amount for the regular price.

BOOK INVENTORY A perpetual system of inventory maintained by adding the value of incoming goods to the value of previous inventory and then subtracting the value of sales, markdowns, and discounts.

BOOK METHOD OF INVENTORY See *book inventory*

BOOK PRICE See *list price*

BOSTON BOX See *Boston Consulting Group Matrix*

BOSTON CONSULTING GROUP MATRIX A method of evaluating a company's product offerings and marketing opportunities developed by the Boston Consulting Group. Products are classified as stars, cash cows, question marks, or dogs and assigned to a space in the four box matrix (the Boston Box). Appropriate strategies may then be developed for the company's entire product portfolio. Also known as the business portfolio matrix and growth/share matrix.

BOSTON CONSULTING GROUP MATRIX

	MARKET SHARE	
GROWTH	HIGH	LOW
HIGH	STAR	QUESTION MARK
LOW	CASH COW	DOG

BOTTOM-UP FASHION See *bottom-up theory*

BOTTOM-UP PLANNING Planning initiated by employees near the bottom of the organizational ladder. Unit objectives and the resources required to attain them are set forth and subsequently transmitted up the organization for evaluation and approval at the decision-making level.

BOTTOM-UP TECHNIQUE See *bottom-up planning*

BOTTOM-UP THEORY A theory of fashion adoption in which young, lower-income persons are seen as the innovators of new styles. Fashion then spreads upward through the various social classes, although in order of adoption the next group may be members of the confident, secure, upper class. The new fashion is then likely to spread widely throughout the population.

BOUTIQUE From the French word meaning "little shop," a boutique may be a small specialty store or an area within a larger store. Emphasis is on merchandise selected for a specific customer, presented in an attractive and unified manner, and accompanied by individualized attention on the part of the sales staff.

BOUTIQUE AGENCY An advertising agency that specializes in writing and designing advertising material and thus focuses on the creative and art aspects of the advertising campaign. Unlike larger, full-service agencies, boutique agencies charge on a per-job basis. Also known as a creative boutique.

BOUTIQUE MERCHANDISING A form of store organization in which related merchandise from a number of departments is brought together in one shop to meet special customer demand.

BOX STORE See *warehouse retailing*

BOYCOTT A term derived from the name of a British agent in 19th century Ireland (a Captain Boycott) which has come to mean 1 in international relations a means of coercion in which one or more nations refuse to deal with another, as, for example, the Arab nations refused to sell to the U.S. during the oil boycott of the 1970s; or 2) in economics, a refusal on the part of certain groups (for example, labor unions) to buy particular domestic or imported products as a means of bringing economic pressure to bear on government or private industry.

BPI See *buying power index (BPI)*

BRANCH A geographically detached unit of a firm which is still an integral part of the business. Branches of companies frequently restrict their activities to the selling function.

BRANCH HOUSE See *manufacturer's branch office*

BRANCH OFFICE See *manufacturer's sales office*

BRANCH STORE In department or other large stores, the smaller retail units owned and operated by the parent store and generally located in the suburbs or in metropolitan area shopping centers.

BRAND A particular product, or line of products, offered for sale by a single producer or manufacturer and made easily distinguishable from other similar products by a unique identifying name and/or symbol. See also *brand name* and *trademark.*

BRAND ACCEPTANCE See *acceptance*

BRAND ADVERTISING See *product advertising*

BRAND AWARENESS See *awareness*

BRAND BUYER See *brand loyalty*

BRAND CHARACTER See *brand personality*

BRAND CONSCIOUSNESS See *awareness*

BRAND DIFFERENTIATION See *product differentiation*

BRAND EXTENSION The practice of marketing new products under well-known brand names in an effort to capitalize on the positive image the parent brand has in the consumer's mind. See also *line extension.*

BRAND EXTENSION STRATEGY A marketing strategy in which a firm uses one of its established brand names on a modified product; i.e., a new line, or on an entirely new product. It is, essentially, a coattails strategy in which new products entering the marketplace are supported by the existing, well-recognized brand name.

BRAND FAMILIARITY The customer's ability to recognize and accept a particular brand of products. Brand familiarity is often divided into five levels: 1) brand rejection; 2) brand nonrecognition; 3) brand recognition; 4) brand preference; and 5) brand insistence.

BRAND IMAGE That perception of a product formed in the mind of the consumer which is the result of the symbols and meanings associated with a particular brand. Advertising is often employed to create a brand image; e.g., automobile advertising on television commonly sells a lifestyle rather than a mode of transportation.

BRAND INSISTENCE An extreme form of brand loyalty in which the customer will search extensively for the desired product or brand and accept no substitute. Consumers who are brand insistent are known as "hard core loyals." Consumers who share their loyalty between two or three brands are said to be "soft core loyals," and those who shift from favoring one brand to another are called "shifting loyals." The least brand insistent consumers, those with no loyalty to any brand, are known as "brand switchers." See also *brand loyalty* and *brand switcher.*

BRAND LOYAL MARKET See *brand loyalty*

BRAND LOYALTY The consistent preference, on the part of the consumer, for one brand over any other, or for one set of brands over others competing in the same category.

BRAND MANAGEMENT See *product management*

BRAND MANAGER See *product manager*

BRAND MANAGER SYSTEM See *product manager system*

BRAND MARK That part of a brand consisting of the signs, colors, symbols, and designs; i.e., those elements which are not words, and are closely identified with the product. Brand marks; e.g., the red tab on the back pocket of Levi Strauss jeans, may also be a part of the firm's trademark. See also *brand, brand name,* and *trademark.*

BRAND MARKETING A strategy in which each of a firm's products is marketed independently, generally under the direction of a brand manager. See also *product line marketing.*

BRAND NAME That part of a brand consisting of the actual letters or words; i.e., that part which can actually be vocalized, which comprises the name of the product or service as distinct from other identifying signs, symbols, and designs incorporated into the overall design. See also *brand, brand mark,* and *trademark.*

BRAND NAME BIAS A tendency on the part of persons being questioned about product use to name a widely advertised brand despite the fact that they may never have bought it. This is generally the result of the respondent forgetting the name of the actual brand purchased and being reluctant to admit it.

BRAND NONRECOGNITION Customers' inability to recognize a brand, though they may recognize the product. This generally occurs because the brand name is not part of the marketing strategy geared to the ultimate consumer, even when it is used by middlemen. Products with brand nonrecognition problems include novelties, school supplies, and other inexpensive goods commonly found in discount stores.

BRAND PERSONALITY A term attributed to the advertising agency Young & Rubicam. A brand's personality is seen to depend more upon what people think about it than upon what it is or what it does. A term distinct from brand image. Sometimes known as brand character.

BRAND POSITION A product's niche in the marketplace. The term "position" refers to the product's relationship to competing brands and is generally measured in terms of how the consumer perceives the various attributes of the brand; i.e., brand position depends on consumer attitudes.

BRAND POSITIONING See *market positioning*

BRAND PREFERENCE In the process of brand acceptance, a middle stage in which the consumer will choose a particular brand over its competitors because of previous favorable experience with the product. However, should the product prove to be unavailable, the consumer is willing to accept a substitute.

BRAND PROLIFERATION The rapid and sometimes excessive growth of similar products within a particular line. Brand proliferation often results from a marketing strategy on the part of large producers who are attempting to dominate shelf space in stores (breakfast foods, detergents, etc.) or to occupy a series of price levels in the marketplace (appliances, automobiles, etc.).

BRAND RECOGNITION A stage in brand acceptance in which consumers remember having heard about or seen a product, even if they have not yet tried it. Such recognition is a company's first objective for a newly introduced product. The effectiveness of advertising and other publicity programs geared to familiarizing the consuming public with such a new product or brand may be tested by either a recognition survey or a recognition test.

BRAND REJECTION Customers' refusal to buy a particular brand of goods because of its poor image or because of previous bad experiences with the brand. Remedies for brand rejection are: 1) change the brand's current image; 2) change the product; 3) change the target segment.

BRAND REPOSITIONING See *repositioning*

BRAND SHARE See *market share*

BRAND STRATEGY The plan employed to create, introduce, and promote a particular brand. Strategies involved include picking a name, selecting an image to project, positioning the product in the marketplace, etc.

BRAND SWITCHER A consumer who shows no loyalty to any brand and who looks instead for the brand that is readily available, is on sale, or is novel. Consumers often maintain brand loyalty for certain items while displaying a willingness to accept substitutes for others. Brand switchers motivated by low price and premiums are said to be "deal prone." This is particularly true in the areas of staple products, such as tuna or toilet tissue, where there is little distinguishable difference between brands, and consumers will often select the brand on sale that particular day. Brand switchers motivated by the desire to try something different are said to be "variety prone." This trait shows up in the snack food industry, for example, where consumers may opt for a new cookie or other taste treat just for the sake of change. See also *brand loyalty* and *brand insistence.*

BRAND SWITCHING See *brand switcher*

BRANDED MERCHANDISE See *brand*

BRANDING The assignment of a brand name to a product or service. Branding is a means of achieving product differentiation in the marketplace. See also *brand, brand name, brand mark, trade name,* and *trademark.*

BRANDSTANDING In advertising and promotion, the tying together of a brand with an event, idea, or issue. The tactic employed generally involves the linking of a brand name (without regard to its particular attributes) to some highly publicized event or other activity; e.g., marathon runners frequently wear numbers which also carry the name of the race's sponsor.

BREACH OF WARRANTY The failure of a manufacturer to honor the warranty issued with a product; i.e., refusal to back up claims concerning proper performance.

BREADTH See *product width*

BREAK BULK See *allocation*

BREAK-BULK CENTER A central distribution point where large shipments of goods (such as carload and/or truckload quantities) are broken down into smaller quantities and shipped to customers closer to the final market. See also *allocation*.

BREAK-DOWN APPROACH A method used to allocate a firm's advertising budget. In the break-down approach, the firm begins with a predetermined total budget, which is then allocated by the person or department in charge of promotions to particular lines of merchandise offered by the firm. See also *build-up approach*.

BREAK-EVEN ANALYSIS A mathematical analysis in which the fixed and variable costs of production are compared to projected revenue in an effort to reveal the break-even point; i.e., that point at which expenses and revenues are balanced.

BREAK-EVEN CHART A graphic representation of fixed and variable costs juxtaposed to total revenue in such a manner that the firm's break-even point is revealed.

BREAKEVEN CHART

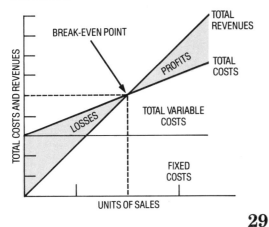

BREAK-EVEN POINT The point at which an enterprise has earned enough money to defray all the fixed and variable costs of operation. Break-even points may be calculated for individual products at specific price points or for an entire business.

BREAKING BULK See *allocation*

BREAKTHROUGH OPPORTUNITY A marketing situation which enables an innovative firm to establish a new marketing strategy, develop and market a new product, or create a new marketing mix. The new strategy will be difficult for others to readily imitate and will, therefore, remain profitable for an extended period of time. The breakthrough opportunity gives the firm, in effect, a temporary monopoly and an edge over competitors. It also helps the firm to capture a large portion of the market share, which may serve to discourage imitators from entering the market. The advantage will remain until competitors decide to meet the innovator in head-on competition. The longer other firms can be discouraged from entering the market, the longer the breakthrough opportunity will remain profitable.

BRIBERY See *commercial bribery*

BROKER An agent or middleman acting as an intermediary to bring the buyer and seller of a product together. Brokers are compensated for their efforts by a fee or commission usually paid by the seller whom they represent. Brokers generally do not take title to merchandise, nor do they have physical possession of the goods. In negotiations they have little authority to extend credit, make terms, or set prices. A broker's principal asset is his knowledge of the market in which he operates. Brokers are sometimes called merchandise brokers or merchandise agents. See also *commission merchant.*

BROKERAGE ALLOWANCE A discount paid to buyers, particularly large organizations such as grocery chains, for performing the broker functions. These organizations request the broker's commission in the form of a price reduction. The practice is technically a violation of the Robinson-Patman Act.

BUDGET A forecasting tool that structures a firm's short-range future plans on the basis of estimated revenues and expenditures expressed in numerical terms. Budgets are often established for a fiscal year. There are several different types of budgets or sub-budgets. A *cash budget* is a forecast of expected cash receipts and disbursements for a specified period of time designed to preclude possible cash-flow problems. The cash budget indicates the firm's cash requirements and its possible need to borrow additional funds by projecting buying and selling patterns for several successive future time periods. A *production budget* is a forecast of the number of units a firm must produce in order to fill expected sales and maintain inventory for a given budget period. The quantitative data used to determine the production budget is derived by adding projected sales to the number of units expected to remain in inventory at the end of the budget period and subtracting the number of units on hand at the beginning of the budget period. A *cost-of-goods-sold budget* is used to determine the price paid for any merchandise required to obtain the sales of the period. It is based on estimates of the cost of materials used in the manufacture of the goods. A *sales budget* sets forth in detail all of a firm's anticipated sales for a given period and makes possible

the allocation of the money and materials which will be needed if the firm is to achieve its sales objectives. Commonly, each product offered will require its own sales budget. The sales budget is based on studies of past sales and estimates of future business conditions. See also *sales expense budget.*

BUFFER INVENTORY See *reserve stock*

BUFFER STOCK See *reserve stock*

BUILD-UP APPROACH A method used to allocate a firm's advertising budget. In the build-up approach, the firm begins by ascertaining the advertising needs of each line of goods offered by the firm, as determined by the person in charge of each line. Any necessary adjustments are made by the individual or group in charge of promotions, and the total is added together to determine the total budget. The firm does not begin with a predetermined total budget as is the case with the break-down approach. A sophisticated form of the build-up approach may be seen in the objective-task method. See also *break-down approach.*

BUILDING METHOD See *objective-task method*

BUILD-UP METHOD See *build-up approach*

BULK-BREAKING See *allocation*

BULK CHECKING The process of checking arriving merchandise by comparing the package markings against the invoice or packing list without actually opening the packaging to verify contents.

BULK FREIGHT See *bulk goods*

30

BULK GOODS 1) Goods such as coal, grain, or gravel which are sold and delivered in loose or unpackaged form. 2) Any large shipment of one item.

BUNDLE OF BENEFITS CONCEPT A theory that customers purchase not only the goods offered by a firm, but also the advantages and capabilities those goods are expected to provide. The real value of the merchandise, therefore, resides in what the goods can do for the consumer, and not in the goods themselves. For example, the purchase of a home computer would be meaningless to the average consumer unless he perceives some real time and labor saving advantages to be gained in the computer's use. If the consumer needs equipment that can help with his income tax, communicate with his bank and pay his bills, allow him to write reports and store records, then he will purchase the home computer and expect it to provide him with those benefits. The same argument may be made for the industrial customer.

BUNDLE OF SERVICES CONCEPT A theory in support of leasing rather than purchasing industrial equipment. The theory takes into account the comparative costs of leasing and buying, including the service and maintenance costs inherent in purchased equipment. According to the bundle of services concept, leased equipment is more cost effective.

BURDEN See *overhead*

BUSINESS ANALYSIS In new product development, efforts made to estimate the profitability of new products before large amounts of money have been spent on their development.

BUSINESS-CONTROLLED PRICING See *administered pricing*

BUSINESS CYCLE The fluctuations in business conditions which occur with some regularity over a period of time. The fluctuations are generally identified as prosperity, recession, depression, and recovery. During the prosperity stage, income and employment are high. During a recession, income, employment, and production begin to decline. If left uncorrected, the recession may become a depression, a period when business activities, employment, and incomes decline rapidly. The recovery that generally follows a depression once again shows an increase in production and employment.

BUSINESS DOMAIN That sector of a market which a firm targets as its business environment. It may be defined in terms of a line of products, a particular group of customers, or some other combination of market factors.

BUSINESS-INDUSTRIAL MARKET See *industrial market*

BUSINESS MARKET See *industrial market*

BUSINESS PORTFOLIO ANALYSIS See *Boston Consulting Group Matrix*

BUSINESS PORTFOLIO MATRIX See *Boston Consulting Group Matrix*

BUY CLASSES See *buyclasses*

BUYBACK A product or service buyback agreement involves the sale of a product (or service) which, in turn, produces other products or services, e.g., the sale of industrial production facilities. Commonly the seller agrees to accept as compensation in part some of the output of the facility. Buyback is a practice found in international marketing where it is regarded as a form of countertrade.

BUYCLASSES The three types of industrial buying: 1) the straight rebuy, 2) the modified rebuy, and 3) new task buying.

BUYER In retailing and wholesaling, an executive responsible for the selection and purchase of merchandise and its ultimate resale at a profit. The term is sometimes applied to industrial or institutional purchasing agents who buy the goods and services required for the operation of their firms or institutions.

BUYER BEHAVIOR See *consumer behavior*

BUYER FOR EXPORT In international marketing, a middleman who buys goods in the domestic market outright and then sells them overseas.

BUYER-SELLER DYAD In personal selling, the buyer-seller dyad is the relationship between a salesperson and a customer, which strongly emphasizes personal, individual attention on the part of the salesperson.

BUYER'S MARKET An economic situation in which an abundance of goods and services are available so that supply exceeds demand. This situation favors buyers and gives them considerable power in the marketplace. See also *seller's market*.

BUYER'S REMORSE See *cognitive dissonance*

BUYING In marketing, the term "buying" commonly refers to the purchase of goods at the wholesale level for resale at the retail level. See also *industrial purchasing*.

BUYING ALLOWANCE A reduction in price on specific goods offered by a producer or manufacturer to a purchaser as an incentive to buy.

BUYING BEHAVIOR See *consumer behavior*

BUYING BY COMMITTEE See *committee buying*

BUYING CENTER In industrial marketing the buying center is made up of those persons who are responsible for purchase decision-making in an organization. They may be the actual users of the products and services, purchasing officers, persons with influence over buying decisions (salespersons, executives, etc.), gatekeepers, etc.

BUYING COMMITTEE In large retail organizations, especially those which handle large numbers of staple products, the buying committee assists individual buyers in making decisions regarding specific merchandise. See also *committee buying*.

BUYING DECISION-MAKING PROCESS See *adoption process*

BUYING DIRECT See *direct selling*

BUYING INFLUENCE See *multiple buying influence*

BUYING LOADER A gift from a manufacturer to a retailer to encourage him to order.

BUYING OFFICE See *resident buying office*

BUYING POWER 1) An organization's capacity to buy large amounts of merchandise, thereby commanding price concessions on the part of suppliers. 2) An individual's capacity to purchase goods or services; i.e., personal income less taxes and other nontax financial obligations plus available consumer credit. 3) The aggregate disposable income for persons living in a particular area or having some common characteristic; i.e., the money income available for purchasing goods and services.

BUYING POWER INDEX (BPI) A measurement developed by *Sales & Marketing Management*, which combines three elements (population, effective buying income, and retail sales) into one index which expresses a market's capacity to buy. The index is calculated as a percentage of the total U.S./Canada market potential.

BUYING PROCESS See *adoption process*

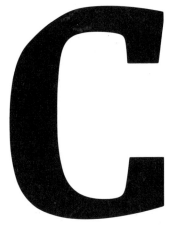

C & F (COST AND FREIGHT) A shipping term meaning that the seller of goods pays the cost of transporting the goods to their shipping point (dock, railroad platform, etc.), the loading charges, and the cost of transporting the goods to their destination. Responsibility for the cost of insurance is transferred to the buyer at the time the goods are loaded aboard the vessel or vehicle.

CAFETERIA BENEFIT PLAN An employee benefit plan in which the employer offers each participating employee a number of options such as disability insurance, medical coverage, tax deferred annuities, dental plans, etc. The employee chooses from this "menu" assembled by the employer those benefits he finds most desirable.

CALL REPORT A log of activity kept by salespersons in which they record the calls they have made during a specified period and in which they record information about their accounts.

CAMPAIGN See *advertising campaign*

CAMPAIGN PLAN A direct mail promotion which extends over a period of time and which is designed to arouse and build interest in an upcoming event or new product. The final mailing is the actual announcement of the event or product. Also known as a teaser campaign.

CANNED APPROACH See *canned presentation*

CANNED PRESENTATION A standardized sales talk memorized by members of the sales force and delivered to customers verbatum.

CANNED SALES TALK See *canned presentation*

CANNIBALIZATION A condition in

which a new product is introduced into the marketplace and sells at the expense of another product in the company's line; i.e., it eats into the profitability of the other product. The opposite of enhancement.

CANNIBALIZING A MARKET See *cannibalization*

CANVASSING Door-to-door or telephone sales technique that involves the solicitation of orders for merchandise which will be delivered at some time in the future.

CAPITAL EQUIPMENT See *capital goods*

CAPITAL GOODS Material property (sometimes called capital-investment goods) in the form of 1) installations such as buildings and major pieces of equipment or machinery, and 2) accessory equipment used in production operations such as materials handling and office equipment. Capital goods are generally expensive, require infrequent replacement (commonly due to wear or obsolescence) and do not become a part of the product being manufactured.

CAPITAL INTENSIVE See *capital intensive industry*

CAPITAL INTENSIVE INDUSTRY An industry which invests heavily in equipment, machinery, and automated devices while using relatively little labor. Expenditures for meeting the requirements of plant and equipment are therefore relatively high. Also referred to as a cost intensive industry. See also *labor intensive industry,* its opposite.

CAPITAL-INVESTMENT GOODS See *capital goods*

CAPITAL ITEMS See *capital goods*

CAPITALISM See *economic system*

CAPTIVE JOBBER See *manufacturer's branch office*

CAPTIVE MARKET Customers, commonly at the retail level, who have little choice about where they shop. For example, the customers of retail or service establishments in hotels or airports where alternative or competitive businesses are relatively inaccessible, constitute a captive market.

CAPTIVE PRODUCT PRICING A pricing strategy used by makers of products which require supplies, accessories, or ancillary equipment for operation. The principal product is moderately priced while the supplies and accessories are given substantial markups.

CAPTIVE WHOLESALER See *manufacturer's branch office*

CARBON-COPY THEORY In personal selling, a theory that new salespersons are best trained by memorizing the techniques of a master salesperson.

CARLOAD See *carload freight rate (C.L.)*

CARLOAD FREIGHT RATE (C.L.) A reduced rail shipping rate allowed to large freight shipments which make up a full carload.

CARRIER See *common carrier, contract carrier,* and *private carrier*

CARRYING COST See *inventory carrying costs*

CARRYOVER EFFECT Any effect that present marketing expenditures, such as advertising expenditures or new package design, may have on future sales. When a time period has elapsed between the expenditure and the visible results of that expenditure, it is known as a delayed response effect.

CARTAGE The fee charged by carriers for hauling freight. The term is used primarily in connection with trucking. When short distances are involved, the term "drayage" is often used instead.

CARTEL In international marketing, an agreement between independent businesses or between governments who produce and market similar products, e.g., petroleum. The essential purpose of cartels is to restrict competition in the marketplace. They frequently engage in such activities as price setting, production quota allocation, assignment of markets, and at times, the distribution of profits.

CASE METHOD OF TEACHING Teaching based on an actual problem faced by a business. Students are required to gather additional information and to form an opinion concerning the action that should be taken.

CASE PRODUCT See *generic product*

CASH-AND-CARRY WHOLESALER A limited service wholesaler who carries merchandise in inventory, which he sells on a customer-pick-up, cash only basis. Commonly found in the grocery business, the cash-and-carry wholesaler offers lower prices than his full-service counterpart.

CASH BEFORE DELIVERY See *cash in advance (CIA)*

CASH BUDGET See *budget*

CASH COW In large business enterprises, cash cows are units which enjoy high earnings but often have low growth potential. Because they generate large amounts of cash, these units are often "milked" to support other divisions of the enterprise, thus the term cash cow.

CASH DISCOUNT A reduction from invoice price granted to a buyer of

goods for prompt payment of his bill. For example, if the terms of the bill are 2/10, net 30, the buyer may deduct 2% from the billed amount if paid within 10 days, otherwise the full amount is due in 30 days. Cash discount does not imply that full cash payment must be made at time of purchase or delivery. See also *dating.*

CASH FLOW The movement of money both into the business, as receipts or revenues, and out of the business, as disbursements, for a given period of time.

CASH FLOW ANALYSIS An examination of the timing of cash receipts and disbursements to identify periods of time in which working capital may be either inadequate to meet the needs of the business or excessive. A cash flow analysis expresses future income and expenditures in a dollar amount, and predicts future cash flow based on an anticipated sales volume. It may be prepared on a weekly or monthly basis for semi-annual or annual projections. The steps in preparing a cash flow analysis include: 1) establishing the period; 2) estimating sales; 3) estimating the anticipated future cash inflows from the estimated sales level; 4) analyzing the expected cash outflow; 5) comparing the estimated inflow with the estimated outflow to determine the net cash gain or loss for the period; and 6) providing an estimated cash balance. The primary use of a cash flow analysis is to help plan the firm's needs for short-term capital.

CASH FLOW STATEMENT An itemized list of cash receipts and disbursements over a particular period of time.

CASH IN ADVANCE (CIA) A term of sale requiring payment to the seller before goods are transferred to the purchaser. No credit is extended and no risk is assumed by the seller. Also called cash before delivery.

CASH ON DELIVERY (C.O.D.) A term of sale requiring payment for goods in cash upon their receipt by the purchaser.

CASH REBATE See *rebate*

CASH SALE A transaction in which the customer pays money for merchandise at the time of purchase.

CASH TERMS An agreement to pay cash for purchased goods, usually within a specified period of time.

CASH WITH ORDER A term of sale requiring that a payment sufficient to cover the cost of the merchandise and delivery accompany the customer's order.

CASUAL EXPORTING Activities of firms which engage in some export business but who do not actively seek it. Also known as accidental exporting.

CATALOG A promotional book or booklet (or electronic data base) in which merchandise is presented to prospective purchasers. Catalogs commonly provide a picture of the item being offered for sale together with descriptive copy and such essential information as price, shipping charges, delivery time, etc.

CATALOG HOUSE See *mail order wholesaler*

CATALOG PLAN See *price agreement plan*

CATALOG RETAILER See *catalog retailing*

CATALOG RETAILING A form of selling in which the retailer provides the consumer with a merchandise catalog by either mailing it to his home or by making it available in a facility maintained by the retailer for that purpose. The consumer may submit his order by mail or by telephone or may fill out an order in the retailer's catalog store. Merchandise ordered is delivered by mail or parcel service.

CATALOG SHOWROOM A warehouse showroom where catalog selling and in-store retailing are brought together. Merchandise is presented in catalogs which the customer consults before giving his order to a clerk; who has the merchandise brought in from the warehouse. Catalog showroom merchants concentrate on nationally advertised name brand products; which they offer at prices below regular retail. Also called a catalog store.

CATALOG SHOWROOM RETAILER See *catalog showroom*

CATALOG STORE See *catalog showroom*

CATCHMENT AREA The geographic region in which the majority of a firm's customers may be found.

CAUSAL RELATIONSHIPS See *causal research*

CAUSAL RESEARCH Marketing research which focuses on cause and effect relationships in the marketplace, e.g., the effect of advertising on the rate at which products sell.

CAUSE MARKETING The application of marketing principles to political, social, educational, charitable, cultural, and religious causes, etc. in an effort to change people's attitudes and, ultimately, their behavior. Not to be confused with cause-related marketing.

CAUSE-RELATED MARKETING Marketing efforts (e.g., corporate sponsorship of the Olympic Games) in which a particular brand or product is linked to a particular cause or special event. The primary objective of cause-related marketing is the generation of revenue, although such activity may result in increased good will on the part of the public. Not to be confused with cause marketing.

CAVEAT EMPTOR A Latin term meaning "let the buyer beware." Intended as a warning to buyers, it implies that purchases are made at the customer's own risk, the seller assuming no responsibility and offering no guarantees.

CAVEAT VENDITOR A Latin term meaning, "let the seller beware." As a legal principle, it implies that the seller is responsible for the quality and quantity of the goods sold. Sometimes called "caveat vendor."

CBD See *Central Business District (CBD)*

CEASE AND DESIST ORDER An order, often emanating from a court or administrative agency, which prohibits the continuance of a particular activity, e.g., the Federal Trade Commission may order a company to cease and desist from a particular marketing practice which has been judged deceptive.

CELEBRITY MARKETING A form of person marketing in which the promotion of entertainers, sports figures, etc. is undertaken by managers, publicity directors, or agencies such as the William Morris Agency. In celebrity marketing, the goals of the marketing campaign are to create, maintain, or alter attitudes toward a particular celebrity or group of celebrities through media appearances, press coverage, and other publicity. See also *person marketing* and *political candidate marketing.*

CELEBRITY TESTIMONIAL A type of promotion in which big-name personalities are used to praise or recommend a particular product, service, idea, or institution. For example, retired professional athletes are often used in beer commercials. Similarly, the same professional athletes may be used to solicit contributions to a charity or to promote prosocial behavior such as not driving while intoxicated.

CELLER-KEFAUVER ANTI-MERGER ACT (1950) An amendment to the Clayton Act (1914); which prohibits the acquisition of any part of the assets of a competing company, as well as its stock, if such an acquisition would substantially lessen competition or tend to create a monopoly. Previously, only the acquisition of the stock of another firm was prohibited if it tended to reduce competition. The legislation was intended to prevent anticompetitive mergers. See also *Clayton Act (1914).*

CENSUS In marketing research, a census is a complete canvas of every member of a population (or universe) under study, as opposed to sampling. Also known as a population survey.

CENTRAL BUSINESS DISTRICT (CBD) In census terminology, central business district refers to that area of a city or town that contains a high concentration of retail businesses, offices, theaters, etc. CBDs are characterized by high traffic flow and often consist of one or more complete census tracts.

In a broader sense the central business district is a city's original retailing center; i.e., what is commonly referred to as downtown.

CENTRAL BUYING In large retail organizations, the concentration of the authority and responsibility for merchandise selection and purchase for a chain of stores or the branch stores of a department store in the hands of the headquarters staff rather than in the individual units. The central buying function is generally located in the flagship store.

CENTRAL MARKET A geographical area containing a large concentration of suppliers. The central market may be a merchandise mart or simply a cluster of suppliers in the same section of a city, such as the garment center in New York. Central markets provide convenient places where buyers and sellers can meet to exchange goods and services.

CENTRALIZED ORGANIZATION In organizational structures, a centralized organization is one in which control of the decision-making processes, power, and authority remains with the central, or parent, organization. For example: in a centralized retail organization, control would be in the hands of the headquarters or flagship store. In multinational marketing, a centralized organization implies that control remains with the parent company in its home country.

CENTRALIZATION See *centralized organization*

CENTS-OFF COUPON See *retailer coupon* and *coupon*

CENTS-OFF DEAL A form of price promotion in which particular consumer products are marked down and prominently labeled to indicate the number of cents reduction, the implication being that the reduction is from the regular retail price. A common practice in the grocery business.

CENTS-OFF OFFER See *cents-off deal*

CERTIFICATION MARK A word or symbol used to designate a product or service as being the holder of some particular certification as to quality, safety, etc. The mark of the Underwriters Laboratory is a common certification mark indicating that a product meets certain safety standards.

CG See *address coding guide*

CHAIN DEPARTMENT STORE See *department store*

CHAIN DISCOUNT See *series discount*

CHAIN PROSPECTING A method used by salespersons to gather new leads by obtaining additional names from current prospects. When the current prospect is a satisfied customer, the leads are called referral leads. Also called the endless chain method.

CHAIN STORE A single unit in a chain store system.

CHAIN STORE SYSTEM A group of stores, usually a dozen or more, commonly owned and centrally merchandised and managed. In the U.S., the largest chains are grocery and automobile service stations. The term has also come to be applied to large mass merchandising organizations (J.C. Penney, Sears), franchise chains (Burger King, McDonald's), and specialty chains (Lerner Shops, etc.). See also *voluntary chain.*

CHANNEL CAPTAIN The organization (usually a manufacturer or wholesaler, but sometimes a retailer) which dominates and controls a channel of distribution. The ability to assume this role is almost always based on economic power. The channel captain assumes leadership within the channel and often sets distribution policy.

CHANNEL CONFLICT In marketing, channel conflict is dissonance between two or more members at different levels of the channel (thus, vertical conflict). It is commonly found when one member of the channel, e.g., a dominant manufacturer, attempts to control the entire distribution system.

Horizontal channel conflict is found when there is dissonance (not to be confused with normal competition) between two or more members of a channel who are operating at the same level. For example, one retailer may feel that another is gaining unfair advantage by intimidating a supplier on which both depend. See also *intertype channel conflict.*

CHANNEL CONTROL See *channel power*

CHANNEL COOPERATION The positive interaction between all members of a channel of distribution, resulting in increased sales and profits for all participants. In general, it is up to the channel captain to win the voluntary cooperation of other channel members. The channel captain may accomplish this by providing advertising materials, training a middleman's sales force, giving financial advice to a channel member, etc. In retailing, retail channel captains assist manufacturers by providing information on consumer preferences and buying patterns. If the channel captain is unsuccessful in fostering voluntary cooperation, it may attempt to coerce its channel members into cooperation by such methods as exclusive dealing, tying agreements, full-line forcing, resale restrictions, reciprocity, price maintenance, price discrimination, and refusal to deal. However, many of these methods are, if not illegal, closely monitored and limited by government regulations. See also *channel of distribution.*

CHANNEL FIT In product marketing, channel fit refers to the degree to which a new product fits into existing channels of distribution. A product is said to have good channel fit when it is simply added to an existing line and does not require the opening up of another channel; e.g., a product which can be sold through the same wholesalers and retailers who handle the company's other products.

CHANNEL FLOWS The various members of a marketing channel (manufacturers/producers, distributors, retailers, customers, etc.) may be connected by one or more forms of movement called flows. These include: 1) physical flow—the actual movement of products or the delivery of services toward the customer; 2) title or ownership flow—the transfer of title to goods from one channel member to another; 3) financial or payment flow—the granting of credit downward in the channel and the movement of payments upward; 4) communication or information flow—includes such activities as the transfer of product information downward, personal selling efforts, and various promotional and advertising campaigns.

CHANNEL INTEGRATION See *vertical integration*

CHANNEL INTERDEPENDENCY A relationship among members of a channel of distribution in which the activities of one member may, to a considerable degree, influence the activities of others.

CHANNEL LEADER See *channel captain*

CHANNEL LEADERSHIP See *channel captain*

CHANNEL LENGTH The various levels of wholesaling middlemen and retailers, etc. taken as a whole. Consumer goods often go through a four-link channel (and sometimes five) employing both the wholesale and retail middlemen on their way from producer to consumer. Industrial goods generally go through fewer channels, as they are often sold directly by the producer to the industrial customer. The length of the channel is affected by the product market characteristics, company characteristics, and the economic environment. A financially strong company, in a healthy economic environment, favors short channels when producing high-priced goods aimed at a small number of customers. This channel length is particularly favorable because there are few legal restrictions impeding the marketing of goods. A financially weak company, in an unhealthy economic environment, favors long channels when producing low-priced goods targeted for mass consumption. This channel length, however, has many legal restrictions.

CHANNEL NUMBER The number of different marketing channels employed by a marketer. The number of different channels varies if the company is selling to entirely different markets or to different market segments. For example, a cosmetic manufacturer such as Revlon sells its high-priced line directly to department stores, but its low-priced products are sold through middlemen to drugstores. The number of channels also depends on geographic regions and the sizes of buyers.

CHANNEL OF DISTRIBUTION A channel of distribution is the route along which goods and services travel from producer/manufacturer through marketing intermediaries such as wholesalers, distributors, and retailers to the final user. A channel may thus be likened to a pipeline or pathway. The firms which participate in this exchange process may themselves be regarded as the distribution channel; i.e., the chain of institutions acting in concert and providing for the flow of goods and services. This flow may involve the physical movement of the product or simply the transfer of title to it. Also known as a distribution channel, a marketing channel, or a trade channel.

CHANNEL OF DISTRIBUTION

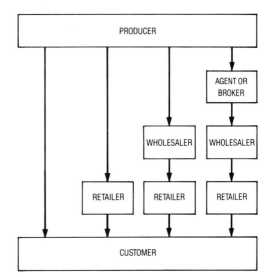

CHANNEL POWER The capacity to make other members of a channel of distribution conform to one's wishes. The member who exerts this power is called the channel captain or channel leader.

CHANNEL VISION A firm's view of the allocation of marketing functions among the members of a channel of distribution and its recognition of places in the channel where there are opportunities for improvement.

CHANNEL WIDTH The number of different outlets or individual firms employed at each level of the channel of distribution. Channel width may be intensive, selling through almost any available wholesale or retail outlet, or exclusive, selling through only one wholesaler or retailer in a given area. Prestige items, such as automobiles, appliances, etc. use exclusive distribution or selective distribution—the use of more than one but fewer than all the firms that might carry a product.

CHIEF MARKETING OFFICER (CMO) In large business organizations, a management level executive responsible for promoting the marketing perspective within the firm and for developing the firm's strategic marketing plan.

CHILD PROTECTION ACT (1966) Federal consumer legislation which banned the sale of hazardous toys and other items intended for use by children. Amended by the Child Protection and Toy Safety Act (1969).

CHILD PROTECTION AND TOY SAFETY ACT (1969) A federal consumer law designed to provide protection from dangerous children's toys, especially those posing electrical or thermal hazards. Updated and amended the Child Protection Act (1966).

CHINESE MARKETING A form of faulty reasoning (based largely on wishful thinking) in which a market is viewed as containing an unrealistically large number of potential customers. The underlying assumption is that the bigger the target market the better. The term comes from a book published in the 1930s by Carl Crow entitled *Four Hundred Million Customers* in which the author claimed that the Great Depression could be ended if the U.S. could simply sell some product to each of the then 400 million Chinese.

CHOICE CRITERIA Those critical attributes employed by a purchaser when evaluating merchandise offered for sale. Among criteria commonly used are convenience of retail outlet, price, quality, etc.

CIA See *cash in advance*

CIF (COST, INSURANCE, AND FREIGHT) A shipping term meaning that the seller of goods pays the cost of transporting the goods to their shipping point (dock, railroad platform, etc.), pays the charges incurred in loading the goods on the conveyance employed, and finally, pays all insurance and transportation costs to the goods' destination. The buyer pays landing costs and all charges incurred in unloading as well as any duties or taxes levied by the importing country.

CIGARETTE LABELING AND PROTECTION ACT (1967) See *Federal Cigarette Labeling and Protection Act (1967)*

CIRCULATION In the print media, circulation refers to the number of copies of a single issue of a magazine or newspaper which are offered for sale or distributed free. Because circulation implies that someone has looked at the publication, the figure for circulation will always be lower than the actual number printed, as a certain percentage of each issue never reaches a reader.

CIRCULATION (PASS-ALONG) See *passalong rate*

CIRCULATION WASTE See *waste circulation*

C.L. FREIGHT RATE See *carload freight rate (C.L.)*

CLASS See *social class*

CLASS RATE The standard rate, established by government regulation, for shipping various commodities. These rates were originally established to guarantee fair prices to all users of both common and contract carriers and to avoid the abuses of railroad shipping prevalent in the 19th century. Class rates are established for shipping certain categories of goods between two geographical points, with distance and weight determining the rate. In general, the greater the distance and the greater the weight, the lower the rate. Conversely, the shorter the distance and the less the weight, the higher the rate. Both commodity rates and exception rates may be used as substitutes for the class rate where appropriate and where allowable by law. See also *commodity rate* and *exception rate*.

CLASSICAL FUNCTIONALISM A strategy in which marketing functions (classically there are eight: buying, selling, transporting, storing, standardizing and grading, financing, risk bearing, and collecting and disseminating marketing information) are viewed as discrete tasks; i.e., they are not integrated into a comprehensive marketing program.

CLASSIFICATION MERCHANDISING In retailing, classification merchandising is the practice of planning the breadth of an assortment on the basis of related types or classifications of merchandise. Data reporting is then controlled by these classifications. The theory behind this practice is that small, homogeneous classes of merchandise are preferable for purposes of control.

CLASSIFIED ADVERTISING In newspapers and magazines, classified advertising refers to those ads placed in special columns arranged by type of product or service. The format and typefaces used in these columns are generally fairly uniform. See also *display advertising*.

CLAYTON ACT (1914) Federal legislation intended to delineate and define acts considered unlawful restraints of trade. The Act outlawed discrimination in prices, exclusive and tying contracts, intercorporate stockholding, and interlocking directorates, where their effect would be to substantially lessen competition and create a monopoly. As such, the Act supplemented the Sherman Antitrust Act (1890). The Act further stipulated that corporate officials found to be in violation of its provisions would be held individually responsible. Labor and agricultural organizations are exempt from the provision of the Act. The Clayton Act was later amended by the Celler-Kefauver Antimerger Act (1950).

CLEARANCE MARKDOWN See *markdown*

CLIENT PUBLIC Those persons who are the direct recipients of the services and products provided by nonprofit organizations.

CLOSE See *closing*

CLOSE OUT See *closeout*

CLOSE RATE The number of actual sales made by a salesperson divided by the number of calls made to potential customers. This is one factor used in the evaluation of salespersons, since it indicates the proportion of successful sales or closings. See also *closing*.

CLOSED BID See *sealed bid*

CLOSED-DOOR DISCOUNT HOUSE A retailer selling goods to consumers who, by virtue of place of employment, membership in a union, or other affiliation, are regarded as "members." Closed-door discount houses charge prices as much as 40% below those found in department stores and depend on high volume and low overhead to make a profit. They carry nationally branded, high quality merchandise for which there is strong consumer demand. Also known as a membership club or wholesale club.

CLOSED SALES TERRITORY See *exclusive distribution*

CLOSED TERRITORY See *exclusive distribution*

CLOSEOUT An offering of selected discontinued goods by the vendor to the retailer at reduced prices. This merchandise has been discontinued because of slow sales, a broken assortment, overstock, the need to make space for a new season, etc. The savings are often passed along to the consumer as a closeout sale, used to generate increased store traffic.

CLOSER See *T.O. man*

CLOSING The step in the sales process when the salesperson must ask the customer to conclude the purchase. Closing techniques include asking for the order, recapitulating the points of the agreement, offering to help write up the order, or indicating what the buyer will lose if the order is not placed immediately. Alternatively, the salesperson may offer some incentive to the buyer, such as a special price or an extra quantity of the goods in question at no extra charge.

CLOSING TECHNIQUE See *closing*

CLOSING THE SALE See *closing*

CLUSTER ANALYSIS See *clustering techniques*

CLUSTER SAMPLE See *area sampling*

CLUSTERING TECHNIQUES In the analysis of marketing research data, clustering techniques are methods used to find usable patterns within sets of data. Patterns may be established for such factors as demographic data, customer attitudes, psychographic data, and purchasing behavior. Using a computer, researchers attempt to search the data for homogeneous groups of people, and then proceed to analyze the data in search of new or improved marketing strategies.

CLUTTER In advertising, clutter (the crowding together of advertising messages in the print and electronic media) results in a loss of advertising effectiveness. Advertisers may avoid clutter by buying more time or reserving more space in the media used. They may also pay a premium for positioning their advertisements in such a way as to avoid clutter. For example, in magazine advertising, the inside front cover is considered a less cluttered position for an ad. Advertisers may also select those media that minimize clutter, refuse to accept piggyback ads, or otherwise regulate the amount of advertising and, hence, the amount of clutter.

CMO See *chief marketing officer*

CMSA See *Consolidated Metropolitan Statistical Area (CMSA)*

C.O.D. See *cash on delivery (C.O.D)*

CODING In market research data analysis, the translation of gathered information into a form (usually numerical) which can be more readily analyzed.

CODING PROCESS See *encoding*

COEFFICIENT OF ELASTICITY See *elasticity of demand*

COEFFICIENT OF INCOME SENSITIVITY A comparison between a product's percentage variation in sales over a number of years and a 1% change in personal disposable income. Used to forecast the effect of a 1% change in available discretionary funds on a product's sales.

COEFFICIENT OF MULTIPLE CORRELATION See *multiple correlation*

COERCIVE RECIPROCITY See *reciprocity*

COGNITION See *cognitive processes*

COGNITIVE COMPONENT In attitude research, particularly in the tripartite view or structural approach, the cognitive component is the knowledge and beliefs a consumer has about a product or service, including evaluative beliefs. It is the intellectual component of attitude. See also *attitude* and *conative component.*

COGNITIVE CONSONANCE The opposite of cognitive dissonance, cognitive consonance is the feeling of satisfaction experienced by a customer at the point of, or immediately following, a decision to purchase. The customer has a feeling of well-being and the sense that the correct decision has been made.

COGNITIVE DISSONANCE Doubt and anxiety suffered by a customer at the point of, or immediately following, a decision to purchase. This dissonance is the result of a conflict between two or more of the purchaser's cognitions (beliefs or perceptions) regarding the purchased product.

COGNITIVE JUDGMENT See *cognitive component* and *cognitive processes*

COGNITIVE PROCESSES Those mental activities which involve thought and reasoning, as, for example, learning and judging.

COHORTS In the study of demographics, cohorts are the members of each of the various age groups that make up the total population.

COLD CALL See *cold canvassing*

COLD CANVASSING Door-to-door or telephone solicitation of orders for merchandise without the benefit of leads or prior appointments.

COLD STORAGE WAREHOUSE A form of public warehouse designed for the storage of perishables requiring refrigeration. For example, butter, furs, and meat products are generally stored in cold storage warehouses. See also *public warehouse.*

COLGATE DOCTRINE (1919) A Supreme Court decision which held that a seller can unilaterally decide the terms under which goods will be sold and can, therefore, refuse to sell to those who do not meet those terms. Intended to curtail the activities of known price-cutting retailers such as discount houses and catalog retailers, its effects have been mitigated in recent years by subsequent decisions. Nevertheless, the basic thrust of the Colgate Doctrine was incorporated into the Robinson-Pathman Act.

COLLECT ON DELIVERY See *Cash On Delivery (C.O.D.)*

COLLEY, RUSSEL H. See *Dagmar*

COLLUSION The coming together of two or more parties in a secret understanding or agreement to the detriment of one or more other parties. Restraint of trade agreements commonly involve collusion.

COLLUSIVE PRICING See *horizontal price fixing*

COMBINATION DRUG STORE See *combo store*

COMBINATION HOUSE A middleman organization which serves the wholesale, retail, and institutional markets.

COMBINATION OFFER A form of consumer fraud involving the sale of a product at a low price tied to the purchase of a continuing service. The sale of food freezers tied to the purchase of frozen foods is a notorious example as the food is frequently of inferior quality.

COMBINATION STORE See *combo store*

COMBINATION SUPERMARKET See *combo store*

COMBINATIONS IN RESTRAINT OF TRADE See *restraint of trade*

COMBINED TARGET MARKET APPROACH A method of market segmentation in which two or more distinct market segments are combined into one larger target market. A single marketing strategy is then used to appeal to the larger group. Combiners, i.e., firms adopting this method, do so in an attempt to increase the size of their target markets, to gain certain economies of scale, to minimize their risks, or to allocate limited resources economically. They try to extend or modify their basic offering to appeal to these combined customers, and rely heavily on promotion to convince each sub-segment that the product will satisfy its needs. See also *market segmentation.*

COMBINER See *combined target market approach*

COMBO STORE 1) An outgrowth of the supermarket, the combo store has a significantly larger share of floor space devoted to higher margin general merchandise. The combo store, although retaining many aspects of the supermarket is, in fact, an incipient full-line discount store. 2) An outgrowth of the large drugstore in which general merchandise is combined with drugs and health and beauty care products. Sometimes called a combination store.

COMMERCIAL 1) Relating to trade, commerce, stores, office buildings, as well as other business activities and properties. 2) A paid advertisement appearing in the broadcast media of radio and television.

COMMERCIAL BRIBERY The illegal attempt to influence business decision-making by offering gifts or favors to the person charged with making the decision.

COMMERCIAL MARKETING The application of marketing strategies, concepts, and techniques to profit-making endeavors as distinct from their use in the nonprofit sector.

COMMERCIAL NAME See *trade name*

COMMERCIAL TRAVELER See *traveling salesperson*

COMMERCIALIZATION The final stage in new product development in which a manufacturer is committed to the production of a new product.

COMMISSARY STORE 1) A store operated by the military (and commonly staffed by civilian employees) for the benefit of military personnel and their dependents. 2) A store operated by a large employer for the benefit of its employees.

Commissary stores generally sell food products and other supplies at prices substantially below those on the open market. Also known as company stores.

COMMISSION A method of compensation in which payments are directly tied to the sales and/or profits achieved by the salesperson. Typically, the salesperson receives a percentage of sales as salary. This is the commission. Various combinations of salary and commissions may be used. In the "salary-plus-commission" method of compensation, the employee receives a straight salary plus a percentage of total sales during a specified period. "Straight commission" denotes a fixed or sliding percentage rate related to the salesperson's sales or profit volume with no straight salary. This method is prominent in the insurance and the securities investment industries. See also *straight commission*

COMMISSION AGENT See *commission merchant*

COMMISSION BUYING OFFICE See *resident buying office*

COMMISSION HOUSE See *commission merchant*

COMMISSION MAN See *commission merchant*

COMMISSION MERCHANT An agent middleman who, although he often has physical control over the goods he sells, does not take title to them. Commission merchants most commonly represent the sellers of such agricultural products as grain, livestock, and produce, which are usually accepted on consignment. They have the authority to negotiate prices and terms of sale on behalf of their principal and may arrange delivery, extend credit, make collections, etc. In this respect the commission merchant has more freedom than the broker.

COMMISSION ON SALES See *commission*

COMMISSION WITH DRAW A method of compensation for salespeople in which payments are based on a percentage of sales but in which regular payments are made from an ac-

count set aside for that purpose (the draw).

COMMITTEE BUYING Purchasing activities collectively performed by a group of buyers on behalf of a multi-unit operation. See also *buying committee.*

COMMODITY Although the term is imprecise, commodities are generally agricultural or mineral products, e.g., wheat, cattle, eggs, cotton, orange juice, silver, hides, coffee, lumber, etc. Occasionally the term may be applied to manufactured goods, but never to services.

COMMODITY APPROACH TO MARKETING An approach to the study of marketing in which the movement of goods from producer to consumer is viewed as a key to understanding the marketing process.

COMMODITY EXCHANGE A nonprofit organization which provides members with a place in which commodities are traded, either among themselves or for others, on a commission basis. The exchange does not engage in buying or selling, but does make and enforce rules and may adjust disputes among member-traders.

COMMODITY PRODUCTS Those products of basic industry which, although they may carry brand names, are not clearly distinguishable from one another in the public eye, e.g., tires, bearings, steel, electronic components, etc.

COMMODITY RATE An allowable deviation from the class rate charged by shippers to their customers. The reduced commodity rate may be awarded to the customer for regular use or for the size of the quantity shipped. However, the commodity rate is still subject to government regulation. See also *class rate* and *exception rate.*

COMMON CARRIER A transportation firm (rail, truck, barge, etc.) engaged in shipping merchandise. Common carriers operate on regular schedules over established routes, charge published standard rates, and are available to all shippers. All are subject to one or more forms of government regulation. See also *contract carrier* and *private carrier.*

COMMON COST See *indirect cost*

COMMON MARKET An association of countries who have reduced or eliminated the trade barriers which existed between them and are parties that share a common external tariff agreement. In addition, common markets generally provide for the free flow of labor and capital from country to country. See also *European Economic Community (EEC).*

COMMUNICATION See *communication process*

COMMUNICATION ADAPTATION A strategy employed in international trade in which a company exports the same products that it manufactures for the domestic market but changes the advertising and other promotional messages which accompany them in the foreign market.

COMMUNICATION PROCESS A process consisting of five components: 1) a source (or sender), 2) an encoding process in which the message is put into a transmittable form, 3) transmission of the message, 4) a decoding process at which time the message is translated into a comprehensible form, and 5) the reception of the message at its destination.

COMMUNICATION PROCESS

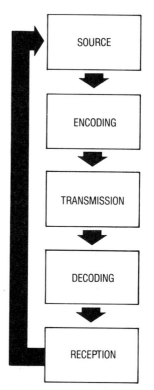

COMMUNICATIONS ACT (1934) See *Federal Communications Commission (FCC)*

COMMUNICATOR See *sender*

COMMUNISM See *economic system*

COMMUNITY SHOPPING CENTER A medium-sized shopping center generally anchored by a variety and/or junior department store and complemented by as many as 50 smaller retail stores and related businesses. Most community shopping centers have a gross leasable area of between 100,000 and 300,000 square feet and require a surrounding population of at least 50,000 to operate profitably. The radius of attraction extends to approximately 10–15 minutes of drive time.

COMPANY DEMAND See *sales potential*

COMPANY IMAGE See *mission identity*

COMPANY MARKETING ENVIRONMENT See *marketing environment*

COMPANY MARKETING OPPORTUNITY A niche in a market perceived by a company as having sales potential.

COMPANY PLANNING See *strategic planning*

COMPANY SALES POTENTIAL See *sales potential*

COMPANY STORE See *commissary store*

COMPARATIVE ADVANTAGE A theory of international marketing in which a country is said to have a comparative advantage when it can produce certain goods (or, for that matter, all goods) more cheaply than another country. In terms of actual trade, however, it is to each individual country's advantage to specialize in the production of those goods which it produces most advantageously; i.e., in which it has a relative advantage, and not in the production of *all* goods. In other words, it is not necessary for a country to have an absolute advantage in order to profitably engage in international trade.

COMPARATIVE ADVERTISING A form of competitive advertising in which specific brands are named and compared in terms of their specific characteristics and attributes. The objective is to demonstrate the superiority of the advertised product. Also known as comparison advertising.

COMPARATIVE COST ADVANTAGE See *comparative advantage*

COMPARATIVE MARKETING In international marketing, the study of the differences and similarities between various national systems regarding supply and demand as well as distribution.

COMPARE-A-PRICE See *unit pricing*

COMPARISON ADVERTISING See *comparative advertising*

COMPARISON SHOPPING A retail trade practice in which one retailer obtains information about his competitor's activities by sending a comparison shopper to the store. Comparison shopping may be carried on by an outside agency organized for that purpose or by the store's own comparison department.

COMPENSATION See *sales compensation*

COMPENSATION DEAL In international marketing, a form of countertrade in which payments are partly in the form of currency and partly in the form of goods.

COMPETITION Although competition may take a number of forms, in its marketing context it is a form of business activity in which two or more parties are engaged in a rivalry for customer acceptance. See also *price competition, monopolistic competition, oligopolistic competition, perfect competition,* and *pure monopoly.*

COMPETITIVE ADVANTAGE A position of superiority one firm may establish over its competitors in the marketplace. The four Ps of marketing are all possible avenues to a firm's finding itself in a favorable marketing situation. See also *four Ps of marketing.*

COMPETITIVE ADVERTISING Advertising which features specific brands rather than broad product categories and which is intended to motivate the consumer to buy the particular product. Also called selective advertising.

COMPETITIVE BID See *sealed bid* and *open bid*

COMPETITIVE BIDDING See *sealed bid* and *open bid*

COMPETITIVE EDGE See *competitive advantage*

COMPETITIVE ENVIRONMENT To any company in the marketplace, the competitive environment is the sum total of other firms marketing products similar to or substitutable for the company's own. For example, to a marketer of sugar, the competitive environment would include all other companies marketing sugar as well as those marketing artificial sweeteners.

COMPETITIVE MONOPOLY See *differentiated oligopoly*

COMPETITIVE PARITY APPROACH TO PROMOTIONAL BUDGETING See *competitive-parity method*

COMPETITIVE-PARITY METHOD An approach to promotional budgeting in which a firm's expenditures are set in proportion to what it believes the competition is spending. The competitive-parity method is widely regarded as a defensive strategy.

COMPETITIVE PARITY TECHNIQUE See *competitive-parity method*

COMPETITIVE SELL See *comparative advertising*

COMPETITIVE STAGE See *maturity stage*

COMPLEMENTARY DEMAND See *joint demand*

COMPLEMENTARY GOODS See *complementary product*

COMPLEMENTARY PRODUCT A product which is accessory to or which in some way supplements another product as, for example, software supplements a computer. See also *accessory equipment.*

COMPLETE SEGMENTATION A form of market segmentation in which each potential customer is treated as an individual rather than as part of an aggregation because each is seen as identifiably distinct from all others. See also *custom marketing.*

COMPLIMENT APPROACH See *praise (or compliment) approach*

COMPONENT PARTS See *fabricating parts*

COMPUTERIZED SHOPPING See *electronic retailing*

CONATIVE COMPONENT In attitude research, particularly in the tripartite view or structural approach, the conative component is the readiness of an individual to purchase a particular product or service or take some other action. It is the active component of attitude. For example, the customer may be very, somewhat, or not at all likely to buy a Honda Civic, take a vacation in the Middle East, or participate in anti-nuclear power plant demonstrations. See also *attitude,* and *cognitive component.*

CONATIVE JUDGMENT See *conative component*

CONCENTRATED MARKETING A marketing strategy in which a firm's resources are devoted to capturing a large share of a narrow market segment.

CONCENTRATION See *assembling*

CONCENTRATION APPROACH See *concentrated marketing*

CONCEPT STATEMENT See *product concept*

CONCEPT TESTING An early stage in the product development process, concept testing attempts to determine consumer reaction to new product concepts before large amounts of money are committed to their production. Typically, potential customers are shown pictures of proposed products and are asked to react to them.

CONCLUSIVE RESEARCH Research studies, often based on such methods as surveys, observation, simulation, and experimentation, which generate large quantities of reliable data. Firms often employ conclusive research in an effort to solve specific problems and employ its results as a basis for decision making.

CONCLUSIVE STUDIES See *conclusive research*

CONDITIONAL SALE See *conditional sales contract*

CONDITIONAL SALES CONTRACT A retail installment contract which requires the buyer to pay monthly payments to a retailer or other creditor. The retailer retains title of ownership until all payments have been made, so that merchandise may be repossessed whenever the buyer fails to meet the terms of the contract. If the repossessed item is resold, the resale price is credited to the customer's balance, but the customer remains liable for the remainder of the balance due.

CONFIDENCE INTERVAL In random sampling, a confidence interval is the range on either side of an estimate which is most likely to contain the actual value with some stated percentage of certainty. The size of the sample determines the percentage of certainty. For example, if a sample of 100 were taken in a random sample concerning a new brand of mouthwash and it was found that 10 percent of the sample preferred the new mouthwash over existing brands, then it may be stated (with 95% certainty) that between 4 and 16 percent of the population actually prefers the new mouthwash.

CONFINED MERCHANDISE In retailing, merchandise sold by a producer or distributor to a limited number of stores so that, in effect, each retailer has exclusive resale rights in his trading area.

CONFISCATION 1) In international marketing, the seizure of foreign owned property by a government without provision for reimbursement of the owners. 2) The seizure of private property by a government, often as a penalty.

CONGLOMERATE See *conglomerate merger*

CONGLOMERATE INTEGRATION See *conglomerate merger*

CONGLOMERATE MERGER A merger of two or more corporations in unrelated industries, such as a cosmetics manufacturer and a children's clothing manufacturer. The two firms need not be on the same level of the channel of distribution. For example, an apparel manufacturer may merge with a retail store, or a car rental agency may merge with a food manufacturer. The companies involved undertake the merger in order to provide a diversity of operations for eachother and to protect their profits from economic fluctuations.

CONGLOMERCHANT See *merchandising conglomerate*

CONGRUENT INNOVATION The development of products which, because they are so slightly changed, are virtually identical to their antecedents. They frequently differ only in terms of higher or lower quality or in that they incorporate a relatively insignificant new feature. Congruent innovation almost never disrupts existing consumptive patterns.

CONJOINT ANALYSIS See *conjoint measurement*

CONJOINT MEASUREMENT A measurement tool used in product planning in which product attributes are analyzed in an effort to determine which are most attractive to potential customers. Also known as benefit structure analysis and trade-off analysis.

CONSCIOUS LEVEL (OF NEED AWARENESS) See *need awareness*

CONSCIOUS PARALLELISM Identical or similar actions taken by two or more firms in the market, especially regarding price changes, which may be seen as collusion. See also *price leader.*

CONSENSUS A judgmental technique for forecasting business results, which is based on the combined opinions of groups of individuals.

CONSIGNEE See *consignment*

CONSIGNMENT Merchandise shipped by a producer to a distributor or retailer with the understanding that the producer retains title to the goods until they are sold. Consignment sales offer the producer the opportunity to control its terms of resale and help overcome dealer resistance to the product.

CONSIGNMENT BUYING See *consignment*

CONSIGNMENT SALES See *consignment*

CONSIGNMENT TERMS See *consignment*

CONSIGNOR See *consignment*

CONSISTENCY OF PRODUCT MIX A firm's product mix has three attributes: width, depth, and consistency. A firm's lines are said to be consistent when they share certain common characteristics such as similar end use, shared distribution channels, common production facilities, etc.

CONSOLIDATED BUYING See *central buying*

CONSOLIDATED METROPOLITAN STATISTICAL AREA (CMSA) Large metropolitan complexes within which individual components, designated as PMSAs, have been defined. These components exhibit a high degree of integration as do, for example, Dade and Broward counties in Florida, which form a PMSA. See also *Metropolitan Statistical Area (MSA)* and *Primary Metropolitan Statistical Area (PMSA).*

CONSORTIA In international marketing, a partnership arrangement similar to the joint venture with the exception that it typically involves a large number of participants and functions in a market in which it was not previously involved. Consortia help to bring together financing and spread risk among more participants.

CONSPICUOUS CONSUMPTION See *veblen goods*

CONSPIRACY IN RESTRAINT OF TRADE See *restraint of trade*

CONSTANT COST See *fixed costs*

CONSTANT DOLLARS A dollar amount modified so that the effects of inflation have been removed. A base year is selected and all subsequent calculations and comparisons are relative to the dollar value in that year. All the resultant dollar values are then constant and comparable. Used in time series analysis, other statistical series, and economics.

CONSTRAINED DECISION MAKING Limitations imposed upon the decision-making discretion of a business, especially as a result of franchise agreements.

CONSUMER See *ultimate consumer*

CONSUMER ADVERTISING Advertising directed to the ultimate consumer, i.e., the general public.

CONSUMER ADVOCATE One who speaks for or represents the interests of the consuming public, particularly with respect to social, economic, and ecological matters.

CONSUMER ANALYSIS See *consumer research*

CONSUMER BEHAVIOR The actions of consumers in the marketplace and the underlying motives for those actions. Marketers expect that by understanding what causes consumers to buy particular goods and services they will be able to determine which products are needed in the marketplace, which are obsolete, and how best to present those goods to the consumer. See also *consumer research.*

CONSUMER BILL OF RIGHTS (1962) Principles stated by President Kennedy in 1962, which outlined the rights consumers should expect from the marketplace and thereby provided the framework for much subsequent consumer legislation. As stated by Kennedy, the consumer is entitled to be safe from injury, to be correctly informed about products, to have a proper forum in which to be heard when problems and complaints arise, to have a choice in the selection of goods and/or services, and to have a voice in the decision-making process through which goods and/or services become available in the marketplace.

CONSUMER CONTEST See *contest*

CONSUMER COOPERATIVE A retail operation owned by its customers and usually incorporated on the basis of one vote for each customer-member. Merchandise is commonly sold at the prevailing market price and profits are divided among the customer-members in proportion to their patronage of the store.

CONSUMER CREDIT The ability of individual consumers to obtain money, goods, or revenues on the strength of their promise to pay at some specified time in the future, generally in installments. Such purchases are thus referred to as being on "time."

CONSUMER CREDIT PROTECTION ACT (1968) A federal statute, passed in 1969 and amended in 1970, which requires finance companies, banks, retailers, and other grantors of consumer credit to reveal to the consumer the true cost of credit, both in terms of annual percentage rates and dollar amounts. The legislation was designed to allow consumers to compare competing sources of credit. The 1970 amendment protects the holder of credit cards from liability if the cards are fraudulently used. Commonly referred to as the Truth-in-Lending Act.

CONSUMER DEAL See *deal*

CONSUMER DECISION PROCESS See *adoption process*

CONSUMER DEMAND The level of desire for goods coupled with the ability to purchase these same goods.

Most frequently applied to the ultimate consumer, but may include industrial, governmental, and institutional customers as well. See also *demand.*

CONSUMER DEMOGRAPHICS Vital statistics of the consuming population including size, age, sex, birth and death rates, location, income, race, education, etc.

CONSUMER DIARY A booklet in which each member of a representative sample of consumers records what he or she is actually viewing on television and/or listening to on radio for one week. The consumers are also asked to provide information about their age, sex, occupation, etc. Use of the consumer diary is intended to give advertisers insight into the make-up of the broadcast media audience.

CONSUMER EFFICIENCY See *theory of consumer efficiency*

CONSUMER GOODS Goods produced for the ultimate consumer and nearly always sold at the retail level. These products are for personal, nonbusiness use and may fall into one of three categories: 1) convenience items (milk, cigarettes, magazines, etc.), 2) shopping items (apparel, automobiles, etc.), or 3) specialty items (gourmet foods, etc.)

CONSUMER GOODS PRICING ACT (1975) Federal legislation that halted all interstate usage of resale price maintenance agreements. This law ended many of the so-called "fair trade" agreements among producers and distributors involved in interstate commerce.

CONSUMER INNOVATOR See *innovator*

CONSUMER JURY See *consumer panel*

CONSUMER LAWS Legislation enacted on the local, state, or national level to protect consumers from unscrupulous business practices. On the federal level in the United States, these laws include the Kefauver-Harris Drug Amendments to the Food and Drug Act (1962), the Wholesome Meat Act (1967), the National Traffic and Motor Vehicle Safety Act (1966), the Child Protection and Toy Safety Act (1969), the Federal Hazardous Substances Labeling Act (1960), the Fair Labeling and Packaging Act (1966), the Consumer Protection Credit Act (1968), the Consumer Product Safety Act (1972), and the Equal Credit Opportunity Act (1976) among many others.

CONSUMER LEGISLATION See *consumer laws*

CONSUMER MARKET The consumer market consists of persons who purchase goods and services for their own use or for the use of persons in their household; i.e., they do not resell the purchased product nor do they use it in some other business enterprise.

CONSUMER MOTIVATION The driving force in an individual that impels him to act in the marketplace. It may be positive or negative depending on how he perceives his needs and goals. See also *motive.*

CONSUMER PANEL In marketing research, a group of individuals brought together for the purpose of determining consumer preferences with regard to products or ideas. The panel members are interviewed collectively and their expressed opinions are tabulated for use in new product development, etc.

CONSUMER-PERCEIVED RISK A consumer's perception of the possible effects, mostly negative, of an incorrect purchase decision. Includes functional risk, physical risk, financial risk, social risk, and psychological risk.

CONSUMER PREMIUM See *premium*

CONSUMER PRICE INDEX (CPI) A measure of the changes in the retail prices of a representative "market basket" of goods and services purchased for day-to-day living by urban consumers. 1967 is the index base year, with current prices expressed in relation to that year. The items making up the "market basket" are of constant quality and quantity. The CPI, which is issued monthly by the U.S. Bureau of Labor Statistics, is limited to measuring the effect of selected price changes on the cost of living, and is not a true cost of living index, which would measure such variables as the total amount families spend to live, how price fluctuations effect the standard of living, or the relative difference in the cost of living between geographic areas. The consumer price index is sometimes called the retail price index or, inaccurately, the cost of living index.

CONSUMER PRODUCT SAFETY ACT (1972) Federal legislation which established the Consumer Product Safety Commission (CPSC). The act stipulates that manufacturers must notify the Commission within 24 hours of discovering that they have produced and sold a product which represents a substantial hazard to consumers. A recall procedure must be instituted by the manufacturer to correct the defect. The Act grants the Commission jurisdiction over most consumer products, the exceptions being those already regulated by another agency such as the Food and Drug Administration. The Commission is authorized to protect con-

sumers by setting standards for product safety, testing products, investigating consumer complaints about defective products, banning dangerous products, and monitoring injuries received from those products. In recent years, such products as cribs for infants have been recalled by the Commission for presenting hazardous defects. See also *Consumer Product Safety Act (1972)*.

CONSUMER PRODUCT SAFETY COMMISSION (CPSC) See *Consumer Product Safety Act (1972)*

CONSUMER PRODUCT SAFETY COMMISSION IMPROVEMENTS ACT (1976) An amendment to the Consumer Product Safety Act (1972) intended to improve the effectiveness of the Commission by providing standards, enforceability, litigation procedures, and funding. See also *Consumer Product Safety Act (1972)*.

CONSUMER PRODUCTS See *consumer goods*

CONSUMER RESEARCH The study of the ultimate consumer to determine the factors that influence purchase decisions involving time, money, and effort in the consumption of goods and services. Consumer behavior includes the related studies of demography, sociology, anthropology, and psychology. Marketers look to consumer research to help them identify their target markets and determine how to market their goods and/or services to those target markets most efficiently. See also *marketing research*.

CONSUMER RIGHTS See *Consumer Bill of Rights (1962)*

CONSUMER RISK See *consumer-perceived risk*

CONSUMER SOCIALIZATION The process by which consumers' form attitudes and opinions within the context of the society around them and develop the skills necessary to become consumers within that society. The process is an on-going one, beginning in childhood and continuing throughout life.

CONSUMER SOVEREIGNTY A concept in marketing in which the consumer is seen as the final arbiter in the marketplace, having the power to decide which products will be successful and which will fail.

CONSUMER STIMULANTS Various promotions and incentives employed to attract the consumer and to stimulate demand. Consumer stimulants may take the form of free samples delivered to the home, cents-off deals and premiums offered at retail, contests and sweepstakes, and other promotional activities.

CONSUMER SURPLUS The difference, as perceived by a consumer, between the value of a purchase and the price he pays for it. A consumer surplus exists if the consumer feels he is getting more than his money's worth and if he would even be willing to pay a somewhat higher price for the same goods.

CONSUMERISM A social movement stemming from the efforts of consumers to promote and protect their own interests in the marketplace. Sometimes organized, sometimes not, these efforts center upon concern for the consumer's rights to safety, information, fair pricing, truthful advertising, and quality control.

CONSUMERS' COOPERATIVE See *consumer cooperative*

CONSUMER'S DECISION PROCESS See *adoption process*

CONSUMER'S SURPLUS See *consumer surplus*

CONSUMPTION PATTERNS The patterns in which consumers use, or do not use, a product. Consumption patterns are commonly employed as a basis for market segmentation.

CONTAINER PREMIUM Packaging for goods which is reusable for another purpose, thus serving as an added inducement for the consumer to purchase the goods. For example, coffee sold in reusable cannisters or wine sold in bottles which can later be used as carafes.

CONTAINERIZATION The consolidation of a number of smaller packages or boxes into a larger standardized container which can be sealed at its point of origin and shipped unopened to its destination. Containerized freight is subject to less damage and pilferage than loose cargo and is cheaper to handle.

CONTAINERIZED FREIGHT See *containerization*

CONTENT LABEL A tag or label affixed in conformance with the requirements of the Federal wool, fur, or textile fiber products acts intended to protect the consumer against the misbranding, mislabeling, and false advertising of furs and other textile products.

CONTEST A sales promotion device in which the participant competes for prizes by submitting an entry which requires a degree of skill or judgment to prepare, e.g., a statement or jingle. Unlike games and sweepstakes, the element of pure chance is eliminated in contests. See also *game* and *sweepstake*.

CONTINGENCY PRICING A payment plan in which a service organization does not receive payment for services performed until the customer's satisfaction can be assured.

CONTINUITY In advertising, the flow of advertising messages over a period of time. In some respects continuity is like a schedule or plan in that it provides some control over the spacing and frequency of ads.

CONTINUITY SERIES In direct marketing, a multi-part product such as a set of books, which is shipped one part at a time to the customer.

CONTINUOUS DEMAND The need and/or desire for goods or services which remains stable for a prolonged time period. See also *demand*.

CONTINUOUS INNOVATION A continuing process by which new products are developed and introduced into the marketplace. Rather than representing some new departure, these new products commonly were already in production and have been slightly altered or improved.

CONTRABAND Merchandise which is forbidden by law to be imported or exported, but which is sometimes smuggled into a country and unlawfully sold.

CONTRACT An agreement between two or more parties which is generally set forth in writing and is enforceable by law. The legality of any contract depends on the following factors: 1) a lawful promise; 2) competent parties; 3) an offer and its acceptance; 4) agreement. The contract must be in writing if it involves a certain amount of money (as determined by the state) or if it extends for more than one year.

CONTRACT CARRIER A transportation company which ships goods for one or more clients on the basis of a legal or business agreement. Unlike the common carrier, the contract carrier does not maintain regularly

scheduled routes. See also *common carrier* and *private carrier*.

CONTRACT FARMING A contractual arrangement between farmers and middlemen or manufacturers in which the farmer receives supplies and/or working capital and the manufacturers or middlemen agree to purchase the farmer's crop, sometimes at a guaranteed price.

CONTRACT HAULER See *contract carrier*

CONTRACT MANUFACTURING 1) In international marketing, a form of joint venture in which a foreign company contracts with local manufacturers in the host country to produce a product. See also *joint venture*. 2) A business arrangement in which one manufacturer produces goods for another manufacturer, a practice common in the apparel industry.

CONTRACT WAREHOUSE A storage facility which combines public and private warehousing services. It is like a public warehouse in that it serves a variety of customers. It differs from a public warehouse, however, in that the arrangements are long term rather than on a month by month basis. The contracts may also include special warehouse services such as packaging or assembly. It provides the stability of a private warehouse, therefore, through long-term leases and special services. Independently owned and operated. See also *public warehouse* and *private warehouse*.

CONTRACTUAL CHANNEL SYSTEM See *contractual vertical marketing system*

CONTRACTUAL VERTICAL MARKETING SYSTEM A system in which independent channel members at two or more levels have entered into formal agreements to coordinate their marketing efforts in an attempt to take advantage of the economies of scale. Contractual vertical marketing systems are generally of three types: 1) voluntary chains, 2) retail cooperatives, and 3) franchise operations. See also *corporate vertical marketing system* and *administered vertical marketing system.*

CONTRACTUAL VMS See *contractual vertical marketing system*

CONTRACYCLICAL PRICING A pricing strategy which runs counter to the usual economic cycle in that during periods of prosperity the firm increases production and reduces prices (because of the high level of demand), and during an economic downturn, reduces production and increases prices (because of reduced demand).

CONTRIBUTION In marketing cost analysis and break-even analysis, contribution generally means the sum of money generated by sales after variable costs have been subtracted. The term may also be applied to the amount of money a unit in a firm contributes toward discharging the firm's overall fixed costs.

CONTRIBUTION-MARGIN APPROACH TO COST ANALYSIS In marketing cost analysis, an accounting system in which only direct expenses are charged to each marketing unit within a firm. The term contribution refers to the amount of money contributed by the unit which is to be applied to the firm's total fixed expenses. Margin refers to that amount of money which is the unit's profit margin, i.e., gross sales less variable costs. The system is particularly useful when a number of alternative courses of action are being compared, since only the costs relating directly to the particular alterna-

tives under consideration are used, while other costs are ignored. The system focuses on variable costs which can be allocated more readily than some fixed costs, especially those fixed costs which do not change over short periods of time and which can, therefore, be omitted from the analysis. See also *full-cost approach to cost analysis* and *marketing cost analysis.*

CONTRIBUTION PRICING A pricing strategy in which, under special conditions (e.g., the promise of a very large order), a firm sets the price of its product lower than that which would cover the full cost of production. Contribution pricing covers the variable costs associated with the production of the specific product and makes a contribution toward meeting the firm's overall fixed costs even though prices at this level may not contribute to the firm's overall profits.

CONTROL In marketing, that aspect of management concerned with monitoring the firm's performance in the marketplace with particular attention given to determining whether or not the basic objectives of the firm are being achieved.

CONTROL AUDIT An examination and evaluation of the results of a marketing plan. A control audit is designed to help identify and correct any deviations from the plan and to monitor the plan's progress. See also *marketing plan, control,* and *marketing audit.*

CONTROLLABLE FACTORS In marketing, those factors over which the firm has significant control, e.g., choice of product, choice of customer, how the product is to be distributed, selling price, overall marketing objectives, etc. Also referred to as controllable variables.

CONTROLLABLE VARIABLES See *controllable factors*

CONTROLLED BRAND A brand of merchandise owned by its manufacturer whose distribution is restricted to a limited number of distributors, generally selected because they are 1) not large enough to support a private brand of their own, and 2) are not in direct competition with one another.

CONVENIENCE FOOD STORE See *convenience store*

CONVENIENCE GOODS Those items usually purchased by the customer in small quantities, at frequent intervals, and with a minimum of comparison shopping. They are usually staples (bread, milk, etc.) or goods needed in an emergency (first aid supplies, small hardware, etc.) or impulse items (candy, magazines, etc.) Because convenience of access is of primary importance to the customer, he is often willing to accept a number of brands as acceptable substitutes for one another.

CONVENIENCE ITEMS See *convenience goods*

CONVENIENCE PRODUCTS See *convenience goods*

CONVENIENCE SAMPLE A method of nonprobability sampling in which the researcher interviews those members of the population most readily available. For example, "man-in-the-street" interviews are a form of convenience sample. See also *nonprobability sampling.*

CONVENIENCE STORE A grocery store, generally small, which carries a limited line of high-demand daily necessities, is open for extended hours, and charges prices higher than a supermarket. Appeals to the customer seeking to avoid the time and effort involved in shopping at a larger store or who is shopping at off hours. Convenience stores are generally placed at highly accessible locations.

CONVENTIONAL CHANNEL A channel of distribution which is loosely organized (as compared to a vertical marketing system) and in which the members are largely autonomous. Most consumer goods follow a conventional channel from manufacturer to wholesaler to retailer to ultimate consumer.

CONVENTIONAL DEPARTMENT STORE See *department store*

COOLING-OFF LAWS Local laws which allow customers a period of time (usually three days) in which to reconsider a purchase, and if they so choose, to cancel the commitment. These laws have been passed to protect consumers from deceptive or high-pressure practices employed by telephone and door-to-door salespeople.

COOP MONEY See *advertising allowance*

COOPERATIVE A term applied to a wide range of organizations, which may include apartment houses, credit unions, mutual insurance companies, electric power distributors, and a number of marketing enterprises which are jointly owned by their members and which were established to take advantage of the economic power inherent in large size.

In marketing, cooperatives include such organizations as consumer cooperatives (usually retail outlets owned by shareholding customers), marketing cooperatives (associations of the producers of certain commodities; e.g., citrus fruit), or supply cooperatives (which sell goods to members at less than open-market prices).

59

Members of cooperatives, who usually own shares in the organization, may be individuals or companies. Cooperatives are distinguished from profit-making ventures in that they render economic services to their members or shareholders on a non-profit basis. In addition, they tend to eliminate at least one merchant middleman in the distribution channel by making purchases a step closer to the producer/manufacturer level.

COOPERATIVE ADVERTISING A strategy in which advertising costs are shared by seller and reseller (commonly manufacturer and retailer). Ads are run at the local level by the retailer and part of the cost is reimbursed by the manufacturer upon receipt of verification that the ads were actually run. This arrangement, because it involves more than one level of the market, is called vertical cooperative advertising. When the cooperative effort is at one level of the market (as with two or more retailers sharing advertising costs) it is called horizontal cooperative advertising. Also known as vertical advertising, dealer-cooperative advertising, and manufacturer's cooperative advertising.

COOPERATIVE BUYING OFFICE See *resident buying office*

COOPERATIVE CHAIN See *retail cooperative*

COOPERATIVE GROUP See *retail cooperative*

COOPERATIVE INTERNATIONAL MARKETING ORGANIZATION A cooperative group composed of several domestic manufacturers who have come together to market their goods abroad. The cooperative organization is partly under the administrative control of its member firms. This type of international marketing middle-man is used frequently by producers of primary products such as fruits, nuts, grains, etc. See also *indirect export.*

COOPERATIVE OFFICE See *resident buying office*

COOPERATIVE RETAILER See *consumer cooperative*

COOPERATIVE STORE See *consumer cooperative*

COOPERATIVE WHOLESALER See *retail cooperative*

COORDINATED ADVERTISING CAMPAIGN See *advertising campaign* and *product line marketing.*

COORDINATION See *integration*

COPY In advertising, copy refers to the words (either written or spoken) which express the message in an advertising piece or commercial.

COPY STRATEGY STATEMENT A description of the objectives, content, support, and tone of the advertising a firm desires for its product. The statement may be directed to either an in-house advertising department or to an advertising agency. In the copy strategy statement, the advertiser also sets out the style, tone, words, and format selected for the message. Since this is done prior to the preparation of the advertising campaign, it serves to give direction to the advertising specialists and inform them as to their client's preferences. See also *advertising message.*

COPY THRUST In advertising and promotion, copy thrust refers to the message to be communicated by the written copy and the accompanying illustrations. It flows directly from the objectives of the promotion, whether it is intended to inform the customer of a sale, or to persuade the customer that the product is worthwhile, etc. See also *advertising objectives.*

COPYRIGHT A grant of property rights to a writer or artist which protects his work from unauthorized sale, reproduction, display, performance, etc. In the U.S., copyright protection is granted under the terms of the Federal Copyright Act. Works created on or after January 1, 1978 are protected for the lifetime of its creator plus 50 years.

CORE MARKET See *brand insistence*

CORE PRODUCT See *generic product*

CORPORATE ADVERTISING See *institutional advertising*

CORPORATE BUYING OFFICE See *resident buying office*

CORPORATE DISTRIBUTION SYSTEM See *vertical integration*

CORPORATE IMAGE The perception of a company formed in the mind of the customer. Corporate image is the revealed personality of the organization.

CORPORATE LICENSING The use of a firm's name to enhance the saleability of a product. For example, the way in which Murjani International employs the Coca-Cola logo on its clothing.

CORPORATE MISSION STATEMENT See *mission statement*

CORPORATE SYSTEM See *corporate vertical marketing system*

CORPORATE VERTICAL MARKETING SYSTEM A system in which a large corporation controls two or more levels of a marketing channel. For example, a manufacturer may own the distribution facilities for his product as well as the retail outlets through which it is sold. See also *administered*

vertical marketing system and *contractual vertical marketing system.*

CORRECTIVE ADVERTISING An advertising message designed to disclaim previous statements. Corrective advertising is sometimes ordered by the Federal Trade Commission (FTC) when an advertisement is deemed to be unfair and/or deceptive. For example, when it was found that Listerine mouthwash did not actually kill germs, the FTC ordered corrective advertising explaining that Listerine does not kill germs, but does fight bad breath. See also *affirmative disclosure.*

CORRELATION ANALYSIS In market factor analysis, a procedure which makes it possible to translate the behavior of variables in the marketing environment into estimates of future sales. Correlation analysis involves the sophisticated manipulation of market factor statistics in an effort to project potential sales for a product or service.

COST 1) The amount spent on producing or manufacturing a commodity. Cost usually refers to money, but may be used in a broader context to include time and effort, etc. 2) The price a vender charges a retailer for goods. 3) In retailing, any money expended to bring merchandise into a store, including the wholesale price of the merchandise, freight charges, etc. See also *price* and *value.*

COST ALLOWANCE A reduction in invoice price made by a manufacturer or supplier to compensate the buyer for an incorrect shipment, goods damaged in transit, delay in delivery, etc.

COST ANALYSIS See *marketing cost analysis*

COST AND FREIGHT See *C & F (cost and freight)*

COST-BASED PRICE STRATEGY
See *cost-plus pricing*

COST BENEFIT ANALYSIS A technique used for sorting out alternatives in order to find that one which will produce the smallest cost-benefit ratio; i.e., the alternative which will provide the greatest benefit (not necessarily expressed in terms of profit) for the lowest expense. Cost-benefit analysis is frequently used in planning government expenditures. Also called crossover analysis, cost-utility analysis, and cost-effectiveness analysis.

COST-BENEFIT RATIO See *cost benefit analysis*

COST-EFFECTIVENESS ANALYSIS See *cost-benefit analysis*

COST, INSURANCE, AND FREIGHT See *CIF (cost, insurance, and freight)*

COST INTENSIVE INDUSTRY See *capital intensive industry*

COST OF DELIVERED PURCHASES See *cost of goods purchased*

COST OF GOODS PURCHASED The net price paid to the vendor for merchandise, plus the price paid for transportation and delivery. In calculating the net cost of delivered purchases, cash discounts are subtracted from the above amount. In calculating the net cost of purchases, cash discounts are subtracted from the original invoice price, without consideration of transportation and delivery fees.

COST OF GOODS SOLD The price paid for any merchandise required to obtain the sales of the accounting period. It generally includes all charges (invoice costs) for goods on hand, goods on order, freight-in charges, and workroom and alteration costs. The cost of goods sold may be calculated either before or after cash discounts have been deducted (or alteration and workroom costs added). The cost of goods sold may also be determined by subtracting the closing inventory at cost from the operating inventory plus purchases at cost.

> Opening inventory (at cost) +
> new purchases for period (at cost) −
> closing inventory (at cost) =
> cost of goods sold

COST-OF-GOODS SOLD BUDGET See *budget*

COST OF LIVING INDEX See *consumer price index (CPI)*

COST OF PURCHASES See *cost of goods purchased*

COST-ORIENTED AUDIT An examination and evaluation of the results of a marketing plan from the point of view of costs and cost-effectiveness.

COST PER THOUSAND (CPM) In advertising, the expense involved in reaching one thousand potential customers with a specific advertisement or advertising campaign.

COST-PLUS PRICING A method for determining selling price based on the cost of manufacture (to the producer) or cost of acquisition (to the distributor or retailer) in which a standard markup is added to the cost figure. Current demand and the competitive situation in the marketplace are not factored into this cost-based pricing strategy.

COST-PUSH INFLATION See *inflation*

COST TRADEOFF The planned increase in one marketing cost (such as transportation) to bring about a decrease in other costs (such as storage). For example, in the attempt to minimize the overall marketing costs, the marketer may find that a more expensive form of shipping (such as air freight) compensates for the fact that the goods will not have to be stored for extended periods of time.

COST-UTILITY ANALYSIS See *cost-benefit analysis*

COUNTERADVERTISING Advertising whose aim is to counter, or contravert, the affect of other advertising. For example, anti-smoking advertising.

COUNTERMARKETING Efforts aimed at eliminating entirely the demand for a product, service, or idea. Countermarketing is generally carried out by parties who find the product in question undesirable or unwholesome. The efforts of the federal government and the American Cancer Society to discourage cigarette smoking are an example of countermarketing. Also known as unselling.

COUNTERPURCHASE In international marketing, a form of countertrade in which the trading parties negotiate two contracts. Under the terms of the first contract the seller receives cash from the buyer. Under the terms of the second contract the seller agrees to buy goods from the original seller at a monetary value equal to that in the first contract; i.e., the original seller, in return for cash payment agrees to become a buyer at some future time (generally within 6 to 12 months).

COUNTERSEGMENTATION A strategy in which the number of market segments targeted by a company are reduced, generally through the elimination of products which have been serving narrow segments of the population.

COUNTERTRADE International business in which some payments are made in the form of goods rather than currency. Countertrade includes four types of transaction: barter, compensation deals, counterpurchase, and buyback.

COUNTERVAILING DUTY A tariff levied on goods entering a country which have been granted an export subsidy or bounty by the government of the exporting country. The countervailing duty is meant to offset the advantage the exporter thus gains in the import market over domestic producers.

COUNTRY STORE See *general store*

COUPON A printed certificate employed by producers, distributors, or retailers as a sales promotion device. The coupon is redeemable by the customer for specified goods or services at a reduced price. Coupons are used to introduce new products, to promote multiple purchases, to encourage the purchase of larger sizes or the trial purchase of smaller sizes, to quickly increase the sales volume of a particular line, to introduce new product features, etc.

COUPONING A promotional strategy in which coupons are employed to achieve two objectives: 1) in the short term, to increase the sales volume of a particular product over a specific period of time, and 2) in the long run, to increase the market share of the promoted product.

COVERAGE The extent to which a medium reaches an audience. In the electronic media coverage includes the number of homes reached by the station's signal. In the print media coverage refers to the ratio of circulation to the total number of individuals, families, or organizations in a geographic area. Sometimes called penetration.

CPI See *Consumer Price Index (CPI)*

CPM See *critical path method (CPM)* and *cost per thousand (CPM)*

CPSA See *Consumer Product Safety Act (1972)*

CREAMING See *skimming*

CREATIVE BOUTIQUE See *boutique agency*

CREATIVE DEMARKETING See *demarketing*

CREATIVE SELLING A sales approach which involves a thorough knowledge of both the product and the ascertained needs of the customer. The product (or service) is demonstrated, explained, and persuasively presented to the customer in such a way as to demonstrate how the product (or service) will satisfy the customer's needs. Considered a high level sales technique, the opposite of routine order-taking.

CREDIT In its marketing sense, credit is the capacity of an individual or organization to buy and sell under a variety of arrangements other than cash-and-carry. An essential component in the concept of credit is faith or trust, i.e., the notion that the person who promises to pay in a given period of time will, in fact, do so.

CREDIT BUREAU An agency that acts as a clearinghouse by collecting and maintaining credit information about individuals or firms and by providing it to members or subscribers.

CREDIT UNION A cooperative financial institution chartered by a state or by the federal government which serves the members of a homogeneous group (the employees of a firm, the members of a union, etc.) Credit unions resemble savings and loan institutions in the services they provide to their members.

CREEPING INFLATION See *inflation*

CRESCENDO METHOD See *snowballing method*

CRITICAL PATH See *critical path method (CPM)*

CRITICAL PATH METHOD (CPM) An analytical process which breaks large projects down into component parts and analyzes the time needed to complete each part. The sequence of individual operations leading to the completion of the whole project is called the critical path. The critical path method provides the manager with an estimate of the least possible amount of time required for completion of the total project, thus enabling him to estimate the time required for production.

CROSS-BRANDING A form of brand promotion calculated to enhance an existing product by drawing on the brand strength of one or more of its ingredients or constituents. For example, advertising for a food product may include reference to a well-known and respected ingredient in an effort to trade on the ingredient's brand equity.

CROSS-CLASSIFICATION MATRIX A device, usually in the form of a grid, employed to isolate specific subdivisions in a market for purposes of segmentation.

CROSS ELASTICITY A concept which relates the change in price of one product to a change in demand for another product. Cross elasticity may be positive, the increase in price for product A may generate increased demand for product B (which may now be a cheaper alternative), or it may be negative—reducing demand for product B (because demand for product B is dependent on sales of product A). Also known as price cross elasticity.

CROSSOVER ANALYSIS See *cost-benefit analysis*

CUE In psychology, and hence in consumer research, a cue is a minor stimulus which guides behavior, often without the conscious awareness of the individual consumer. A cue helps determine when, where, and how the consumer responds to products and services in his/her environment. The advertisements seen or heard by the consumer, the exposure of the consumer to the good or service, and the attitudes of other people toward the good or service are all cues that influence the consumer's decision to buy.

CULTURE From a marketing standpoint, culture most directly relates to the way people behave in the marketplace. Culture is, as anthropologist A.L. Kroller has stated, "a set of patterns, of and for behavior, prevalent among a group…" which includes the group's laws, customs, norms, and institutions.

CUMULATIVE ADOPTION CURVE See *adoption curve*

CUMULATIVE QUANTITY DISCOUNT A discount based on all purchases made during a specified period from a producer, manufacturer, or wholesaler. The objective is to encourage repeat orders on the part of buyers. Also called a deferred or patronage discount.

CURIOSITY APPROACH A technique used by a salesperson in the first few minutes of contact with a prospect. The salesperson presents the prospect with an unexpected question or gadget to arouse the prospect's immediate interest and curiosity. See also *approach*.

CUSTODIAL WAREHOUSER See *field warehouser*

CUSTOM HOUSE BROKER An individual or firm specializing in the expeditious clearance of imported goods through U.S. Customs. Custom house brokers are licensed by the Treasury Department and are employed by importers who do not have representation at the port of entry of their goods. Sometimes known as customs brokers and (because they may assume additional duties) foreign freight forwarders.

CUSTOM MARKETING A form of marketing in which the target customers are completely segmented, i.e., each customer is so distinct from all others that he must be treated as an individual. A unique marketing mix is developed for each customer.

CUSTOM MARKETING RESEARCH FIRM See *marketing research firm*

CUSTOM PRICE See *customary price*

CUSTOMARY PRICE A price which, because it has not changed in a long time, has become traditional or customary. Inflation has made customary prices virtually impossible to maintain, but in the past such items as postcards, soft drinks, and candy bars had such stable prices that the consuming public came to expect them to remain constant. Sometimes referred to as a custom price.

CUSTOMER Any person or firm who is the actual or intended purchaser of goods and/or services from a store or other marketer. The term is sometimes reserved for those patrons who make frequent and systematic purchases.

CUSTOMER DIVISION OF AUTHORITY See *market division of authority*

CUSTOMER PROFILE The demographic and psychographic characteristics of a firm's customers.

CUSTOMER SAMPLING See *sampling*

CUSTOMER SERVICE LEVEL In physical distribution, the customer service level is a measure of a firm's ability to deliver what the customer wants quickly and dependably. A higher service level may be desirable in highly competitive environments (such as pure competition or oligopoly) where it may allow the firm to increase its market share without changing its products, prices, or promotions. An increase in the customer service level, however, may increase total costs, since it may require additional distribution points, warehousing facilities, and inventory costs.

CUSTOMER SERVICE STANDARDS In the distribution of goods, the quality of the service that a firm's customers can expect to receive. These standards include the receipt of the goods in undamaged condition, speedy and reliable delivery, availability of items ordered, and accuracy in order filling. In general, most companies try to meet or exceed the standards set by their competitors, since service is another way in which similar firms may compete.

CUSTOMER SERVICES As a business activity, customer services may be regarded as either an attribute of the product itself or as a part of the selling process. At the industrial level, customer services generally involve the installation, repair, and maintenance of the vendor's product, but prompt deliveries, accuracy in filling orders, and the availability of merchandise are also regarded as significant services. In retailing, services include delivery, gift wrap, credit, and other activities performed by the retailer for the customer's convenience which are not directly related to the sale of a specific product within the store.

CUSTOMS BROKER See *custom house broker*

CUSTOMS DUTY See *tariff*

CUSTOMS UNION An association of countries which have agreed to reduce or eliminate the trade barriers existing between them and who have, in addition, agreed to levy a tariff on goods imported from countries outside the union.

CYCLICAL DEMAND Demand for products and services which is responsive to changes in the country's economic cycles.

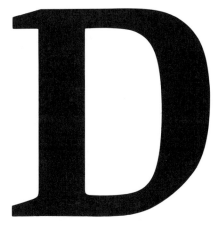

DAGMAR A method developed in the 1960s by Russell H. Colley for determining the effectiveness of advertising. The process lists 52 possible advertising goals and outlines criteria by which each may be measured. Colley presented his theory in his *Defining Advertising Goals for Measured Advertising Results* (1961), from which Dagmar derives its name.

DATA Information of a concrete nature, such as statistics or measurements, which is used as a basis for reasoning and decision making.

DATA BANK See *database*

DATA REDUCTION That step in marketing research in which collected data is summarized so that it may be analyzed.

DATABASE An information system, generally a computer, in which a variety of factual data is organized and stored and made available for quick retrieval.

DATING On invoices, dating refers to the time period during which discounts may be taken by a reseller customer (typically a retailer) as well as to the date on which the total dollar amount on the invoice becomes due. See also *cash discount.*

DATING PERIOD See *dating*

DEAL Usually at retail, a temporary special offering of merchandise, either in the form of a price reduction (cents-off deal, etc.) or as multiple units at a special price.

DEAL PRONE See *brand switcher*

DEALER An individual or firm which sells merchandise without altering it. The term is most frequently applied to retailers, e.g., automobile dealer, but is sometimes used synonymously with wholesaler or distributor.

DEALER BRAND See *private brand*

DEALER-COOPERATIVE ADVERTISING See *cooperative advertising*

DEALER-LISTING ADS See *manufacturers' dealer-listing ads*

DEALER LOADER 1) A gift from a manufacturer to a middleman to encourage him to order. 2) A retail point-of-purchase fixture provided by a manufacturer or supplier and generally placed near the register or checkout counter to display merchandise. Sometimes called a display loader.

DEALER-SERVICE SALESPERSON See *manufacturer's salesperson*

DECAY CURVE In product development, a decay curve is a graphic representation of the survival rate of new product ideas. As each item is subjected to screening and analysis, development, and testing more and more products are dropped from further consideration until only a small percentage ever reach the commercialization stage.

DECAY MODEL See *advertising sales-response and decay model*

DECAY RATE See *advertising sales-response and decay model*

DECENTRALIZATION See *decentralized organization*

DECENTRALIZED ORGANIZATION In an organizational structure, a decentralized organization is one in which authority and responsibility have been distributed to the greatest possible number of members, departments, or employees at the lowest possible level of the organizational hierarchy. For example, in multinational marketing, a decentralized organization implies that many of the marketing and other decision making processes reside in the individual local firms and subsidiaries in the host countries, rather than with the parent in the home country.

DECEPTIVE ADVERTISING See *deceptive practice*

DECEPTIVE PACKAGING The packaging of products offered for sale in a manner calculated to deceive the purchaser, e.g., large boxes only partially filled with merchandise.

DECEPTIVE PRACTICE Business practices calculated to deceive the consumer. Most deceptive practices fall into one of two categories: 1) deceptive advertising and promotion, and/or 2) fraudulent and confusing selling practices.

DECEPTIVE PRICING Pricing tactics which are calculated to deceive or confuse the purchaser. Included are all misrepresentations of credit terms as well as the use of fraudulent reference prices and other deceptive markdown practices.

DECEPTIVE PROMOTION A promotional practice calculated to deceive or mislead the consumer. The misrepresentation of price or performance is common in deceptive promotions.

DECISION-MAKING UNIT (DMU) In purchasing, that person or persons responsible for deciding what is to be purchased for the firm.

DECISION PROCESS See *adoption process*

DECISION SUPPORT SYSTEM (DSS) A type of management support system based on interactive computerized information retrieval. Managers access a central computer's processing unit through a terminal or personal computer, input their data, and have the data processed for immediate results. See also *marketing information system (MIS)*

DECISION TREE In marketing planning, a method of graphically depicting a series of alternative courses of action in the shape of a tree with each branch of the tree representing a possible decision along with its projected outcome. Decision trees aid managers in visually understanding an array of alternatives.

DECLINE STAGE The next to last stage in the life cycle of a product (it precedes abandonment) when sales are in decline and profits more difficult to achieve. See also *product life cycle (PLC)* and *retail life cycle*.

DECODER See *decoding*

DECODING The translation of a message from the form in which it was transmitted into a form comprehensible to the recipient.

DEFENSIVE PRICING A strategy in which a company prices its products so as to protect (or defend) established products or market share, e.g., a new product may be introduced at a price higher than another of the firm's products so as not to cannibalize it.

DEFERRED BILLING See *forward dating*

DEFERRED DISCOUNT See *cumulative quantity discount*

DELAYED DATING See *forward dating*

DELAYED-QUOTATION BIDDING A pricing strategy employed in the industrial market in which the final price of the product or service is not set until the item is either complete and/or delivered. Delayed-quotation bidding is most common in large projects involving extensive development time.

DELAYED RESPONSE EFFECT See *carryover effect*

DELIVERED PRICE A price quotation at wholesale or retail level which includes the cost of delivery. This price strategy is also known as freight allowed pricing.

DELPHI METHOD See *delphi technique*

DELPHI TECHNIQUE An expert-opinion method of arriving at business forecasts. A group of experts or knowledgeable individuals is polled under the assumption that their reactions will be predictive of the broader population. The experts place their individual predictions on paper, compare the results, and repeat the cycle until a consensus is reached. At each new estimate, a company analyst reviews and revises the results. Also known as the "jury of executive opinion" technique.

DEMAND The concept demand has two components. On the one hand, purchasers must have a need or desire for the product or service offered for sale and, on the other hand, must be willing and able to pay the price asked by the seller. This condition (in which the buyer can actually fulfill his needs) is known as effective demand.

DEMAND ANALYSIS In a broad context, demand analysis involves an examination of the factors which govern the sale and use of a product or service, e.g., such factors as economic conditions, price, scarcity, and buying habits. In a more narrow context, demand analysis is concerned with explaining changes in the demand curve and the relationship between price levels and demand in the marketplace.

DEMAND-BACKWARD PRICING A method of setting prices which starts with what is considered an acceptable final (retail) price and works backward to what a producer can actually charge. The producer determines how much may be spent on producing the item by starting with this acceptable final price and subtracting both the margins which channel members typically expect and the average or planned marketing expenses. Demand-backward pricing, to be effective, requires demand estimates, since the quantity demanded will affect production costs. The producer must also determine whether quality will play a significant role in demand, or if improved quality may be sacrificed to reduce costs of production. Also known as demand-minus pricing.

DEMAND CURVE A schedule, generally represented as a graph, depicting the relationship between a series of prices for a product and the demand for the product in the marketplace. Also known as a demand schedule.

DEMAND CURVE

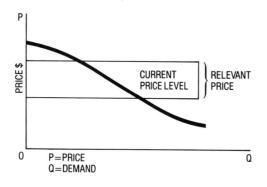

P=PRICE
Q=DEMAND

DEMAND EXPANSIBILITY Demand for a product or service which can be increased through the use of advertising alone. No change in price or any other variable is necessary to affect the change.

DEMAND-MINUS PRICING See *demand-backward pricing*

DEMAND-ORIENTED PRICING A strategy used in setting retail prices based on the level of demand for the product on the part of the customers. Merchandise for which there is strong demand will carry a higher price than merchandise for which there is relatively weak demand.

DEMAND-PULL INFLATION See *inflation*

DEMAND SCHEDULE See *demand curve*

DEMARKETING A marketing strategy calculated to reduce rather than increase demand for a product or service. Demarketing efforts are usually confined to periods of product shortage, e.g., American oil companies discouraged gasoline consumption during the Arab oil boycott. Sometimes called creative demarketing.

DEMOGRAPHIC SEGMENTATION A method of market segmentation based on geographic location (such as world or national region, population density, city size, etc.) or shared socioeconomic characteristics (such as age, sex, religion, education, income, etc.). See also *geographic segmentation, socioeconomic segmentation,* and *market segmentation.*

DEMOGRAPHICS The vital statistics of a population, including the size of the group and the age, sex, birth and death rates, location, income, occupation, race, education, etc. of its members. See also *market segmentation.*

DEMOGRAPHY The study of populations of human beings, including vital and social statistics.

DEMONSTRATION 1) In the sales process, a demonstration is the involvement of the potential customer in the presentation by the salesperson. The salesperson allows the customer to use, test, or experiment with the product. See also *dramatic approach.* 2) In retail selling, a demonstration is a form of in-store sales promotion in which one or more individuals explain to customers how a product is used and show how the product may be useful in the customer's own life. At times the demonstrator may be employed by a manufacturer rather than the store.

DEMONSTRATION ADVERTISING A form of advertising in which the attributes of a product are actually demonstrated and which frequently emphasizes the competitive strengths of the product.

DEPARTMENT MANAGER In retailing, the department manager is the individual responsible for running a particular selling area in a store. In some stores, the department manager may be involved in both the buying and selling of merchandise. In other more centralized organizations, however, the department manager is primarily involved in the presentation of merchandise, supervision of personnel, and customer service.

DEPARTMENT STORE A large-scale retailing institution which sells a wide variety of goods including hard lines and which, with some exceptions, provides its customers with extensive services. The department store takes its name from the units (departments) in which related kinds of merchandise are grouped for purposes of promotion, service, and control. Although the traditional department store with its downtown flagship and its emphasis on fashion and service (exemplified by such stores as Macy's, Marshall Field, and the May Co.) is the most clearly recognized form of department store, there are other retail organizations which fall into this category. Included are departmentalized specialty stores with their narrower assortment of goods concentrated at the high end in

terms of price and fashion (for example Lord and Taylor, Neiman-Marcus), and chain department stores, which include the great mass merchandisers with their common format (Sears, J.C. Penney) and which have taken on many of the aspects of the traditional department store even though the profit base is the entire store rather than the individual department. The discount department stores (K-mart, Wal-Mart) characterized by low margins and self-service, sell merchandise in such great varieties that they also may be regarded as department stores. Store ownership groups round out the category (for example, Federated Department Stores, Allied Stores). These organizations, generally unknown to the public, pull together a number of department stores and their branches into a single centrally managed (but individually merchandised) retailing group. See also *chain store system, promotional department store, junior department store, specialty store, department store ownership group, discount store.*

DEPARTMENT STORE CHAIN See *department store ownership group*

DEPARTMENT STORE OWNERSHIP GROUP A retailing organization in which the member stores (usually once independent department stores) are centrally owned and controlled in terms of broad policymaking, but which are operated and merchandised autonomously. The individual stores and their branches operate under their original names and the general public is seldom aware of their affiliation with the group. Also known as a department store chain.

DEPRECIATION The reduction in value of property due to wear and tear or the passage of time. Depreciation may be clearly observable as in the rusting away of machinery, or it may be less easily detectable as in the eroded value of fashion goods held too long in inventory.

DEPRESSION See *business cycle*

DEPTH See *product depth*

DEPTH INTERVIEW A technique used in motivation research which uses an informal open discussion to uncover unconscious motives and to delve beneath the superficial answers of the participants. See also *motivation research.*

DEREGULATION The systematic discontinuance of laws and regulations which once controlled business activities but have subsequently been deemed undesirable. For example, the deregulation of the airline industry allowed airlines to compete on the basis of rates and charges, whereas they had previously been forced to compete on the basis of peripheral services to customers. Similarly, the Motor Carrier Act (1980) deregulated the trucking industry, so that private carriers were permitted to solicit back haul merchandise for the first time in nearly fifty years.

DERIVED DEMAND Market demand for a product which can be traced to the demand for another product. Most derived demand is, finally, traceable to consumer demand.

DESCRIPTION BUYING In industrial buying, the practice of purchasing a product on the basis of a written or verbal description of the product without first inspecting it. Description buying is facilitated by guarantees of quality in the form of grading, branding, and buying by specification. For example, accepted government standards of grading produce allow these goods to be sold without further inspection or sampling by wholesalers or retailers.

DESCRIPTIVE LABEL See *label*

DESCRIPTIVE RESEARCH Market research calculated to yield information about a particular problem, e.g., how consumers behave under specific marketplace conditions or how one can identify the users of a given product.

DESK JOBBER See *drop shipper*

DETAILER 1) In retailing, a missionary salesperson who sets up vendor displays in stores and maintains the inventory of the product. 2) In the health care field, a manufacturer's representative who contacts physicians and other professionals to promote the products (drugs, etc.) of his employer.

DETAILING See *detailer*

DETERMINING DIMENSIONS The needs and preferences of the customer which affect the purchase of a specific product type or specific brand in the marketplace. Such factors as a product's value as a status symbol, color of the product, demographic characteristics of the customer, behavioral needs, attitudes, the degree of a customer's urgency for satisfaction of his/her needs, and brand name are examples of determining dimensions. See also *qualifying dimensions.*

DEVALUATION A reduction in the value of a nation's currency, undertaken by the government of that nation, in relation to other currencies or to gold. A devaluation may be undertaken to bring a nation's currency more into line with other currencies in an effort to facilitate international trade by making exported goods more affordable to foreign consumers. See also *revaluation.*

DIFFERENTIAL ADVANTAGE The advantage one firm holds over its competitors because of its wide range of experience, greater resources, higher level of competence, superior reputation, familiarity to the consuming public, etc.

DIFFERENTIAL PRICING A form of demand-oriented pricing commonly applied to markets which can be divided into segments—some in which demand for the product or service is elastic and some in which demand is inelastic. Marketers attempt to sell at a high price in market segments having inelastic demand and at a lower price in segments having elastic demand.

DIFFERENTIATED MARKETING A marketing stratey in which a manufacturer produces a number of related products, each with a narrow segment of the total market as its target. The manufacturer attempts to build sales by addressing various segments of the market individually rather than by marketing a single product for all customers. See also *undifferentiated marketing* and *market segmentation*.

DIFFERENTIATED OLIGOPOLY A condition in the marketplace characterized by 1) the presence of a relatively small number of competing firms who are 2) selling similar, but not identical, products. One or two producers are large enough to set prices on an industry-wide basis, e.g., the automobile industry.

DIFFERENTIATION In organizational structure, differentiation is the structuring of jobs in such a way as to allow for specialization of functions and provide greater efficiency within the organization. The larger the organization, the greater the opportunity for differentiation. In large companies, the marketing task may be differentiated into such specialized units as commercial research, advertising and promotion, application development, sales, and customer service.

DIFFUSION See *diffusion process*

DIFFUSION CURVE See *adoption curve*

DIFFUSION OF INVOCATION See *diffusion process*

DIFFUSION PROCESS The process by which a product is adopted in successive stages by members of a target market. Consumers are generally classified as innovators (the first group of customers to buy a product), early adopters, members of the early and late majorities, laggards, and finally, non-adopters (those who do not buy the new product). This classification is implemented in an effort to describe the behavior of consumers as a product is diffused through the marketplace. See also *adoption process*.

DIFFUSION PROCESS

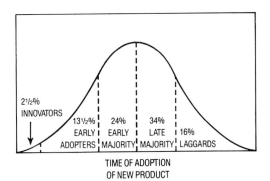

2½% INNOVATORS
13½% EARLY ADOPTERS
24% EARLY MAJORITY
34% LATE MAJORITY
16% LAGGARDS

TIME OF ADOPTION
OF NEW PRODUCT

DIRECT ACTION ADVERTISING See *product advertising*

DIRECT CHANNEL OF DISTRIBUTION See *direct selling*

DIRECT COMPETITOR A firm competing head-to-head with another firm, generally offering potential customers similar or identical products or services.

DIRECT COST Costs involved in doing business which can be directly ascribed to a particular product or to an

73

organizational unit. Commonly, materials and supplies, wages, and overhead are regarded as direct costs which vary with the volume of production. See also *overhead, fixed cost, variable cost,* and *indirect cost.*

DIRECT DERIVATION In market factor analysis, a procedure which makes it possible to translate the behavior of variables in the marketing environment into estimates of future sales. Direct derivation involves the relatively non-technical examination of statistics in an effort to project the market potential for a product or service.

DIRECT DISTRIBUTION See *direct selling*

DIRECT DISTRIBUTION CHANNEL See *direct selling*

DIRECT EXPENSE See *direct cost*

DIRECT EXPORT A method of exporting goods in which the domestic firm handles its own exporting, independent of any international marketing middlemen. Direct export may be achieved through the use of a domestic-based export department or division within the firm, an overseas sales branch or subsidiary, traveling export sales representatives, or through foreign-based distributors or agents.

DIRECT EXPORTING See *direct export*

DIRECT INVESTMENT A company's investment in foreign-based manufacturing facilities, rather than entering into competition with local foreign manufacturers. This form of direct export provides the company with cost economies such as cheaper labor and/or raw materials, government investment incentives, and freight savings. Direct investment also leads to a bet-

ter image of the investing company in the host country, closer ties to the government of the host country, better relationships with suppliers and distributors, and better control over its investment than may be possible with other forms of direct export. See also *direct export.*

DIRECT MAIL The use of the postal service to arouse the interest of consumers in a product or service being offered for sale. In a sense, direct mail efforts may be regarded as a form of advertising (in contrast to mail order retailing, which is a method of doing business). Direct mail may be employed to prospect for new customers or to maintain contact with existing ones. Sales letters, postcards, circulars, and catalogs are frequently used in direct mail activities.

DIRECT MAIL ADVERTISING See *direct mail*

DIRECT MANUFACTURER'S OUTLET See *factory outlet*

DIRECT MARKETING Marketing via direct mail, telephone retailing, mail order retailing, catalog retailing, mail order ads and inserts (preprints) in magazines, door-to-door retailing, and such electronic media as two-way cable television. Direct marketing efforts are calculated to elicit a direct response on the part of potential customers. See also *direct selling.*

DIRECT MARKETING ASSOCIATION (DMA) An association of firms using and producing direct mail and direct response advertising. The association studies attitudes toward direct marketing, sponsors institutes and workshops, and serves as an industry liaison with the government in Washington, D.C. DMA provides a "Mail Preference Service" for consumers wishing to increase or decrease the amount of advertising mail they receive, and a "Mail Order Action Line" to help resolve consumer complaints about mail order purchases. DMA publishes *Direct Line* (monthly), *Direct Marketing Journal* (bimonthly), *Special Reports,* (quarterly), an annual *Membership Roster,* and the *Direct Mail/Marketing Manual.* The association is based in New York City.

DIRECT MARKETING ASSOCIATION CATALOG COUNCIL (DMACC) A professional association of catalog houses, printers, list brokers, and related firms and individuals. The DMACC serves important legislative and educational functions for its membership, and represents the industry in Congress. DMACC headquarters are located in New York City.

DIRECT MARKETING CHANNEL See *direct marketing*

DIRECT MARKETING EDUCATIONAL FOUNDATION (DMEF) An association of individuals, businesses, and organizations working to promote college-level education in direct marketing. The association sponsors seminars, and institutes for both students and faculty. It also sponsors summer student internship programs, regional institutes for faculty, and visiting executive programs. DMEF publishes educational materials, course outlines, and career pamphlets.

DIRECT MARKETING MINORITIES OPPORTUNITES (DMMO) A New York based association dedicated to educating and training minority employees for careers in direct marketing. The association places minority candidates in direct marketing firms. It also offers referrals, support groups, and continuing education programs. DMMO publishes a quarterly

newsletter entitled *Direct Marketing Minority Opportunities.*

DIRECT-MAIL SHIPPER See *drop shipper*

DIRECT PROMOTION See *personal selling*

DIRECT PURCHASE See *direct selling*

DIRECT RESPONSE MARKETING See *direct marketing*

DIRECT RESPONSE RETAILING See *mail order retailing*

DIRECT-SALES RESULTS TEST A test designed to measure the effectiveness of advertising or other promotional activities by calculating the increase in revenue achieved by each dollar of promotion expenditure.

DIRECT SELL A type of advertising message which focuses on a single unique product benefit and hammers it home to the target audience through constant repetition. This approach is often used in conjunction with product demonstrations such as the superior absorbency of certain paper towels, the extra-strength relief of a pain reliever, and the inability of coffee drinkers to distinguish between fresh-brewed coffee and certain instants. Not to be confused with direct selling. See also *image sell,* which is its opposite.

DIRECT SELLING A relatively imprecise term having two principal meanings: 1) At the industrial level, direct selling is generally taken to mean selling from producer/manufacturer to final user without recourse to middlemen—neither wholesalers nor retailers. This arrangement is also known as a zero-level channel or a direct-to-user channel. 2) At the retail level direct selling commonly refers to such activities as telephone sales, door-to-door selling, or in-home parties. See also *direct marketing*.

DIRECT-TO-USER CHANNEL See *direct selling*

DISAGGREGATED MARKET A market in which the customers are all so distinct from one another that no aggregates may be formed. Such markets are said to be completely segmented.

DISCONTINUOUS INNOVATION The development of products which are so new and innovative that they have no clearly discernible antecedents. An entirely new market must be developed for these products.

DISCOUNT A reduction from list or marked price similar to an allowance granted by a seller to a buyer. Discounts are most commonly granted to induce the buyer to pay for his purchases quickly (cash discount), to buy substantial amounts of merchandise (quantity discount), to perform certain middleman functions in the distribution channel (trade discount), or to place orders during the time of year when business is slow (seasonal discount). See also *trade discount*.

DISCOUNT DEPARTMENT STORE See *promotional department store*

DISCOUNT HOUSE See *discount store*

DISCOUNT RETAILER See *discount store*

DISCOUNT STORE A retail establishment which operates on very low margins in order to offer merchandise at prices well below the recognized market level. The discount store emphasizes self-services. Typically volume oriented, it is distinguished primarily by its emphasis on price and value. The magazine *Discount Merchandiser* restricts the term discount store to retail outlets of at least 10,000 square feet doing an annual volume of $1 million. See also *promotional department store*.

DISCREPANCY OF ASSORTMENT The difference between the lines made by the producer and the assortment wanted by the consumer. Wholesalers and retailers compensate for this discrepancy by putting together an appropriate product mix for their customers. See also *assorting*.

DISCREPANCY OF QUANTITY The difference between the number of goods it is economical for a producer to make and the quantity normally wanted by the consumer. Wholesalers and retailers in the channel of distribution compensate for this discrepancy by regrouping the goods into increasingly smaller quantities through allocation. See also *allocation*.

DISCRETIONARY BUYING POWER See *discretionary income*

DISCRETIONARY EXPENDITURES See *discretionary income*

DISCRETIONARY INCOME That portion of a person's earnings which remains after taxes have been paid, contracted payments made, and the necessities of life purchased. The individual has a certain amount of discretion as to how the balance shall be spent. Such expenditures are called discretionary expenditures.

DISCRETIONARY PERSONAL INCOME See *discretionary income*

DISCRIMINATORY PRICING The sale of goods or services at different prices to different customers. Pricing is discriminatory when it is calculated to give one party an unfair advantage over another. Discriminatory pricing is illegal under the provisions of the Robinson-Patman Act when it reduces competition in interstate commerce.

DISECONOMIES OF SCALE Cost increases and other operating disadvantages arising out of large scale operations. For example, a business may grow so large (as in the case of General Motors) that size in itself attracts the notice of government regulators.

DISPERSION See *allocation*

DISPLAY The impersonal, visual presentation of goods or ideas. Display is frequently employed in the retail trade in store windows and interiors to facilitate customer examination and selection of merchandise. See also *visual merchandising.*

DISPLAY ADVERTISING In newspaper advertising, display advertisements are those which feature illustrations and other visual devices as well as words.

DISPLAY LOADER See *dealer loader*

DISPLAY MERCHANDISING See *visual merchandising*

DISPOSABLE INCOME Earnings which remain after income and other taxes and mandatory payments have been deducted. Roughly equivalent to "take home pay."

DISPOSABLE PERSONAL INCOME See *disposable income*

DISSATISFIER See *motive*

DISSOCIATIVE GROUP A reference group from which an individual makes an effort to disassociate himself; e.g., from a particular social class or ethnic group.

DISSONANCE See *cognitive dissonance*

DISTINCTIVENESS STAGE See *fashion cycle*

DISTRIBUTION In a broad sense, those activities involved in physically transferring goods from the point at which they are produced to the point of their consumption. Functions in the distribution process include transportation, warehousing, wholesaling, and retailing. Distribution may best be understood as that part of the marketing process which follows production; i.e., those activities taking place after there is a physical product to distribute. At the manufacturing level, distribution sometimes includes selling and advertising functions as well as order processing, customer service, and delivery. At retail, distribution refers to the movement of merchandise within the organization; e.g., from distribution center to store, from stock room to department, etc. See also *physical distribution (PD).*

DISTRIBUTION CENTER See *break-bulk center*

DISTRIBUTION CHANNEL See *channel of distribution*

DISTRIBUTION COST ANALYSIS An analysis of the costs incurred, both direct and indirect, in selling a company's products. Such a study is calculated to reveal which salespeople are most productive, which products are most profitable, and other data useful in managing the marketing effort.

DISTRIBUTION INTENSITY A measure of the exposure a product is given at wholesale or retail. The more outlets, the more intense the distribution.

DISTRIBUTION INTENSITY RESPONSE FUNCTION See *response function*

DISTRIBUTION PLANNING Planning efforts calculated to facilitate the storage and transfer of products as they move from producer to consumer.

DISTRIBUTION STANDARDS In customer service, standards of performance with respect to response time, delivery time, accuracy in order-filling, depth of inventory, etc.

DISTRIBUTION STRATEGY The decision to market goods through a particular channel to achieve the most economic or cost-effective result. See also *channel of distribution* and *distribution.*

DISTRIBUTION STRUCTURE The sum of all the distribution channels existing in an industry.

DISTRIBUTION SYSTEM RESPONSIVENESS In physical distribution, the responsiveness of the system is the degree to which it can react to a change in demand; i.e., a system is judged responsive if it can increase the flow of products quickly when demand increases.

DISTRIBUTION WAREHOUSE See *break-bulk center*

DISTRIBUTOR A broad, generic term often used synonymously with wholesaler and, more specifically, with general merchandise wholesaler. The term carries the additional meaning of "exclusive sales representative" in some segments of manufacturing. See also *wholesaler, manufacturer's agent, general merchandise wholesaler,* and *industrial distributor.*

DISTRIBUTOR BRAND See *private brand*

DISTRIBUTOR WITHOUT A YARD See *drop shipper*

DISTRIBUTOR'S BRAND See *private brand*

DISTRICT OFFICE See *manufacturer's branch office*

DIVERSIFICATION Diversification in marketing may take a number of forms. A firm may introduce new products into existing markets or it may introduce existing products into new markets. In a complete departure, it may introduce new products into new markets. Some diversification is accomplished through mergers and acquisitions. The object of diversification is almost always expansion with a concurrent increase in profits.

DIVERSION IN TRANSIT A practice in rail transportation in which the final destination of goods is determined after they have left the shipping point. As long as the route involves no backtracking, the shipper receives the regular carload rate from the railroad. This practice allows producers of goods, especially perishables, to move them in the general direction of their markets before a final destination is known.

DIVESTITURE The selling off of some of their businesses by large companies, usually for economic reasons but occasionally upon the insistence of the government (as was the case with A.T.&T. in the early 1980s).

DMA See *Direct Marketing Association (DMA)*

DMACC See *Direct Marketing Association Catalog Council (DMACC)*

DMEF See *Direct Marketing Educational Foundation (DMEF)*

DMMO See *Direct Marketing Minorities Opportunities (DMMO)*

DMU See *decision-making unit (DMU)*

DOG A business unit or product which has proved unprofitable and which is viewed as having little future potential.

DOMESTIC-BASED EXPORT AGENT An independent international marketing middleman used in indirect export. The domestic-based export agent negotiates foreign purchases for the domestic manufacturer and receives compensation in the form of a commission. Trading companies are one form of domestic-based export agents. See also *indirect export.*

DOMESTIC-BASED EXPORT DEPARTMENT In direct exporting, the part of a domestic firm whose activities are directed toward selling goods abroad. This is a self-contained unit of the producer and does not involve the use of an independent international marketing middleman. The department may eventually evolve into a division or a subsidiary of the producer. See also *direct export.*

DOMESTIC-BASED EXPORT DIVISION See *domestic-based export department*

DOMESTIC-BASED EXPORT MERCHANT An independent international marketing middleman used in indirect export. The domestic-based export merchant buys the manufacturer's product and sells it abroad. See also *indirect export.*

DOMESTIC-BASED EXPORT SUBSIDIARY See *domestic-based export department*

DOMESTIC-ONLY ORIENTATION A marketing strategy which excludes all foreign business, both import and export.

DOMESTICATION A process in which foreign businesses are forced to give up control of their operations by the government of the host country. The final step in the domestication process is the outright ownership of the corporation's property by nationals.

DOOR-TO-DOOR RETAILING Retailing in which the selling is done directly to the consumers in their own homes. Products sold door-to-door are often those which the customer has not been actively seeking out (such as encyclopedias, vacuum cleaners, etc.).

DOOR-TO-DOOR SELLING See *door-to-door retailing*

DOUBLE SEARCH Marketplace activity characterized by consumers looking for products they need and producers looking for customers—each is searching for the other.

DOWNWARD-FLOW THEORY See *fashion adoption process*

DPI See *disposable income*

DRAMATIC APPROACH A technique used by a salesperson in the first few minutes of contact with a prospect. The salesperson presents an eye-opening demonstration of how the good or service works. Often the prospect may be involved in the demonstration. See also *approach.*

DRAWING ACCOUNT See *commission with draw*

DRAYAGE See *cartage*

DRIVE In psychology, and hence in consumer research, a drive is a strong stimulus that necessitates action. For example, an individual may have a drive to succeed in a professional career. When such a drive is directed toward a particular object that will help realize (and thus reduce) the drive, it becomes a motive. Thus, the same individual may attend college in his/her chosen field in order to achieve success. The drive to succeed has now become the individual's motive to attend college. Marketers investigate the drives that motivate customers to determine how their products may be used to help the customer realize the drive and how best to present and promote their products to the customer. Thus, in the same example, an apparel manufacturer may gear a promotion to "dressing for success" as a way of marketing clothing geared to the success-driven consumer.

DROP SHIPMENT 1) A shipment of goods arranged by a limited-service wholesaler called a drop shipper. 2) In retailing, the term refers to merchandise shipped by a manufacturer to the individual branch stores of a chain or department store organization rather than to a warehouse or distribution center.

DROP SHIPMENT WHOLESALER See *drop shipper*

DROP SHIPPER A limited-service wholesaler who, although he takes title to the goods he sells, never actually has them in his possession. Drop shippers commonly sell bulk products like sand and gravel, coal, or building materials. They receive orders from customers and then find a suitable manufacturer or supplier who ships the goods directly to the customer. The supplier bills the drop shipper who, in turn, bills the customer. Also known as a desk jobber or drop shipment wholesaler.

DRUG LISTING ACT Federal legislation which provided the Food and Drug Administration (FDA) with access to information on drug manufacturers so as to protect consumers.

DRUGSTORE A retail establishment which traditionally was a place where drugs and medicines were prepared and dispensed according to a physician's written prescription. As drugstores evolved, they added proprietary drugs, health and beauty aids, medical supplies, books and magazines, cigars and cigarettes, small appliances, etc. to the mix of products they stocked.

DRY GOODS See *soft goods*

DSS See *decision support system (DSS)*

DUAL ADAPTATION A strategy employed in international marketing in which the product offered for export is different from the domestic product and which is promoted differently in the foreign market.

DUAL CHANNEL OF DISTRIBUTION See *dual distribution*

DUAL DISTRIBUTION The use of more than one channel of distribution to reach customers at different levels of the marketplace. For example, a manufacturer may sell to large customers directly, but to smaller ones through a wholesaler. Or he may sell through his own retail outlets while, at the same time, selling through other retailers. Conflict may arise when more than one channel is used to reach the same market segment. Also called multiple channels and multichannel marketing. See also *vertical integration,* and *dual marketing.*

DUAL MARKETING The practice of selling the same or similar products to both individual consumers and to industrial or institutional customers. For example, automobile manufacturers sell cars to individuals through franchised dealers (retailers) while, at the same time, selling fleets of new cars to auto rental firms. See also *dual distribution.*

DUAL-TARGET MARKET In nonprofit marketing, nonbusiness organizations are seen as functioning in a dual-target market; i.e., on the one hand they have to address the sources of their funds (donors, government agencies, organized charities, etc.) and on the other hand must provide for their clients and other recipients of their services.

DUMPING Price discrimination in international trade which results in like goods being sold at different prices in the home market and in one or more foreign markets. Dumping is being practiced when goods are sold in a foreign market at a price which does not cover production costs or at a price which is below that charged in the home market. For example, a producer might sell a product in a foreign market at a predatory price level and make up the difference through profits on sales at a higher price in the home market. Dumping is a strategy sometimes employed by exporting firms to capture a foreign market and is viewed as a threat by domestic producers of the same or substitutable products.

DUPLICATED MEDIA AUDIENCE See *reach*

DURABLE GOODS Tangible capital or consumer goods having a relatively long useful life (sometimes arbitrarily put at three years).

DUTY See *tariff*

DYAD See *buyer-seller dyad*

DYNAMICALLY CONTINUOUS INNOVATION The development of products which are either completely new or which are substantially altered versions of existing products. Innovation of this type is generally attributable to changes in the lifestyles and expectations of consumers, and may bring with it considerable disruption in consumption patterns.

EARLY ACCEPTOR See *innovator*

EARLY ADOPTER In the diffusion process, early adopters are consumers who are among the first to purchase a new product or service. They frequently have high social status, occupy leadership positions, and are anxious to keep up with the latest trends and fashions. They are, however, not as willing as innovators to take risks.

EARLY FOLLOWER See *early majority*

EARLY MAJORITY In the diffusion process, the early majority constitutes those consumers in the mass market who have relatively high social status and who are receptive to innovation. The early majority adopts new products and services at an above average rate.

EBI See *effective buying income*

EC See *European Economic Community (EEC)*

ECONOMETRIC ANALYSIS In causal research, econometric analysis is the attempt to project sales or other activities by constructing an econometric model and simulating a future outcome. The model uses two or more regression or similar analyses to simulate future events on the basis of past relationships.

ECONOMETRICS See *econometric analysis*

ECONOMIC APPROACH TO PRICING An overall economic strategy in which price levels are viewed as being determined by the interaction between supply and demand in the marketplace.

ECONOMIC EMULATION STAGE See *fashion cycle*

ECONOMIC ENVIRONMENT The interaction of all phases of the economy in which a marketer conducts business. Such factors as national income, economic growth, recession, inflation, and depression must be taken into account by the marketer since they affect the success or failure of the firm's marketing strategy. For example, during a period of recession, depression, or rapid business decline customers curtail their purchases or stop buying a product completely. This will cause the marketing strategy to fail, no matter how well-planned it may be. Similarly, the shortage of natural resources needed by the marketer (such as energy resources) will affect the manner in which the marketer conducts business. For example, an energy crisis will cause consumers to seek out and purchase more fuel-efficient automobiles, or use their automobiles less for trips to shopping malls and other retail establishments. The availability of the natural resources or raw materials needed in the production of a product will also affect the marketer. For example, during World War II, when available silk was needed to produce parachutes, hosiery manufacturers were forced to switch to nylon for women's stockings. See also *technological environment.*

ECONOMIC FORECASTING The use of changes in the national and international business climate to predict the effects of those changes on specific industries. For example, changes in the Gross National Product (GNP) are said to affect changes in U.S. automobile sales. When the GNP increases (indicating prosperity), auto sales are said to rise accordingly. Commonly used predictors or indicators are the GNP, the unemployment rate, the increase (or decrease) in average weekly hours worked, the increase (or decrease) in the employment cost per man hour, gross private domestic investment, corporate profits, housing starts, interest rates, disposable personal income, consumer price indexes, and retail sales, etc. These indicators are compiled and published in the United States both by the government and by outside organizations such as banks, brokerage houses, and universities. Economic forecasting may be used to predict impending changes in the demand for both consumer and industrial goods. See also *forecasting.*

ECONOMIC INFRASTRUCTURE See *infrastructure*

ECONOMIC MAN See *economic man theory*

ECONOMIC MAN THEORY A view of consumer behavior which postulates that price is the primary motivating factor in consumer purchase decisions. The theory maintains that people compare choices in terms of cost and value received in an attempt to maximize their satisfaction.

ECONOMIC NEEDS Those customer needs which are concerned with making the best use of limited resources (from the customer's own point of view). These needs include convenience of product use, efficiency of product operation or use, dependability of the product, reliability of service, durability, improvement of earnings, improvement of productivity of property, and economy of purchase or use. Economic needs govern how and why customers select certain product features over others.

ECONOMIC ORDER QUANTITY (EOQ) The optimum size of an order, calculated to minimize carrying and procurement costs, especially the cost of frequent re-ordering, while maintaining sufficient quantities to meet the average level of demand. An EOQ model is the technique used to balance the costs of holding inventory against the costs involved in placing orders.

ECONOMIC ORDER QUANTITY (EOQ)

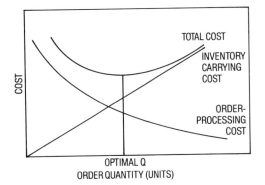

ECONOMIC ORDER QUANTITY MODEL See *economic order quantity (EOQ)*

ECONOMIC SHOPPER See *economical shopper*

ECONOMIC SYSTEM The manner in which an economy is organized to utilize scarce resources to produce goods and services and to distribute them for consumption. The economic system of any given society will reflect that society's goals and the nature of its political institutions. Nevertheless, all economic systems must develop some method to decide what and how much is to be produced and distributed as well as by whom, when, and to whom. Planned economic systems are those in which government planners decide what and how much is to be produced and distributed by whom, when, and to whom. Socialist and communist economic systems function in this manner. In market-directed economic systems, such as capitalism, the individual decisions of producers and consumers make the decisions for the economy as a whole. In a pure market-directed economy, also known as a free-market economy, consumers determine a society's production by their choices in the marketplace without government intervention.

ECONOMICAL SHOPPER A consumer who is particularly sensitive to price, quality, and merchandise assortment and who shops for the best value available.

ECONOMIES OF SCALE Cost reductions and other operating advantages accruing from efficient, large scale production. Such economies are generally reflected in lower unit prices.

ECONOMY See *economic system*

ECONOMY PACK Several products, wrapped together and sold at a lower price than if each were sold separately, to provide a saving to the consumer. The economy pack most often comes directly from the producer, but middleman organizations sometimes repackage merchandise to create an economy pack.

ECONOMY SIZE A large quantity of a product, such as detergent, sold in a single large package to provide the consumer with a lower per unit price.

ECR See *point-of-sale (POS) perpetual inventory control system*

EDITING In marketing research data analysis, editing is that step which precedes coding and which involves checking collected information for omissions, errors, irrelevancies, etc.

EDM See *electronic direct marketing*

EEC See *European Economic Community (EEC)*

84

EFFECTIVE BUYING INCOME (EBI) A measurement developed by *Sales & Marketing Management* (magazine) which is the equivalent of disposable personal income, i.e., it represents wages and salaries and other income (rents etc.) less federal, state, and local taxes and other deductions such as contributions toward insurance coverage, pension systems, etc. EBI is a bulk measurement of market potential and is viewed as most effective when employed in making generalizations about a market's capacity to buy.

EFFECTIVE DEMAND See *demand*

EFFORT SCALE In consumer behavior studies, the effort scale is an attempt to graphically represent the amount of time and effort consumers are prepared to expend in shopping for a particular product.

EFT See *electronic funds transfer (EFT)*

EGO-BOLSTERING DRIVE In consumer motivation, an ego-bolstering drive is a psychological buying motive characterized by the need to enhance one's personality, prestige, and self-image while avoiding ridicule. See also *psychological buying motive.*

EGO-INVOLVED PRODUCTS Products in which the consumer feels he has an emotional or psychological stake. Most designer merchandise, which in some way satisfies a need, may be regarded as ego-involved.

EGOISTIC NEEDS An equivalent term for the fourth level in Maslow's hierarchy.

80-20 PRINCIPLE A rule of thumb stating that approximately 80% of a firm's business is generated by approximately 20% of its customers.

EKB THEORY See *Engel-Kollat-Blackwell (EKB) theory*

ELASTIC DEMAND See *elasticity of demand*

ELASTIC SUPPLY See *elasticity of supply*

ELASTICITY The adaptability of a market and its ability to respond to a change in price. Elasticity is calculated as the percent change in the quantity demanded divided by the percent change in price.

$$\text{Elasticity} = \frac{\%\text{ change in quantity demanded}}{\%\text{ change in price}}$$

See also *elasticity of demand.*

ELASTICITY COEFFICIENT See *elasticity of demand*

ELASTICITY METHOD A system of basing a firm's advertising appropriation on supply and demand curves. The average cost of any additional expenditure is compared with the average return on increased profit, indicating the point beyond which advertising is uneconomic.

ELASTICITY OF DEMAND A concept that relates quantities of goods sold to changes in price. Normally, demand for goods will vary inversely to price, other factors remaining constant. For example, if a 1% decrease in price produces an increased demand of *less* than 1%, demand is said to be inelastic. Conversely, if a 1% decrease in price produces increased demand of *more* than 1%, then demand is said to be elastic. If a 1% decrease in price produces exactly 1% in increased demand, a condition of unitary elasticity is said to exist.

ELASTICITY OF EXPECTATIONS The ratio that exists between the predicted future percent change in price and the most recent current change in price.

ELASTICITY OF SUPPLY An economic concept that relates the supply of goods to their market price; i.e., as the price of goods advances, producers are inclined to respond by producing more, thus increasing the supply in the marketplace. If, however, supply does not respond to an increase in price it is regarded as inelastic.

ELECTRONIC BANKING NET-WORK See *electronic funds transfer*

ELECTRONIC CASH REGISTER (ECR) See *point-of-sale (POS) perpetual inventory control system*

ELECTRONIC DIRECT MARKET-ING (EDM) An interactive system, such as two-way cable television, in which the concept of direct marketing is combined with the electronic media (television, radio, and the telephone). EDM is calculated to elicit a direct response on the part of potential customers. See also *telemarketing* and *electronic retailing*

ELECTRONIC FUNDS TRANSFER (EFT) In retailing, the use of automated electronic equipment, such as computer terminals, to move money directly from the customer's account to the retailer's account at the point-of-sale or service.

ELECTRONIC RETAILING The use of electronically transmitted information to facilitate consumer shopping without the need to enter a store. Electronic retailing is a form of direct marketing in which telephone lines connected to home computers, television sets equipped with special decoders, and interactive cable television are employed to transmit information to the consumer. The potential buyer views a "menu" combining text and still graphics which includes all merchandise being offered for sale. If the consumer decides to purchase, a number is entered on a keyboard (or, in some systems, a telephone call is made to a central location) and the item is ordered.

Another form of electronic retailing employs transactional discs (either in the store or placed in remote locations) equipped with video-disc players or other electronic equipment on which the customer may view a merchandise "menu." Sales are commonly executed through the use of a keyboard or by an in-store clerk.

Although some systems bypass the traditional retailer completely—the manufacturer sells directly to the consumer—electronic retailing is generally viewed as an adjunct to in-store shopping rather than a replacement for it.

ELECTRONIC SHOPPING See *electronic retailing*

EMBARGO The most stringent form of trade restriction or quota under which specific products are barred from entering a country.

EMBOURGEOISEMENT The theory, now out of vogue, that affluent workers in industry adopt middle-class standards, life styles, and purchasing patterns as the result of their higher earnings.

EMERGENCY GOODS Products purchased only when the need is very great.

EMOTIONAL APPROACH See *imaginative approach*

EMOTIONAL BUYING MOTIVE Any factor which contributes to a customer's impulse to buy certain merchandise which is rooted in the customer's self-image and personal feelings rather than in logical thought. See also *motive* and *rational buying motive.*

EMPATHY The ability to put oneself in another's place. In marketing, this allows the perceptive marketer to anticipate a customer's reaction to appeals and campaigns.

EMPIRICAL CREDIT SYSTEM A method for determining the creditworthiness of applicants. It is based on creditors' experience with borrowers and attributes points to traits describing the applicant (such as previous credit history, whether the applicant owns or rents a dwelling, length of employment, salary, etc.).

EMPLOYEE BENEFIT Any of the non-wage forms of employee compensation. May include paid sick leave, holidays and vacations, group medical and dental insurance, retirement programs, etc.

EMPLOYEE DEVELOPMENT A program designed to upgrade employees through training. The program may aim to improve the performance of employees at their present jobs or to qualify them for advancement within the organization.

EMPLOYEE HANDBOOK A manual of facts and instructions provided to the employees of a business. May include the history and philosophy of the firm, regulations, policies, procedures, benefits, dress code, etc. Often used in the orientation of new employees.

EMPLOYEE INDOCTRINATION See *employee orientation*

EMPLOYEE ORIENTATION A period in which all new employees are familiarized with the policies, history, and operations of the business as well as the responsibilities of their particular jobs. The employees are also introduced to employee benefits and opportunities for advancement during the orientation period. An orientation booklet is provided by some firms. The booklet may contain details about the firm's history, development, organization, and policies as well as general information about the firm's operations and facilities. Employment policies and practices are often spelled out. Intended to give the new employees insight into the company, what is expected of them, and what they may expect in return.

EMPLOYER A person or company which hires others to work for wages, salary, or commission.

EMULATION STAGE See *fashion cycle*

ENCODER See *encoding*

ENCODING In communications, the process of putting plain language into an easily transmitted symbolic form.

END OF MONTH TERMS In the dating of invoices, an agreement indicating that cash discounts and net credit periods begin at the end of the month the goods were shipped. Invoices dated on the 25th of the month or later are generally treated as if dated on the first day of the next month.

END-USE APPLICATION SEGMENTATION In industrial marketing, the subdivision of a market on the basis of how the product is to be used by its purchaser.

END-USE PRODUCT See *consumer goods*

ENDLESS CHAIN METHOD See *chain prospecting*

ENGEL, ERNST See *Engel's laws*

ENGEL-KOLLAT-BLACKWELL (EKB) THEORY A theory of buyer behavior in which the individual's psychological makeup (his personality, emotions, attitudes, etc.) is believed to affect his mental processes and thus his behavior in the marketplace.

ENGEL'S LAWS A 19th century theory of spending behavior developed by Ernst Engel, a German statistician. Engel postulated that as a family's income increases, it spends a smaller percentage of that income on food, about the same percentage of that income on housing and household operations, and a larger percentage of that income on other (less essential) items. This theory was a precursor to Maslow's hierarchy.

ENHANCEMENT A condition in which a new product is introduced into the marketplace and which increases the sales rates of one or more other products in the company's line. The opposite of cannibalization.

ENTRAPMENT STUDY A technique employed in marketing research in which the purpose of the study is not revealed to the respondent.

ENTREPOT A commercial center which receives and redistributes goods and which is free of import duty and/or maintains bonded warehouses. London, Amsterdam, and Rotterdam's Europort are examples of entrepots.

ENTREPRENEUR A person who organizes, launches, and directs a business undertaking such as a new business, a new product, or a new production process.

ENVIRONMENTAL DYNAMICS See *marketing environment*

ENVIRONMENTAL OPPORTUNITY In a marketing context, a part of the business environment in which there is an unmet need for products or services which a company may exploit.

EOM DATING See *end of month terms*

EOQ See *economic order quantity (EOQ)*

EOQ MODEL See *economic order quantity (EOQ)*

EQUAL CREDIT OPPORTUNITY ACT (1975–1977) Federal legislation prohibiting the denial of credit to any applicant on the basis of age, sex, marital status, national origin, race, religion, receipt of payments from public assistance programs, and/or childbearing intentions. The Act went into effect in stages from 1975 to 1977. It further stipulates that creditors must provide each unsuccessful applicant with reasons for denial of credit, that married people may request separate accounts, and that alimony and child care payments must be considered as income.

EQUILIBRIUM POINT In supply and demand, the point at which the quantity and the price of a good or service that sellers are willing to offer equals the quantity and price that buyers are willing to pay for that good or service. Graphically, the equilibrium point may be represented as the point at which the supply curve and the demand curve intersect. The price of a particular good or service so determined is known as the equilibrium price. See also *supply curve* and *demand curve*.

EQUILIBRIUM PRICE See *equilibrium point*

EQUIPMENT See *installed equipment* and *accessory equipment*

EQUITY THEORY A method of explaining employee motivation which assumes that individuals must see a relationship between the amount of work they perform (input) and the rewards they obtain (outcome).

ERRATIC DEMAND The need and/or desire for goods or services which is unstable and unpredictable over a protracted period.

ESCALATOR CLAUSE In pricing practice, a clause in an agreement which permits a producer or manufacturer to increase his prices based on a specified formula such as the cost-of-living index.

ESTABLISHED TRENDS A pattern of increased demand for specific merchandise by style, color, material content, price lines, etc. as indicated by customer preference reflected in sales or by consumer research.

ESTIMATED LIABILITY The projected costs to be incurred for uncertain, variable obligations such as repairs under warranty.

ETHICAL SHOPPER A customer who feels obligated to patronize small stores or local businesses to help them stay in business and is willing to sacrifice the potential price and assortment benefits available in larger stores or chains in order to do so.

ETHNIC MARKET A group of customers defined by race, country of origin, language, etc.

ETHNOCENTRICISM The belief that one's own cultural values are, or should be, the norm. Ethnocentrism is exemplified in the self-reference criteria in which one's values are taken as a reference point for all others.

EUROPEAN COMMUNITY (EC) See *European Economic Community (EEC)*

EUROPEAN ECONOMIC COMMUNITY (EEC) The European common market resulting from the Treaty of Rome, 1957. Members include France, the United Kingdom, the Federal Republic of Germany, Italy, the Netherlands, Belgium, Luxembourg, Ireland, Denmark, and Greece. Aims include the sharing of common agricultural practices, free movement of labor and capital between members, and a unified transportation system. Most tariffs between members were dropped by 1970. Also known simply as the European Community (EC) or the Common Market.

EVALUATIVE CRITERIA In consumer behavior, those aspects of a product or service which a consumer considers during the process of weighing alternative courses of action.

EVEN-LINE PRICING A method of ascribing whole number selling prices to merchandise to give the impression of high-end retailing. For example, a retailer using even-line pricing would charge $100 for an item rather than $99.95. See also *odd-line pricing.*

EVEN PRICES See *even-line pricing*

EVENTS Nonpersonal communications such as news conferences, grand openings, etc. designed to communicate particular messages to target audiences. See also *nonpersonal communication channels.*

EVOKED SET In consumer behavior, evoked set refers to the specific brands a buyer will consider when shopping a product category; i.e., customers commonly do not consider *every* possible choice or alternative when making buying decisions. Evoked sets are relatively small compared to the total number of choices in the marketplace. See also *inert set* and *inept set.*

EX DOCK (NAMED PORT OF IMPORTATION) A term of sale indicating that the quoted price includes the cost of the goods and all costs necessary to bring the goods to the named port. Includes duty, if any.

EX WORKS A shipping term indicating that the seller of goods is responsible only for making the goods sold available at his factory, or works. The buyer is responsible for loading the goods on whichever vehicle he provides and for transportation to the final destination.

EXCEPTION RATE A freight rate charged by shippers to their customers. The exception rate is a deviation from the class rate allowed under special circumstances, though still subject to government regulation. It may be either higher or lower than the class rate and applies to both contract and common carriers. In general, lower exception rates may be charged to encourage competition or otherwise aid the shipping industry. Higher rates are allowed for special services, such as express or overnight delivery. See also *class rate* and *commodity rate*.

EXCEPTION REPORT In a marketing information system, a report to an executive of some circumstance or occurrence in the system which exceeds predetermined levels. For example, a manager may not be concerned with the level of sales as long as they do not increase or decrease by more than a preestablished percentage. If they exceed these limits he is automatically sent an exception report.

EXCHANGE 1) In marketing, an exchange occurs when two or more parties trade products for products (swapping or barter) or products for money (buying or selling). 2) In retailing, the substitution of one item for another, usually returned merchandise. 3) A place where securities, commodities, etc. are traded.

EXCHANGE CONTROL A method used by some governments to regulate foreign trade. The government controls the amount of currency exchanged by requiring firms that earn foreign currency (exchange) through exporting to sell this currency to a central bank or control agency which serves as a clearinghouse. Similarly, importers must buy their foreign currency from the same central clearinghouse.

EXCHANGE FUNCTIONS The buying and selling activities in the marketing process which result in the exchange of title to goods or services. Exchange is regarded as one of the basic marketing functions.

EXCHANGE RATE The price of one country's currency expressed in terms of another country's currency or gold. For example, a U.S. dollar is worth a certain number of British pounds sterling, Canadian dollars, French francs, Japanese yen, etc. The exchange rate is not a constant, and fluctuates on a daily basis as currencies are traded in international money markets.

EXCLUSIVE AGENCY METHOD OF DISTRIBUTION See *exclusive distribution*

EXCLUSIVE DEALING A form of exclusive distribution in which the middleman or retailer, having an exclusive distributorship granted by a manufacturer or supplier, is prohibited from carrying competing lines.

EXCLUSIVE DEALING AGREEMENT See *exclusive dealing*

EXCLUSIVE DISTRIBUTION A form of distribution in which a product or service is offered for sale to only one distributor or retailer in a particular territory. The manufacturer or producer thus gives the exclusive right to resale to a single organization. See also *confined merchandise*.

EXCLUSIVE OUTLET SELLING See *exclusive distribution*

90

EXCLUSIVE TERRITORY See *exclusive distribution*

EXCLUSIVES Merchandise produced for one or a limited number of resellers.

EXECUTIVE Any person whose function is to administer or manage the affairs of a business or other organization. Executives are generally expected to provide leadership by directing, motivating, and guiding the work of individual employees and departments and causing others to follow their lead.

EXECUTIVE LEADERSHIP See *executive*

EXECUTIVE PANEL SURVEY A technique used to estimate demand for a product. The individuals surveyed are all involved in some aspect of the marketing process, such as executives with experience in marketing similar or related products.

EXEMPT CARRIER A form of transportation (rail, highway, river, etc.) which has been granted an exemption from certain regulations by the localities in which it operates when certain specified products are being moved. For example, a barge line may be exempt from all local laws except for those governing safety when it is transporting a commodity like wheat.

EXHIBIT APPROACH See *product* (or *exhibit*) *approach*

EXPECTED NET PROFIT See *expected profit concept*

EXPECTED PRICE The level at which the customer expects a product or service to be priced; i.e., expected price represents what the customer thinks a product or service is worth.

EXPECTED PROFIT CONCEPT A strategy employed by firms engaged in competitive bidding. The profit which might be expected to accrue from each bid price is calculated in the knowledge that the probability of an acceptable bid decreases as projected profit increases.

EXPECTED VALUE A concept used in selecting alternative courses of action. The expected value of an alternative is an average of all the conceivable consequences of that alternative with each consequence being assigned a probability percentage. When applied to the marketing of new products, the expected value concept facilitates the sorting out of the many probabilities existing in the marketplace.

EXPENSE Any cost incurred in the course of running one's own business, doing one's work, etc. Expenses are subtracted from the gross margin to get the net profit.

EXPENSE GOODS See *expense item*

EXPENSE ITEM Any short-lived good or service which may be charged off as it is used, usually in the year of purchase. See also *capital goods*.

EXPERIENCE CURVE A graphic representation of a marketing reality; i.e., that those firms having the highest share of the market will have an advantage over their smaller competitors because of their learning advantage, greater specialization, economies of scale, etc.

EXPERIENCE CURVE PRICING A strategy used in pricing manufactured goods in which the selling price is calculated on the basis of projected costs at the time of production rather than on costs prevailing during the planning stages.

EXPERIMENT A technique for gathering primary data in which variables are manipulated in such a way that cause and effect relationships become apparent. Experiments provide a basis for small-scale trial runs before the firm totally commits itself to a course of action.

EXPERIMENTAL GAMING A method of research which utilizes a simulated environment to observe behavior.

EXPERIMENTAL METHOD See *experiment*

EXPERIMENTAL RESEARCH See *experiment*

EXPERT CHANNEL A personal communication channel consisting of independent experts making statements to target customers.

EXPIRATION DATE In food retailing, the last date on which perishable merchandise may be sold.

EXPLICIT COSTS Expenditures such as wages, utilities, supplies, etc., which are clearly stated and readily observable. They appear on the accounting record as costs and are charged against the operation of the business. See also *implicit costs.*

EXPLORATION STAGE In new product development, the initial stage during which ideas for new products are either searched out or internally generated by a firm.

EXPONENTIAL SMOOTHING In time-series analysis, exponential smoothing is the practice of making predictions on a weighted average of experiences. Experiences are weighted with regard to their occurrence in time, with the most recent experience given more weight than the others. For example, if a firm's cigarette sales for the four previous months had been 6,000, 5,000, 7,000, and 7,500 cartons, respectively, the forecast for the coming month would be above 7,500 cartons.

EXPORT 1) To send or transport goods to another country or countries especially for the purpose of sales. 2) An export is any item sent to another country or countries.

EXPORT AGENT See *foreign-based export agent*

EXPORT BROKER An agent middleman involved in international trade, performing the functions of a broker for domestic firms exporting their goods to foreign markets. The export broker brings buyers and sellers together and essentially provides information to each of them, connecting the needs of the buyers to the available goods of the supplier. See also *agent middleman, domestic-based export merchant,* and *import broker.*

EXPORT COMMISSION HOUSE A commission merchant involved in international trade, or selling domestic goods in a foreign market. The export commission house handles goods shipped to it by sellers, completes the sales, and sends the money to each seller. The export commission house is reimbursed for its services by means of a commission paid by the seller. See also *commission merchant.*

EXPORT COMMISSION MERCHANT See *export commission house*

EXPORT DISTRIBUTOR See *foreign-based export distributor*

EXPORT DUTY A tax (or tariff) levied on a country's exports generally employed by nations which are heavy exporters of raw materials. Export duties are designed to protect and encourage domestic industries or simply to raise revenue.

EXPORT-MANAGEMENT COMPANY An independent international marketing middleman which manages a company's export activities in indirect exporting and is paid a set fee. See also *indirect export.*

EXPORT SALES REPRESENTATIVE In direct export, the export sales representative is a domestic-based salesperson sent abroad at intervals to find foreign customers for the producer. See also *direct export.*

EXPORTING The sale of goods or services to customers in foreign countries.

EXPOSURE The degree to which an advertising message is actually perceived by members of the target audience. For an ad to be exposed it must be more than simply seen—it must be noticed to an extent that there is some measurable impact.

EXPRESSED WARRANTY See *warranty*

EXPROPRIATION The seizure of foreign owned property by a government with some provision for the reimbursement of the owners.

EXTENDED PRODUCT Those tangible and intangible elements which accompany a product or service. Included are warranties, service contracts, supplies, and such intangibles as the status and prestige associated with ownership of the product.

EXTENDED TERMS Additional time allowed the buyer of goods to pay an invoice.

EXTENSIBLE MARKET A market which has room for expansion, either through an increase in per capita consumption or by attracting more first-time customers.

EXTENSIVE DISTRIBUTION See *intensive distribution*

EXTENSIVE MARKET OPPORTUNITIES Opportunities in the marketplace for new growth which generally involve a company in activities not previously part of its marketing effort. For example, a company may develop an entirely new product line to appeal to its existing customers.

EXTENSIVE PROBLEM SOLVING In consumer behavior, extensive problem solving is the effort taken to understand one's needs and how to satisfy them. This is particularly applicable when a need is completely new to the individual consumer. See also *limited problem solving.*

EXTERNAL MARKETING ENVIRONMENT See *marketing environment*

EXTINCTION PRICING See *predatory pricing*

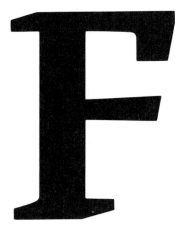

FABRICATING MATERIALS Component products which have been processed past the raw material stage, e.g., pig iron, cement, flour, etc. before they are incorporated into a finished product. Unlike fabricating parts, fabricating materials usually change form as they are further processed.

FABRICATING PARTS Manufactured components which become part of a larger finished product; e.g., an automobile battery or coat buttons. Despite the fact that fabricating parts are incorporated into another product, they do not change form. See also *fabricating materials.*

FACE-TO-FACE SELLING See *personal selling*

FACILITATING AGENCIES IN MARKETING Businesses which provide services essential to the marketing process but which neither take title to the product nor engage directly in the buying or selling function. These organizations (financial institutions, transportation companies, exchanges, marketing research firms, insurance companies, etc.) provide assistance to marketing channel members but, unlike wholesalers and retailers, they are not actually a part of the channel.

FACILITATING FUNCTION See *facilitating marketing function*

FACILITATING MARKETING FUNCTION Any activity which assists marketers in the performance of the universal marketing functions. Facilitating marketing functions include standardization, grading, risk taking, financing, and the gathering of market information. See also *facilitating agencies in marketing.*

FACILITATORS See *facilitating agencies in marketing*

FACTOR A financial institution which buys at discount the accounts receivable of other businesses. The transaction provides the business with ready cash. The factor makes a profit by collecting the outstanding debts while at the same time bearing the risks of uncollectable accounts. See also *market factor.*

FACTOR ENDOWMENT In the international marketing theory called "comparative advantage," the advantage rests, at least in part, on factor endowment; i.e., resources such as labor, land, natural resources, capital, etc., which provide the advantage in the first place. See also *comparative advantage.*

FACTOR METHOD A method used to forecast sales by establishing a relationship between the company's sales and some other variable (or factor). Past sales (or industry sales) × variable = sales forecast. Several variables may be used together for greater forecasting accuracy.

FACTORING The sale of the accounts receivable of a business to a financial institution, e.g., a bank or factor. The buying institution purchases the accounts at a discounted rate but assumes all losses resulting from uncollectable debts. The business profits from this arrangment by having access to ready cash.

FACTORY OUTLET Originally a manufacturer-owned store located at the factory site through which unwanted inventory (overruns, closeouts, irregulars, etc.) could be unloaded at greatly reduced prices without offering competition to the manufacturer's retail customers. Now these stores commonly sell in-season first-quality merchandise of more than one manufacturer and are often located in factory outlet malls which compete directly with traditional retailers. Also known as outlet stores. See also *manufacturer's store.*

FACTORY PACK See *banded pack*

FACTORY-POSITIONED WAREHOUSE A facility in which goods may be stored. The factory-positioned warehouse is located near the place of manufacture and may be used to store raw materials and fabricating parts to be used in production, or to store finished goods waiting to be shipped.

FACTUAL APPROACH A technique used by a salesperson in the first few moments of contact with a prospect. In this approach, the salesperson turns an interesting fact connected with the product or service being sold into an enticing opening sentence. See also *approach.*

FAD A style or product that is accepted quickly by large numbers of consumers but which enjoys short-lived popularity and passes into oblivion in a relatively short time.

FAIR DEBT COLLECTION PRACTICES ACT (1978) Federal legislation prohibiting the use of abusive, deceptive, and unfair debt collection practices. The legislation is essentially a list of specific practices that creditors or collection agencies may not use.

FAIR CREDIT REPORTING ACT (1970) Federal legislation which permits any credit applicant who is rejected for credit on the basis of adverse information supplied by a credit bureau to be notified of the reasons for such a rejection. The applicant may examine the credit file and have it corrected. Adverse credit information may not be used if it is more than 7 years old, and information that is only

3 months old must be verified before it is used. The Act is designed to control the practices of credit bureaus in their determination and distribution of credit ratings, protect credit applicants from the effects of erroneous information that a credit bureau may have in its files, and provide applicants with the opportunity to inspect their own files so as to counter any misinformation contained therein.

FAIR PACKAGING AND LABELING ACT (1966) Federal legislation enabling the Federal Trade Commission (FTC) and the Food and Drug Administration (FDA) to take action against the use of false or misleading matter on labels, the omission of ingredients, the omission of net quantity and size of serving information on food products, and the use of misleading shapes and sizes in packaging. Also known as the Truth-in-Packaging Act.

FAIR TRADE See *resale price maintenance*

FALLING DEMAND See *faltering demand*

FALTERING DEMAND That point in the product life cycle when demand for a product or service begins to wane, i.e, when purchasers have less need and/or desire for the product.

FAMILY BRAND A line of products offered for sale by a single producer all of which carry the company's brand name, logo, or similar identifying design. Also known as family packaging or as a blanket brand.

FAMILY LIFE CYCLE (FLC) Those stages through which a family passes from formation to dissolution including single persons, young married couples, couples with children, couples without children at home (the so-called empty nest), and finally single persons again (i.e., solitary survivors).

FAMILY PACKAGING See *family brand*

FARM PRODUCTS Raw materials produced by farmers, such as cotton, hogs, eggs, and milk. These are unprocessed goods that are handled as little as needed to move them to the next step in the production process. They become part of a physical good when they are processed in the form of textiles, frozen or canned foods, etc. This is in contrast to produce, which refers to fresh fruits and vegetables sold at retail.

FAS (FREE ALONG SIDE) A term used in shipping agreements meaning that the seller of goods pays the freight charges on a shipment up to the point where the goods are placed on the dock alongside the ship (or train or truck). At that point title to the goods passes to the buyer who pays all costs associated with delays in loading or damage to goods.

FASHION Those styles (clothing, automobiles, etc.) which are currently most popular are said to be in fashion, i.e., they are widely accepted by consumers at one or more levels of the market. Since styles constantly change in response to consumer demand for the new, it may be said that fashion is, in fact, change—that fashion is not some thing so much as it is an on-going process.

FASHION ADOPTION PROCESS The mechanism by which fashions are diffused throughout a population. There are three theories of fashion adoption: 1) the downward-flow (or trickle-down) theory in which adoption and diffusion are seen as flowing from higher socioeconomic classes downward to the lower classes; 2) horizontal-flow (the mass-market theory) in which fashions are believed to move from group to group in the same social class; e.g., opinion leaders within the large middle class have as much influence on fashion adoption as do leading members of the upper class; 3) the upward-flow theory in which generally younger people (and sometimes young people of relatively low socioeconomic levels) are seen as influencing fashions as they quickly adopt new styles which will later be diffused up the class structure. See also *diffusion process* and *fashion cycle*.

FASHION CYCLE A theory, similar to the product life cycle, in which styles are seen to appear and rise in popularity, flourish, peak, and finally decline and disappear. The cycle may be seen as having three stages: 1) the introductory or distinctiveness stage (in which some consumers seek and are willing to pay for products different from those accepted by the majority; i.e., new and innovative fashions); 2) the acceptance or emulation stage (in which a particular style catches on due to the desire of other consumers to imitate the original users; and 3) the regression or economic emulation stage (in which many consumers desire the fashion and manufacturers mass produce the product at low cost. This continues until the market passes through the growth and maturity stages and rapidly moves into sales decline). See also *product life cycle (PLC)*.

FASHION LIFE CYCLE See *fashion cycle*

FASHION OBSOLESCENCE See *planned obsolescence*

FAST FREIGHT SERVICE In physical distribution, fast freight service refers to the use of special, fast trains for the shipment of perishable goods, goods in urgent demand, or high-value items.

FCC See *Federal Communications Commission (FCC)*

FCN TREATIES See *friendship, commerce and navigation (FCN) treaties*

FDA See *Food and Drug Administration (FDA)*

FEATURES APPROACH TO SELLING See *benefit approach*

FEDERAL CIGARETTE LABELING AND ADVERTISING ACT (1967) Federal legislation intended to protect consumers from the hazards of cigarette smoking. The Act requires that cigarette packaging and advertising bear specific health warnings.

FEDERAL COMMUNICATIONS ACT (1934) See *Federal Communications Commission (FCC)*

FEDERAL COMMUNICATIONS COMMISSION (FCC) The federal agency responsible for administering the Communications Act of 1934 and subsequent related legislation regarding the licensing of television and radio broadcasters. The Commission also exercises control over the practices of the broadcasters, in an effort to ensure they operate for the public interest, convenience, and necessity. This control has frequently extended to advertising practices.

FEDERAL FOOD AND DRUG ACT (1906) Federal legislation which prohibited the manufacture, sale, or transportation of adulterated or fraudulently labeled foods and drugs in interstate commerce. The Act was replaced by the Food, Drug and Cosmetic Act (1938), amended by the Food Additives Amendment (1958) and the Kefauver-Harris Drug Amendments to the Food and Drug Act (1962). Also called the Pure Food and Drug Act (1906).

FEDERAL HAZARDOUS SUBSTANCES LABELING ACT (1960) Federal legislation requiring manufacturers to place warning labels on all items containing dangerous household chemicals.

FEDERAL TRADE COMMISSION (FTC) A regulatory agency of the federal government charged with policing anti-monopoly laws. In the 1970s, the FTC emerged as a protector of consumer rights by regulating children's advertising, cigarette package labeling, the funeral industry, etc. See also *Federal Trade Commission Act (1914)*.

FEDERAL TRADE COMMISSION ACT (1914) Federal legislation which established the Federal Trade Commission (FTC) and empowered it to enforce the Sherman Antitrust Act (1890), the Clayton Act (1914), and subsequent related legislation. The Act made it illegal for anyone to commit an unfair or deceptive act of commerce or to engage in deceptive business practices. Amended by the Wheeler-Lea Act (1938).

FEEDBACK 1) In communications, the response to a decoded message transmitted back from the receiver to the sender. 2) More generally, responses fed back from consumers in the marketplace.

FERTILITY RATE The birth rate expressed as the number of children per woman.

FIELD SALES MANAGER Lower level sales manager generally at the district or regional level. The field sales force reports to the field sales manager.

FIELD WAREHOUSER A specialized public warehouse organization which provides cash for goods on hand. The field warehouser holds some of a manufacturer's finished goods as its own property. In exchange, it issues warehouse receipts to the manufacturer. The warehouse receipts may be used as collateral to borrow money. This is a particularly valuable service to manufacturers whose goods are not yet sold. The manufacturer's own warehouse is used to avoid the expense of transporting the goods, and the seller retains title. Control of the goods, however, passes to the field warehouser. Also known as a custodial warehouser.

FIGHTING BRAND An individual brand used to meet the competition while the company's other, higher quality, better known, and more expensive brand is protected. See also *individual brand*.

FILL-INS Goods purchased for resale to fill gaps in the inventory of regular merchandise which has been sold out.

FIMA See *Financial Institutions Marketing Association (FIMA)*

FINAL CONSUMER See *ultimate consumer*

FINANCIAL FLOW See *channel flows*

FINANCIAL INSTITUTIONS MARKETING ASSOCIATION (FIMA) An association of individuals involved in marketing, public relations, sales, advertising, and/or consumer research in the banking industry. The Chicago based association publishes *Financial Marketing* (monthly) and *Marketing Alert* (bimonthly), an annual *Membership Directory*, and specialized manuals and books.

FINANCIAL OBJECTIVES The profit and return on investment sought by a company in the current year as expressed in the marketing plan.

FINANCIAL RATIOS The series of ratios used to measure a company's productivity, solvency, liquidity, and other items on the company's balance sheet. The ratios indicate trends in these financial areas and provide a means of comparing companies within an industry. The financial ratios are grouped into two types: 1) those that summarize an aspect of the business operation for a period of time (generally one year) and 2) those that summarize an aspect of the company's financial position of a given moment in time.

FINANCING See *financing function*

FINANCING FUNCTION A facilitating marketing function by which funding is provided to manufacture, transport, sell, buy, and store products.

FISHYBACK A coordinated transportation arrangement in which truck trailers are loaded directly onto ships. This use of containerization helps eliminate costly and time-consuming unloading and reloading of the goods being shipped. See also *containerization.*

FIT See *channel fit*

FIXED COST Those costs involved in operating a business which do not fluctuate in direct relation to production levels or sales volume. Fixed costs vary over a period of time but are relatively independent of short-term changes in output. Included are rent, property taxes, plant and equipment depreciation, interest on bonds, etc. Also called fixed expenses, standby costs, constant costs, and period costs. See also *overhead, variable cost, direct cost,* and *indirect cost.*

FIXED EXPENSES See *fixed cost*

FIXED-SUM-PER-UNIT AP-PROACH A method of computing a promotional budget by allocating a fixed amount of money for each unit produced or sold.

FLANKER PRODUCT A new product related to an already established companion product and bearing the same brand name. For example, a new hair conditioner bearing the same name as an established shampoo would be an appropriate flanker product, as would a shaving cream with the same name as an established brand of razors. The introduction of flanker products may be used to help boost the sales of the mature product.

FLC See *family life cycle (FLC)*

FLEA MARKET Originally an outdoor bazaar in which vendors offered cheap secondhand goods for sale to the public. Flea markets now may be held indoors and goods offered for sale may be new first-quality merchandise selling well below regular retail prices.

FLEXIBLE BREAK-EVEN ANALYSIS A form of business analysis used to project the performance of a product in the marketplace at various price points. Break-even analysis reveals the number of units of a product that must be sold for total revenue to equal total product cost. Flexible break-even analysis allows the market researcher to estimate the expected sales volume at a number of different prices.

FLEXIBLE-PRICE POLICY See *flexible pricing*

FLEXIBLE PRICING A variable pricing policy which allows for bargaining between buyer and seller as well as for the adjustment of prices to conform to peaks and slumps in the normal business cycle. Flexible prices are commonly found in the industrial market but occur at the retail level in the used car, appliance markets, etc.

FLOOR PLAN FINANCING A form of short-term financing commonly used by retailers of big ticket items such as home appliances, boats, and automobiles. The retailer borrows money from a lending institution and uses it to pay the vendor (a manufacturer or distributor) for the goods at time of receipt. The lending institution holds title to the goods as collateral and is repaid by the retailer as the goods are sold.

FLOOR PLANNING See *floor plan financing*

FLOW-THROUGH CONCEPT A concept in warehousing in which the rapid movement of the warehoused goods is given priority. Flow-through is most generally applied to distribution centers in an effort to quickly meet customers' needs.

FLUCTUATING DEMAND In industrial marketing, the volatile demand for industrial goods and services, particularly for new plants and equipment. This demand is generally regarded as less stable than the demand for consumer goods and services. See also *accelerator principle*.

FMI See *Food Marketing Institute (FMI)*

FOB (FREE ON BOARD) A term used in shipping agreements meaning that the buyer of goods pays the freight charges from the FOB point (the point of origin), e.g., the factory, port-of-entry, etc. Title to the merchandise passes to the buyer at the FOB point, for example, at the time the goods pass the ship's rail.

FOB (FREE ON BOARD) FACTORY A shipping agreement in which the seller of goods places them on a carrier at the factory site at no charge to the buyer (thus "free on board"). The buyer assumes title to the goods as soon as they are on board the carrier and pays the freight from the factory to destination.

FOB FACTORY PRICING See *FOB (free on board) factory*

FOB ORIGIN PRICING See *FOB (free on board) factory*

FOB PLANT See *FOB (free on board) factory*

FOB PLANT-FREIGHT ALLOWED See *freight absorption pricing*

FOB SHIPPING POINT See *FOB (free on board) factory*

FOCUS GROUP See *focus group interview*

FOCUS GROUP INTERVIEW A form of indirect interview used in marketing research. In a focus group interview, a small group of consumers is invited to participate in a spontaneous discussion in the hope that the discussion will reveal the participants' real feelings about a product or services.

FOOD AND DRUG ACT (1906) See *Federal Food and Drug Act (1906)*

FOOD AND DRUG ADMINISTRATION (FDA) The federal agency responsible for monitoring the purity of foods, food additives, and drugs in interstate commerce. Maintains a testing program to insure this, and enforces penalties against misbranding, adulteration, and other related offenses. Created by the Federal Food and Drug Act (1906).

FOOD BROKER A manufacturer's agent who specializes in the distribution of grocery items. Food brokers call on grocery wholesalers and large retailers on behalf of their clients and are directly involved in marketing strategy, planning, and promotion of the goods they carry.

FOOD MARKETING INSTITUTE (FMI) A Washington, D.C. based association of grocery retailers and wholesalers. The association represents the industry to both the government and to consumers. FMI conducts research, collects statistical data, and maintains a library. It publishes *Washington Report* (weekly) and *Issues Bulletin* (monthly), as well as three important annual publications, *Supermarket Industry Financial Review, Facts About New Supermarkets,* and *Food Marketing Industry Speaks.*

FORECASTING The practice of predicting future demand in the marketplace over a given period of time. Both subjective and statistical methods may be used. See also *sales forecasting* and *economic forecasting*.

FOREIGN-BASED AGENT See *foreign-based export agent*

FOREIGN-BASED EXPORT AGENT In direct export, a foreign company which sells the goods on behalf of the exporting company. The agent may have either exclusive or general rights to represent the exporter in that country. See also *direct export*.

FOREIGN-BASED EXPORT DISTRIBUTOR In direct export, a company located in the host country that buys and owns goods from the exporter. See also *foreign-based export agent* and *direct export*.

FOREIGN FREIGHT FORWARDER See *custom house broker*

FOREIGN LICENSING See *licensing*

FOREIGN TRADE ZONE (FTZ) A city (frequently a seaport) designated by a country which may receive foreign goods to store and further process them without the importer paying import duties unless the goods actually enter the country. Foreign trade zones facilitate international trade in that exporters can ship from the zone where large quantities of goods are stored to other countries without being involved in the country's trade restrictions—the zone is, in fact, an enclave free of these regulations. Also known as a free trade zone or free port.

FORM UTILITY The usefulness (or consumer satisfaction) derived from the physical transformation raw materials undergo in processing or manufacture. Form utility may be regarded as the economic utility derived from the actual physical product.

FORMULA PRICING A pricing strategy in which final price is established through the use of a formula, e.g., price may be set at three times cost without consideration of any other variables or with competitive conditions in the marketplace.

FORWARD DATING Refers to the payment due date on invoices for merchandise. The payment due date is moved forward by the manufacturer or supplier in an effort to make the terms of sale more attractive to the retailer. This tactic is frequently employed to encourage retailers to buy large quantities of merchandise to meet anticipated high demand, e.g., during the Christmas selling season.

FORWARD INTEGRATION A marketing system in which a producer or manufacturer owns or controls the distribution channels (up to, and sometimes including, retail outlets) through which his product passes on its way to the ultimate consumer.

FORWARD INVENTION In international marketing, the development of new products for foreign markets.

FORWARD MARKET SEGMENTA-TION A means of identifying segments of a population using such attributes as race, nationality, age, education, psychological traits, lifestyle characteristics, etc. The underlying assumption is that groups, or market segments, which share certain attributes will react homogeneously to marketing efforts.

FOUL-WEATHER PRICING A pricing strategy in which a company charges so little for its product that it is sold at no profit or, in extreme cases, production costs are not even met. This strategy is employed on the short-term in an effort to keep a company in business during times of economic crisis.

FOUR Cs In automatic vending, the products which represent 80% of sales; i.e., cigarettes, candy, coffee, and cold drinks.

FOUR Os The basic characteristics of a market; i.e., objects (what is purchased), objectives (why the product or service is purchased), organization (who is the purchaser), and operations (how the purchaser operates).

FOUR Ps OF THE MARKETING MIX The four Ps are a device to aid in remembering the four principal variables in the marketing mix: 1) product—the right product matched to the right market; 2) place—reaching the market through adequate distribution channels; 3) promotion—informing the target market of the product; and 4) price—setting a competitive price. Also known as the promotional quadrangle.

FRANCHISE See *franchising*

FRANCHISING In general, franchising may be regarded as a vertical marketing system in which a manufacturer or service organization confers upon an individual or firm the privilege of marketing a product or service.

Thus, franchising is seen as a system or method of doing business in which the franchisor and franchisee have entered into a contractual relationship which involves clearly established rights and responsibilities.

Franchise organizations take four basic forms: 1) those which are part of a limited distribution system for particular products, e.g., automobile dealerships, gasoline stations; 2) wholesaler sponsored retail outlets, e.g., certain drugstore and automobile parts stores; 3) wholesaler licensing systems, e.g., soft drink bottlers, beer distributors; and 4) retail outlets which carry the trade name of a nationally known organization and which commonly provide a service, e.g., fast food restaurants, car rental agencies.

Automobile dealerships, gasoline service stations, and soft-drink bottlers account for roughly 75% of all franchise sales.

FREE ALONGSIDE See *FAS (free along side)*

FREE COMPETITION See *perfect competition*

FREE GOODS Merchandise offered at no additional charge by a manufacturer or distributor to a reseller (usually a retailer) as a reward for placing a large order. Free goods are usually given in lieu of a special discount and are treated as price concessions by the Federal Trade Commission.

FREE MARKET See *economic system*

FREE MARKET ECONOMY See *economic system*

FREE MERCHANDISE See *free goods*

FREE ON BOARD See *FOB (free on board)*

FREE ON BOARD FACTORY See *FOB (free on board) factory*

FREE PORT See *foreign trade zone (FTZ)*

FREE TRADE ASSOCIATION An association of countries that agrees to reduce or eliminate the trade barriers which exist between them.

FREE TRADE ZONE See *foreign trade zone (FTZ)*

FREIGHT ABSORPTION A pricing policy in which the seller of goods absorbs some or all of the cost of shipping his products to their destination in an effort to maintain a competitive selling price in the local marketplace. Also called freight equalization.

FREIGHT-ABSORPTION PRICING See *freight absorption*

FREIGHT ALLOWED PRICING See *delivered price*

FREIGHT EQUALIZATION See *freight absorption*

FREIGHT FORWARDER A transportation intermediary who consolidates the small shipments of a number of manufacturers into carload or truckload lots to take advantage of the lower rates offered by common carriers.

FREIGHT ON BOARD see *FOB (free on board)*

FREQUENCY In advertising, the number of times an audience is exposed to a message.

FREUD, SIGMUND See *motive*

FRIENDSHIP, COMMERCE, AND NAVIGATION (FCN) TREATIES International agreements which, among a number of other things, cover a wide range of commercial matters such as marketing practices in the trading partner's country, agreements on duties and other taxes, foreign exchange, travel, communications, etc.

FRINGE MARKET That segment of a firm's customers who are outside the firm's core market; i.e., who patronize the firm on an occasional basis. See also *brand insistence* for a definition of the hard-core market.

FTC See *Federal Trade Commission (FTC)*

FTZ See *foreign trade zone (FTZ)*

FULL-COST APPROACH TO COST ANALYSIS A method of cost analysis in which all functional costs, including fixed and common costs, are allocated in some way to products, customers, or other similar categories. This allows analysts and marketing managers to find the profitability of various customers, products, etc. by subtracting costs from sales. See also *contribution-margin approach to cost analysis* and *marketing cost analysis.*

FULL COST PRICING A relatively rigid pricing strategy in which all the variable and fixed costs of a product or service are covered by its sale price.

FULL DEMAND A condition in the marketplace in which purchasers want and are willing to pay for all the products which are being produced.

FULL DISCLOSURE A practice in which all relevant data about a product is made available to the consumer so that an informed purchase decision can be made. Full disclosure is one of a number of consumer protections against deceptive practices.

FULL-FUNCTION WHOLESALER See *full-service wholesaler*

FULL-LINE DISCOUNT STORE See *promotional department store*

FULL-LINE FORCING A trade practice in which a manufacturer forces wholesalers and retailers to buy his entire line of merchandise (including the less saleable items) if they are to sell any of his products.

FULL-LINE PRICING A pricing strategy which takes into consideration the way prices for individual products in a line relate to the prices of other products in the line. In general, an effort is made to present buyers with a logical pricing system, e.g., General Motors prices its automobiles in a predictable manner from the least expensive Chevrolet to the most expensive Cadillac.

FULL-LINE STRATEGY A marketing strategy in which a seller offers a wide variety of products for sale in an effort to broaden his customer base.

FULL-SERVICE WHOLESALER A wholesaling middleman who, in addition to taking title to the goods he resells, often takes physical possession of the merchandise. Full-service wholesalers usually operate warehouses and provide their customers with delivery services, extend credit, and assist the customer with accounting, inventory, and marketing information.

FUNCTIONAL ACCOUNT A functional account is one which indicates the purpose for which the expenditure was made. In marketing such accounts may include marketing research, sales and sales promotional activities, order processing, shipping, warehousing, bookkeeping, etc. Sometimes referred to as a marketing function account.

FUNCTIONAL APPROACH TO MARKETING An approach to the study of marketing in which such functions as sales, distribution, advertising, etc. are viewed as a key to understanding the marketing process. The investigator studies how each of these functions works and from these findings generalizes about the larger marketing picture.

FUNCTIONAL DISCOUNT See *trade discount*

FUNCTIONAL OBSOLESCENCE See *planned obsolescence*

FUNCTIONAL WHOLESALER See *full-service wholesaler*

FUNCTIONS OF MARKETING See *marketing functions*

GAME A sales promotion device in which the participant competes for prizes by engaging in an activity which does not require skill, e.g. winning numbers may be revealed on a rub-off card. Pure chance determines who wins. Some games have a continuity element, i.e., they have been set up so as to encourage the participant to enter more than once. See also *contest* and *sweepstake*.

GATEKEEPER In industrial purchasing, generally an individual who controls the flow of information within an organization. Persons wishing to sell to the organization must find a way to get their message past the gatekeeper (often the firm's purchasing agent).

GATEKEEPER PHENOMENON See *gatekeeper*

GATT See *General Agreement on Tariffs and Trade (GATT)*

GENERAL ADVERTISING See *national advertising*

GENERAL AGREEMENT ON TARIFFS AND TRADE (GATT) A multilateral trade treaty entered in force January 1, 1948 with 23 signatories which sets down reciprocal rights and obligations for member countries. GATT has as a principle goal the reduction of tariffs and the removal of trade barriers between its contracting parties. Headquartered in Geneva, Switzerland.

GENERAL ELECTRIC STRATEGIC PLANNING APPROACH A company-wide approach to marketing planning which takes a number of factors (market growth, competition, market share, profitability, margins, technology, etc.) into account in order to set corporate strategies and objectives.

GENERAL LINE WHOLESALER A full-service wholesaler who carries one or two lines of merchandise in full assortments and who, for the most part, supplies single-line retailers; e.g., a general-line hardware wholesaler will have as his customers hardware stores.

GENERAL MERCHANDISE DISTRIBUTOR See *industrial distributor*

GENERAL MERCHANDISE STORE A retail establishment carrying a wide variety of merchandise in some depth. Department, discount, and variety stores as well as mail order houses may be regarded as general merchandise stores.

GENERAL MERCHANDISE WAREHOUSE A form of public warehouse which may store any type of manufactured goods. See also *public warehouse*.

GENERAL MERCHANDISE WHOLESALER A full-service wholesaler who maintains a broad inventory of a number of unrelated products (such as non-perishable groceries, plumbing supplies, hardware, soft goods, etc.). Although they sometimes sell to manufacturers, they are mainly suppliers for smaller stores and non-commercial organizations. See also *wholesaler*.

GENERAL PRODUCT MANAGER The executive who functions as the supervisor of a number of product managers and who, in addition, is responsible for coordinating their plans and programs and for submission to the firm's marketing manager.

GENERAL STORE A small, undepartmentalized version of the general merchandise store, this retail establishment is commonly found in rural areas and sells food, clothing, farm implements, garden supplies, hard-

ware, and other highly utilitarian items.

GENERIC BRAND Something of a misnomer, inasmuch as a brand is a product made distinguishable from other similar products by a unique identifying name and generics lack just such a name. In common usage, generic brand refers to unbranded products. See also *generic product* and *generic name*.

GENERIC DEMAND See *primary demand*

GENERIC MARKET A market in which vendors offer substitute products which are different physically or conceptually. Markets are viewed broadly and from the customer's perspective. For example, there are several different ways of satisfying a customer's need for status. Vendors in the generic market aim to satisfy the customer's need (in this case, status) rather than focus on the differences between the individual products which will satisfy this need. Thus, quite different products may compete with each other in the same generic market. In the generic status market, for example, luxury cars compete with cruises, furs, jewelry, etc. Each of these products will confer the desired status, and so may be viewed by the customer as substitutes for each other. See also *product market* and *market*.

GENERIC NAME The letters or words used to describe a particular kind or type of product, i.e., a product's common name as distinct from its brand name. Generics are common in the pharmaceutical industry where drugs are sold under their common chemical name as well as under brand name. See also *generic product*.

GENERIC PRODUCT 1) A product sold under a common name rather than a brand name. Generic products are merchandised in a "no frills" manner, given little advertising support, and are sold at a lower price than branded items. 2) In a broader sense, the generic product is not the item itself, but a concept which includes the expectations the buyer has with regard to the product, i.e., the benefits the consumer sees the product embodying.

GENERIC PRODUCT ADVERTISING Advertising which features a product type, without identifying a brand name or company. This type of advertising is undertaken to stimulate primary demand for a class of products. See also *primary demand.*

GENTLEMEN'S PRICING A form of pricing generally found in the professions. For example, a physician may charge a flat $1,000 fee for performing an operation, making no effort to actually cost out the price in terms of hours worked, skill level employed, etc.

GEOCENTRISM A form of organization, found in some multinational marketing firms, in which the marketing effort focuses on the whole world, rather than on any particular nation or region. No single national market is preferred over others. Employees, including management personnel, are hired from diverse backgrounds and nationalities.

GEOGRAPHIC DIVISION OF AUTHORITY In marketing management, a form of organization in which line authority is organized along geographic lines, i.e., management is set up on a regional basis, often in an effort to promote better supervision.

GEOGRAPHIC SEGMENTATION A method of market segmentation based on the geographic location of the target group. The target market may be subdivided by world region (continent, developing countries, East, Far East, West, Soviet Bloc, etc.), national region (East, Mid-West, Far West, etc.), population density (urban, suburban, rural), and city size. See also *market segmentation.*

GEOGRAPHIC SEGMENTATION FACTORS See *geographic segmentation*

GIFT-GIVING APPROACH See *premium* (or *gift-giving) approach*

GLOBAL MARKETING See *international marketing*

GNP See *gross national product (GNP)*

GOALS The definite mission of an organization, i.e., the achievements the organization wishes to attain, the desired end of organizational activity. See also *objectives* and *advertising goals.*

GOALS DOWN-PLANS UP PLANNING A form of planning in which managers at the top of the organizational hierarchy set corporate goals and then communicate them downward to the various operating units within the organization. These units develop plans for the achievement of the goals and communicate these plans upward for management's approval.

GOFFMAN MODEL A view of consumer behavior based on the sociology of Irving Goffman in which the consumer is seen as a role player and the goods he is shopping for are seen as props in a play. The buyer is thus viewed as a player in a drama of his own making.

107

GOING-RATE PRICING A "collective wisdom" approach to pricing strategy in which a firm bases the prices of its products less on what it costs to make them and more on what their competitors are charging or on what the firm believes its customers may be willing to pay.

GOOD See *product*

GOODS-SERVICES CONTINUUM A means of visualizing the distribution between goals and services. The continuum is graphically represented as a spectrum with pure goods at one end (a bottle of shampoo, for example) and a pure service at the other (a haircut, for example). As one moves along the continuum one moves from the tangible to the intangible.

GOVERNMENT MARKET That part of the industrial market which is in the public sector. Included are all levels of the federal, state, and local government and their many branches, agencies, and authorities.

GRADE LABEL A label on a product which indicates its quality. See also *label.*

GRADING The sorting of goods into quality classifications, e.g., meat, men's suits, and cotton are all graded according to predetermined quality standards.

GRAY MARKET Consumer and industrial products sold outside a manufacturer's authorized distribution channels. Unlike the black market, which is involved in illegal trade, the gray market is generally supplied by distributors or retailers who direct goods from their regular marketing channels to manufacturers outlets in a manner within the limits of the law. Gray market goods are sometimes called parallel imports.

GREEN RIVER ORDINANCE A law passed by a local government to restrict door-to-door selling. The name is derived from Green River, Wyoming, one of the first places to pass such an ordinance.

GRID See *market grid*

GROSS MARGIN The difference between the total cost of goods and their final selling price. Gross margin may be expressed as net sales less the cost of goods sold. Since markdowns, shortages, and discounts have been deducted in computing gross margin, the figure is not the same as maintained markup. Gross margin is often used synonymously with the term gross profit. The former term is more usually found in retailing and the latter in manufacturing usage.

GROSS NATIONAL PRODUCT (GNP) The total value (at current market prices) of all goods and services produced by a nation over a specified period of time (commonly one year).

GROSS PROFIT Total receipts less the cost of goods sold, but before selling and other operating expenses and income taxes have been deducted. Gross profit is often used synonymously with gross margin, but gross profit is more commonly used in the manufacturing sector, gross margin more commonly in retailing.

GROSS SALES Sales revenue before deductions have been made for returns and allowances, but after sales and excise taxes have been deducted. It represents the total amount charged to all customers during the accounting period. When returns and allowances are deducted, the resultant figure is the vendor's net sales. See also *net sales.*

108

GROWTH/SHARE MATRIX See *Boston Consulting Group Matrix*

GROWTH STAGE That stage of the product life cycle during which demand for the product picks up momentum and competitive products are introduced into the marketplace. During the growth stage, production increases and profits rise until competition begins to drive down prices.

GUARANTEE A statement, either written or implied, by the seller of merchandise, in which assurances are made concerning the proper performance of the product and which stipulates the corrective measures which will be taken should it not perform properly. Also referred to as a guaranty. See also *warranty.*

GUARANTY See *guarantee*

H

HAGGLE Bargaining or wrangling between buyer and seller over price or other matters affecting trade. Also called *higgle.*

HALO EFFECT The transfer of consumer trust and loyalty from one of a manufacturer's products to another. The halo effect is more likely to occur when both products share a brand name. See also *brand* and *brand loyalty.*

HARD CORE LOYALS See *brand insistence*

HARD CORE MARKET See *brand insistence*

HARD SELL Vigorous personal selling generally directed at the reluctant customer.

HARVESTING See *milking*

HAZARDOUS SUBSTANCES LABELING ACT (1960) See *Federal Hazardous Substances Labeling Act (1960)*

HEAD-ON POSITIONING A market positioning strategy in which two products which are nearly identical compete with one another directly.

HEAVY HALF That segment of the marketplace which represents numerically half of the consumers in the population, but which contains by a large majority most of a firm's actual customers.

HEDGING In commodity marketing, a buying and selling practice in the futures market calculated to protect the purchaser against unfavorable price changes. Some commodities are purchased at current market prices and some are purchased on the commodity futures market at a speculative price for delivery at a later time. The hedge lies in the purchaser's expectation that a change in one price will be accompanied by a compensatory change in the other price.

HEDONIC GOODS Consumer goods whose attractiveness lies principally in that they give the purchaser pleasure.

HERZBERG, FREDERICK See *motive*

HETEROGENEOUS SHOPPING GOODS Shopping goods perceived by the customer as different in quality and suitability. For example, clothing and household furnishings are considered heterogeneous shopping goods. Style and quality play a significant role in the customer's decision to buy these and similar items. Price is of lesser significance. See also *shopping goods* and *homogeneous shopping goods*.

HEURISTIC IDEATION TECHNIQUE (HIT) An invention of Edward M. Tauber of the Carnation Company who called the technique "a systematic procedure for new product search." Words which describe existing products are separated and reassembled in new combinations in an effort to generate ideas for new products. The term heuristic is employed to suggest that the technique involves a process of discovery.

HIDDEN BUYER In purchasing, a person other than the purchasing agent who, through his power to specify the characteristics of a product, is the real buyer. Technicians, managers, and others within an organization may have the capacity to exert such influence.

HIDDEN COST Any of the costs of doing business that cannot be recorded by an accountant and so do not show up on a firm's balance sheet or income statement. For example, the losses resulting from a customer's failure to

reorder and cancellations of orders are considered hidden costs.

HIDDEN SERVICE SECTOR Services which are to some extent concealed because they are provided by firms which are also manufacturers. For example, manufacturers of photocopiers also provide supplies and maintenance service.

HIERARCHY OF BEHAVIOR EFFECTS See *hierarchy of effects*

HIERARCHY OF EFFECTS Those stages (beginning with unawareness and ending with purchase of the product) through which consumers pass when responding to a firm's promotional efforts. In order, they are: awareness, knowledge, liking, preference, conviction, and purchase.

HIGGLE See *haggle*

HIT See *heuristic ideation technique (HIT)*

HOLDING COST See *inventory carrying costs*

HOME COUNTRY ORIENTATION A marketing orientation in which a firm gives domestic business top priority, making little or no effort to developing markets overseas.

HOMOGENEOUS SHOPPING GOODS Shopping goods perceived by the customer as basically the same. The customer is willing to substitute one brand for another and seeks the lowest price. Thus a slight price cut can significantly increase sales volume, and price competition tends to be keen. See also *shopping goods* and *heterogeneous shopping goods*.

HORIZONTAL CHANNEL CONFLICT See *channel conflict*

HORIZONTAL CHANNEL INTEGRATION See *horizontal integration*

HORIZONTAL COMPETITION Competition between channel of distribution members at the same channel level, e.g., in retailing, department stores in head-to-head competition. Not to be confused with channel conflict.

HORIZONTAL COOPERATIVE ADVERTISING See *cooperative advertising*

HORIZONTAL COOPERATIVE PROMOTION Promotional efforts sponsored by two or more members of a distribution channel who are operating at the same level. For example, a number of manufacturers may cooperatively sponsor events in support of American participation in the Olympic Games.

HORIZONTAL DIVERSIFICATION An effort to increase sales (primarily to current customers) through the introduction of products unrelated to the firm's existing line.

HORIZONTAL-FLOW THEORY See *fashion adoption process*

HORIZONTAL INDUSTRIAL MARKET A broad market for industrial goods—one which includes a number of industries. Products sold in horizontal markets have a relatively wide range of potential customers.

HORIZONTAL INTEGRATION The ownership, achieved by acquisition or internal expansion, of additional business units at the same channel of distribution level. Retail organizations often expand through horizontal integration, either adding units or buying up other retail organizations.

HORIZONTAL PRICE FIXING Resale price maintenance agreements between firms at the same level of the market, e.g., collusive agreements between two or more manufacturers of the same product to fix prices at an artificially high level. Generally, horizontal price fixing has as its objective higher profits and/or the restriction of competition.

HOST COUNTRY ORIENTATION An overseas marketing orientation in which a firm's overseas subsidiaries are often managed by local people and are thus more responsive to the needs of the local consumer.

HOUSE AGENCY An advertising agency owned or controlled by a single firm which commonly provides service only to that firm.

HOUSE MARK See *family brand*

HOUSE-TO-HOUSE RETAILING See *door-to-door retailing*

HOUSEHOLD According to the U.S. Bureau of the Census, a household comprises "all persons who occupy a housing unit, that is, a house, an apartment, or other groups of rooms, or a single room that constitutes separate living quarters. A household includes the related family members and all the unrelated persons, if any, such as lodgers, foster children, wards, or employees who share the housing unit. A person living alone or a group of unrelated persons sharing the same housing unit as partners is also counted as a household." Quoted from the *Statistical Abstract of the U.S.*

HOWARD-SHETH (H-S) THEORY A theory of buyer behavior in which consumer buying is treated as rational and systematic behavior. The Howard-Sheth theory attempts to describe the processes occurring in an individual between the time stimuli (advertising messages, etc.) are received and some form of buying response is initiated.

H-S THEORY See *Howard-Sheth (H-S) theory*

HUMOROUS SELL An advertising message that jokes about the product being sold. This technique was very much in vogue in the late 1960s and early 1970s. Also called the soft sell.

HYPERINFLATION See *inflation*

HYPERMARCHÉ See *hypermarket*

HYPERMARKET A European retailing development ("hypermarché" in France) which brings food and general merchandise together in a warehouse atmosphere. These stores include elements of the traditional discount operation as well as those of the supermarket and may be as large as 200,000 square feet. Merchandise carried is almost always high volume sellers, as the operation depends on moving very large quantities of goods to turn a profit. See also *superstore.*

HYPODERMIC NEEDLE MODEL A largely discredited theory of mass communication which held that the mass media have a direct, immediate, and powerful effect on the people receiving the media message. The people were seen as helpless victims whose attitudes and behavior were influenced by the mass media messages, much as if they had been injected with a hypodermic needle. The theory was superseded first by the two-step flow model and later by the multistep flow model. See also *two-step flow model* and *multistep flow model.*

HYPOTHESIS A theory or proposition tentatively accepted to explain certain facts or relationships, make predictions about the future, and to provide a basis for further investigation (in which case it is often referred to as a working hypothesis). Researchers develop hypotheses from observation and intuition, then go on to test each hypothesis scientifically.

**I-AM-HERE-TO-HELP-YOU AP-
PROACH** A technique used by a
salesperson in the first few minutes of
contact with a prospect. This approach involves a direct, enthusiastic
offer of help in increasing profits, productivity, etc. (for industrial clients)
or household efficiency, personal
money management effectiveness,
etc. (for the ultimate consumer). See
also *approach.*

ICEBERG PRINCIPLE In the evolution of marketing performance, the
iceberg principle states that much
valuable information is not represented adequately in summary data—
that such summary data, in fact, is
only the tip of the iceberg and that
only detailed figures will reveal the
submerged information.

IDEA APPROACH A technique used
by a salesperson in the first few minutes of contact with a prospect. In this
approach, the salesperson opens with
a helpful new idea to interest the prospect. The idea should illustrate how
the goods or services will increase the
prospect's profits, productivity, etc.
See also *approach.*

IDEA MARKETING The application
of marketing principles in an effort to
promote ideas, issues, causes, etc.
Idea marketing may be carried on by
profit and nonprofit organizations.

IDEAL MARKET EXPOSURE The
degree to which a product receives
exposure to potential customers so
that it is sufficiently available to meet
customer needs without exceeding
them. Exceeding customer needs by
providing additional exposure of the
product is seen as adding unnecessar-
ily to the total marketing cost of the
product. See also *exposure.*

IDEAL SELF See *self-image*

IDEAL SELF-CONCEPT See *self-image*

IDEAL SELF-IMAGE See *self-image*

IDEAL STOCK See *balanced stock*

ILLEGAL GOODS The sale of unlawful goods, e.g., stolen property, certain drugs, firearms under certain circumstances, etc.

IMAGE Mental perceptions or impressions held by an individual about himself, about others, or about products or services. How a customer sees himself and the way he fits into his environment influences his behavior in the marketplace. See also *store image* and *self-image*.

IMAGE ADVERTISING See *image sell* and *institutional advertising*

IMAGE BUILDER PRICING A practice generally found in retailing in which one product in a line is offered at a substantially higher price than the rest of the products in the line in an effort to enhance their image in the minds of consumers. For example, the Corvette helps stimulate sales for all the models in the Chevrolet line.

IMAGE BUILDING Advertising and other promotional efforts intended to influence customers' perceptions of a firm. For example, a business may engage in activities which enhance its reputation for being socially responsible. See also *institutional advertising*.

IMAGE MARKETING The application of marketing principles to the enhancement of the image of a person or organization; i.e., the alteration of the public's perception of the person or organization.

IMAGE SELL A type of advertising message which focuses on creating and conveying a particular image for the product or service being advertised. For example, the use of popular retired athletes in beer commercials is meant to convey an image of masculinity and success. See also *association advertising format*.

IMAGINATIVE APPROACH In advertising copy, an imaginative approach is one which concentrates on the possibilities for self-fulfillment and life-enrichment to be derived from the good or product. For example, if you buy the toothpaste you'll get the fancy sports car and the pretty girl. Also called an emotional approach, it is calculated to take advantage of the customer's emotional buying motive. See also *emotional buying motive*.

IMI See *International Marketing Institute (IMI)*

IMITATIVE COMBINER A firm which uses the combined target market approach to market its goods to an already-established combination of sub-markets. The imitative combiner seeks to offer an improved marketing mix to the target market established by the innovative combiner. The products so developed tend to resemble or even duplicate the innovator's product. See also *combined target market approach* and *innovative combiner*.

IMITATIVE SEGMENTER A segmenter which tries to offer an improved marketing mix to meet the needs of a target market already identified by an innovative segmenter. The products so developed tend to resemble or even duplicate the innovator's product. See also *segmenter* and *innovative segmenter*.

IMPACT PRICING See *penetration pricing*

IMPERFECT COMPETITION See *monopolistic competition*

115

IMPLICIT COSTS Those expenses in a business which are less obvious and accountable than explicit costs, but which may affect the overall profitability of the business. They may include the owner's salary (even if the actual money is not paid out) or the rental value of the building (even if it is owned by the business, since it is not being rented out to others).

IMPLIED WARRANTY See *warranty*

IMPORT 1) To bring or transport goods into a country especially for the purpose of sales. 2) An import is any item brought into a country.

IMPORT AGENT In international trade, a manufacturer's agent involved with the importation of foreign goods. The import agent sells similar products for several noncompeting foreign manufacturers in the domestic market and receives a commission on what is sold. See also *manufacturer's agent.*

IMPORT BROKER In international trade, an import broker is an agent middleman who brings buyers and sellers together for the purpose of selling foreign goods in a domestic market. Import brokers provide the domestic buyers of imported goods with information about the availability of such goods. They also provide potential importers with information about the needs of the domestic buyers. See also *agent middleman* and *export broker.*

IMPORT COMMISSION HOUSE A commission merchant involved in international trade, functioning to sell foreign goods in the domestic market. The import commission house handles goods shipped to them by foreign sellers, completes the sales, and sends the money to the seller. The import commission house is reimbursed for its services by means of a commission paid by the seller. See also *commission merchant.*

IMPORT QUOTA See *trade quota*

IMPORTANCE-PERFORMANCE ANALYSIS A marketing research tool employed to identify strengths and weaknesses in a company's performance as they are perceived by customers or potential customers. Results are plotted on a two-dimensional grid in an effort to give marketing managers an indication of how their products are regarded in the marketplace.

IMPORTING See *import*

IMPULSE BUYING Consumer purchases made without prior planning, generally on the basis of the immediate appeal of the merchandise and its proximity to the point-of-sale.

IMPULSE MERCHANDISE Items which, because of their immediate appeal to the customer, are purchased without prior planning or long consideration.

IMPULSE PURCHASE See *impulse buying*

IN-PACK PREMIUM A free gift or other item placed within the package of the item being promoted by the manufacturer. For example, the "prize in every package" inside each box of Cracker Jacks.

IN-TRANSIT MIXING In transportation, a practice in rail shipping in which shippers are allowed to unload carload lots of goods at a warehouse, mix the goods into new carload lots, reload the cars, and ship to their destination without incurring additional charges for the stopover privilege.

INAME See *International Newspaper Advertising and Marketing Executives (INAME).*

116

INCOME See *personal income*

INCOME SEGMENTATION The subdivision of a population on the basis of the earnings of each segment.

INCOME STATEMENT See *profit and loss statement*

INCREMENTAL REVENUE The increase or decrease in revenue which results from the addition or subtraction of a unit of sales or from the advance or decline of price.

INCREMENTAL TECHNIQUE A strategy used in budgeting for promotional purposes in which the current budget is based upon previous expenditures and upon the firm's expectations of future business. Depending on the planner's feelings, money is either added to, or subtracted from the previous year's budget.

INDEPENDENT BUYING OFFICE See *resident buying office*

INDEPENDENT RETAILER See *independent store*

INDEPENDENT STORE Typically owned and operated by an individual, family, or partnership, the independent store is not a part of a chain organization or ownership group, although it may be a member of a voluntary chain. These retail outlets are often general stores or limited-line stores.

INDEPENDENT WHOLESALER See *wholesaler*

INDEXATION See *indexing*

INDEXING A strategy employed to mitigate the effects of inflation by tying increases in wages, taxes, interest rates, etc. to changes in a price index; i.e., as prices advance and retreat a variety of escalators are used to bring other aspects of the economy into line. For example, Social Security payments may be tied to fluctuations in the consumer price index.

INDIRECT-ACTION ADVERTISING See *indirect advertising*

INDIRECT ADVERTISING An advertising program designed to stimulate future buying decisions and sales over an extended period of time rather than an immediate purchase. The program does so by emphasizing the advantages of a product or service and suggesting that the consumer keep this in mind when the need for the product or service does arise. For example, much advertising by funeral homes is geared to having the firm's name in the consumer's mind at some future date when funeral services are required. Also called indirect action advertising.

INDIRECT CHANNEL OF DISTRIBUTION The movement of products from manufacturer through independent middlemen to the ultimate consumer or industrial user. The employment of middlemen in the channel of distribution leaves the producer with somewhat less control over distribution and with less contact with customers.

INDIRECT COMPETITION A form of business activity in which potential customers for a firm's product satisfy their needs by buying a totally different product or by buying nothing at all; e.g., a labor-saving device may go unpurchased when cheap labor is readily available.

INDIRECT COST Costs involved in doing business which cannot be directly related to a particular product or service or to a particular organizational unit. Included in this category are such expenses as the cost of heat and light, administrative expenses, building depreciation, etc. Also known as common cost. See also *overhead, fixed cost, variable cost,* and *direct cost.*

INDIRECT EXPENSE See *indirect cost*

INDIRECT EXPORT A method of exporting goods which involves the use of independent international marketing middlemen to enter the foreign market. These middlemen include the domestic-based export merchant, the domestic-based export agent, cooperative international marketing organizations, and the export management company. A firm interested in indirect marketing, may use any of these middlemen to reach the foreign market.

INDIRECT EXPORTING See *indirect export*

INDIRECT PROMOTION Those forms of sales promotion that are more impersonal than personal selling. For example, advertising, branding, and packaging are all forms of indirect promotion. See also *sales promotion.*

INDIVIDUAL BRAND A particular product offered for sale by its producer under a unique brand name, i.e., none of the manufacturer's other products carry the same name.

INDIVIDUAL BRANDING See *multiple branding*

INDIVIDUAL OFFERINGS In a firm's product mix individual offerings are single products.

INDOCTRINATION See *sales force indoctrination*

INDUCTIVE STATISTICS See *inferential statistics*

INDUSTRIAL ADVERTISING Advertising by producers of industrial goods or by providers of business services directed to purchasing agents or other industrial buyers.

INDUSTRIAL BUYING See *industrial purchasing*

INDUSTRIAL CONSUMER See *industrial market*

INDUSTRIAL DISTRIBUTOR Mainly a wholesaler of goods to producers and manufacturers rather than to retailers, the industrial distributor may provide his customers with a wide range of services including calls by salespersons, the extension of credit, the stocking of large assortments, delivery, etc. These establishments, depending on where they operate in the industry, are also known as mill supply houses, industrial supply houses, and general merchandise distributors. See also *wholesaler* and *general merchandise wholesaler.*

INDUSTRIAL GOODS Products whose end use is at the manufacturing level, i.e., those which will be incorporated into other products, or which are used in making other products. Included are raw materials, machinery, tools, components, and supplies necessary in the manufacturing process.

INDUSTRIAL MARKET The industrial market consists of all those organizations which are involved in production, manufacturing, providing services, wholesaling, and retailing, together with the many levels of government and a wide variety of institutions; i.e., all potential customers with the exception of individuals buying goods for themselves or their immediate families.

Most products purchased in the industrial market are used to produce a commodity, manufacture a product, deliver a service, or are consumed in the day-to-day operation of the organization. Also known as the business market. See also *producer market, government market,* and *institutional market.*

INDUSTRIAL MARKETING Those activities which result in the sale of goods or services at the organizational level of the marketplace; i.e., at the production, manufacturing, wholesaling, institutional, governmental, or retailing levels. Organizational consumers either incorporate the products they buy into other products, use them in the course of their operations, or resell them.

INDUSTRIAL PRODUCTS See *industrial goods*

INDUSTRIAL PURCHASING The buying of goods and services at the business, industrial, or institutional level. Most industrial purchasing is carried on by professionals skilled in negotiating prices and buying in large quantities. Also known as procurement. See also *buying.*

INDUSTRIAL STORE See *commissary store*

INDUSTRIAL SUPPLY HOUSE See *industrial distributor*

INDUSTRIAL USER See *industrial market*

INDUSTRY FORECASTING The practice of predicting sales expectations for a class of products (such as shampoos) rather than a particular product (such as Prell shampoo). Industry forecasting is based on the amount of industry-wide marketing activity as well as the prevailing social and legal climate of the marketing area. The goal of industry forecasting is to predict the share of income that consumers are willing to spend on a product rather than save or spend elsewhere.

INELASTIC DEMAND See *inelasticity*

INELASTICITY The relative insensitivity of a product's sales volume to changes in price. A product which has inelastic demand does not motivate its marketer to cut the price, since sales revenue per unit of product decreases more rapidly than unit sales increase. This, however, is a relative concept. For example, a small change in the prices of gas heat will not significantly affect the market for natural gas, and the demand may be said to be inelastic. A major decrease in the price of natural gas, however, may cause consumers to switch to gas heat, use more of it, and thus increase demand. In the second case, the demand for natural gas may be said to be elastic.

INEPT SET In consumer behavior, inept set refers to those specific brands which, for one reason or another, the buyer excludes from consideration when shopping a product category. See also *evoked set* and *inert set.*

INERT SET In consumer behavior, inert set refers to those specific brands to which the buyer exhibits indifference when shopping a product category. See also *evoked set* and *inept set.*

INFERENTIAL STATISTICS Statistical tools used in marketing research in order to project the findings of a sample to a large population. Probability theory, inferential statistics (or inductive statistics as they are sometimes called), may be used to reduce random error.

INFLATION An economic condition notable for rising prices so that a set dollar amount buys less than it did previously. Normal inflation is considered to be up to 3% annually. Creeping inflation denotes modest increases in the general price level at a rate of 4–9% annually. Rapid inflation is said to exist when rising prices cause consumers' real incomes to shrink and thus leads to changes in consumer attitudes and behavior. An economic climate in which the general price level has risen to the double digit level is called strong inflation. Runaway inflation exists when there are steep increases which may go up to 100% (as it has in Argentina, Brazil, Mexico, and Israel at various times). Finally, hyperinflation is rapid, uncontrolled inflation such as that affecting Germany from 1920–1923.

Hyperinflation is marked by prices changing so rapidly that they cannot be trusted from day to day, or even hour to hour. In such an economic climate, the national currency becomes virtually worthless. Inflation may be fed by a situation in which the demand for goods and services exceeds the supply, thus raising prices. This is known as demand-pull inflation. However, inflation may also be caused by increases in the costs of production (such as wages), even without any excess demand. This type of inflation is known as cost-push inflation, and the increase in the cost of production is known as the wage-price spiral.

INFLUENCER In industrial purchasing, the influencer, although he does not make the final buying decision, has input during the preliminary discussions regarding the transaction, generally on the strength of some technical expertise.

INFORMATION FLOW See *channel flows*

INFORMATION SEARCH An activity by which consumers gather product information and weigh alternatives. The search may be carried out internally, i.e., by the consumer consulting his memory for relevant information collected in the past, or it may be carried out externally, i.e., through the examination of advertising, discussions with friends or salespeople, etc.

INFORMATION UTILITY The usefulness (or consumer satisfaction) derived primarily from advertising and promotion efforts on the part of a marketer. For example, billboards along a highway have information utility when they inform the motorist of available services.

INFORMATIVE ADVERTISING A form of advertising which figures heavily in the pioneering stage of new product development and other situations in which the aim is to build primary demand. Informative advertising serves to tell customers about a new product, suggest new uses for a product, inform the market of a price change, explain how the product works, describe available services, correct false impressions, reduce consumers' fears, and to build a company image.

INFRASTRUCTURE A term used in international marketing. Infrastructure refers to a country's essential facilities and services, such as its transportation and communications system or its banking and financial system, (i.e., those facilities which make marketing activities in the country possible).

INITIAL INDOCTRINATION OF SALES FORCE See *sales force indoctrination*

INITIAL MARKON See *initial markup*

INITIAL MARKUP When expressed in dollars, initial markup is the difference between the cost price of merchandise and its first retail price.

When expressed as a percentage, it is computed as the difference between cost price and first retail price divided by retail price. In both cases markdown and stock shortages are not counted in the computation. Initial markup is sometimes referred to as original markup, initial markon, or markon.

INNER-DIRECTED A person guided primarily by goals and ideals stemming from his/her own value system rather than by the opinions of others. Inner-directed people are often considered nonconformists by their peers. See also *other-directed.*

INNOCENT RECIPROCITY See *reciprocity*

INNOVATION DIFFUSION See *diffusion process*

INNOVATION STAGE See *retail life cycle*

INNOVATIONS In the product development process, innovations are changes in or additions to a firm's product line which the consumer will generally perceive as new. Innovations fall into two categories: 1) minor innovations—products the firm, did not previously produce but which already existed in the marketplace, and 2) major innovations—products which have not been produced before by any firm. See also *congruent innovation, continuous innovation, dynamically continuous innovation,* and *discontinuous innovation.*

INNOVATIVE COMBINER A marketing firm using the combined target market approach to identify a new combination of sub-markets. Innovative combiners are often followed into the marketplace by a number of imitators. See also *imitative combiner* and *combined target market approach.*

INNOVATIVE MATURITY A stage at the end of the product life cycle in which the product is either repositioned or modified to extend its lifespan. Tactics employed include finding new uses for the product, encouraging more frequent use by current customers, and attracting new customers by expanding the market for the product.

INNOVATIVE SEGMENTER A segmenter that seeks out new submarkets, identifies unsatisfied needs, and attempts to develop a marketing mix to reach the new segment. Innovative segmenters are often followed into the marketplace by a number of imitators seeking to utilize the newly identified market segment for their own products. See also *imitative segmenter* and *segmenter.*

INNOVATOR In the diffusion process, the innovator is the first consumer to accept and adopt a new product, service, or idea. Innovators tend to be young, high in social and economic status, and willing to take considerable risk in adopting new trends and fashions. Also known as an early acceptor.

INPUT-OUTPUT MODEL A technique employed in an effort to measure and forecast fluctuations in supply and demand in the industrial market. The model is based on the relationship between industries in which the output of one is purchased by the other industries in the marketplace (goods and services becoming their input).

INSIDE ORDER-TAKER See *order-taker*

INSPECTION BUYING In industrial buying, the practice of purchasing a product only after every item has been carefully examined. This method is used primarily for products that are

121

not standardized and require inspection. For example, one-of-a-kind products such as cars and buildings must be inspected.

INSTALLATIONS See *installed equipment*

INSTALLED EQUIPMENT Capital equipment which is generally fixed, long-lasting, and expensive such as the plant machinery used to manufacture a firm's products. Installed equipment does not become a part of the finished product and is thus distinct from materials and components used in manufacture. Also referred to as major equipment and installations.

INSTALLMENT CREDIT A consumer credit arrangement between retailer and customer, generally implemented for the purchase of expensive durable goods. Unlike revolving credit, the installment plan usually involves a formal contract which is secured by a down payment. The customer agrees to pay the balance at periodic intervals, each installment including interest and service charges which represent revenue for the retailer. Under this plan the store retains title to the merchandise until it is fully paid for, thus leaving the way open for repossession if it should be necessary.

INSTITUTIONAL ADVERTISING Advertising intended to enhance the prestige, image, and reputation of a firm or institution rather than to promote a specific product or to induce an immediate response on the part of the target audience. Institutional advertising (sometimes called corporate advertising) has as its principal purpose the promotion of good will on the part of the organization by 1) informing the public of the role the organization plays in the community, and 2) representing the organization as being responsible and civic minded regarding such issues as energy conservation, environmental quality, etc. See also *public relations advertising*.

INSTITUTIONAL APPROACH TO MARKETING An approach to the study of marketing in which attention is given to the various types or organizations involved in the marketing process (manufacturers and producers, wholesalers, retailers, etc.) in an effort to understand the marketing system.

INSTITUTIONAL MARKET The institutional market consists of a wide variety of organizations, many of them non-profit, including schools, churches, hospitals, etc. The institutional market is a part of the larger industrial market. See also *industrial market, producer market,* and *government market*.

INSTITUTIONS IN MARKETING See *marketing institutions*

INSTRUMENTED STORE A retail outlet in which information gathered and analyzed by computers has determined the optimum layout and shelf-space. Inventory control, ordering, and related functions are also determined by information gathered by computers, usually through point-of-sale scanning. See also *point-of-sale (POS) perpetual inventory control system*.

INTANGIBILITY OF SERVICES A concept which embodies the notion that most services are not tangible—that they have no physical properties, that they have no existence until they are performed.

INTANGIBLE RESOURCES With reference to a business organization, intangible resources include the firm's reputation in the marketplace, the relationship it maintains with customers, the quality level of its products or services, etc.

INTEGRATED MARKETING A strategy in which all of a company's marketing efforts are handled by a single organization, generally a large advertising agency (sometimes called a superagency). These agencies are equipped to provide services such as direct mail, coupons and other promotions, publicity releases, and public relations activities as well as traditional advertising.

INTEGRATION In business organizations, particularly large, complex firms, integration is the attempt to coordinate all the functions of the firm into a cohesive whole so that all functions and specializations work toward the same goal. This effort is particularly important when timing and consistency are significant, as they are in marketing firms. Some larger organizations employ integrators whose primary function is to coordinate demand and supply, packaging programs, and customer service functions. Integrators are expected to maintain the balance between production and sales, long-term and short-term goals, and similar counterpoising influences while resolving interdepartmental conflicts. See also *horizontal integration* and *vertical integration.*

INTEGRATIVE MARKET OPPORTUNITIES Opportunities in the marketplace for new growth which generally involve new production or different levels of distribution. See also *backward integration, forward integration, vertical integration,* and *horizontal integration.*

INTEGRATOR See *integration*

INTENSITY OF DISTRIBUTION Intensity is said to be increased as the number of outlets (wholesale and retail) are increased.

INTENSIVE DISTRIBUTION A marketing strategy in which goods are placed in the maximum number of retail outlets by the manufacturer or distributor, thus giving the product the widest possible exposure to the public. Also known as mass distribution and extensive distribution.

INTENSIVE MARKET OPPORTUNITIES Opportunities in the marketplace which may be further developed by a company through more aggressive marketing activities. For example, a company may increase sales by persuading existing customers to buy more of the firm's product, by persuading current customers of competing products to switch to the firm's brand, by improving the distribution through such means as vertical integration, etc.

INTERACTING SKILLS The skills used by marketing managers to influence others to implement the firm's marketing strategy. These skills include motivating employees of the firm as well as others on whom the firm relies (such as marketing research firms, advertising agencies, dealers, wholesalers, agents, etc.). For example, managing conflict within a channel of distribution is one area in which the marketing manager must utilize interacting skills. See also *allocating skills, monitoring skills,* and *organizing skills.*

INTERDEPENDENT PRODUCT PRICING See *product line pricing*

INTERINDUSTRY COMPETITION Competitive activity in the marketplace between large industries, particularly those which manufacture complementary products, e.g., the textile and apparel industries.

INTERMEDIARY See *middleman, retailer,* and *wholesaler*

123

INTERMEDIATE CUSTOMER A generic term for any buyer between the producer of the basic raw materials that are used to make the product and the ultimate consumer. Manufacturers, wholesalers, retailers, and other middlemen are all intermediate customers.

INTERMODAL SERVICES In transportation, such coordinated services as piggyback and fishyback which combine two or more modes of transportation, e.g., truck trailers on railroad flat-cars.

INTERNAL DATA Marketing information derived from a firm's own internal records. Included are such accounting records as profit and loss statements and financial ratios, sales revenues and costs, inventory data, etc. Also known as operating data.

INTERNAL INVENTORY TRANSFER In plant operations, the movement of semi-finished goods through the manufacturing process.

INTERNAL MARKETING Management strategies for employee development, particularly for those employees involved in selling. The intent of internal marketing is to improve the organization's relations with its customers.

INTERNATIONAL DEPARTMENT That part of a firm charged with the conduct of foreign operations.

INTERNATIONAL FRANCHISING See *licensing*

INTERNATIONAL MARKETING There are two basic forms of international marketing: 1) operations carried on in the home country, which produce goods to be exported and marketed in a foreign country; and 2) operations in foreign countries which produce goods in that country for sale there. Some foreign operations are wholly-owned subsidiaries of the parent company while others may be joint or licensed ventures or contract manufacturing operations.

INTERNATIONAL MARKETING INSTITUTE (IMI) An association of marketing executives which conducts summer programs both in the United States and abroad geared to improving the marketing skills of its membership. IMI maintains both a placement service and a library. It publishes a newsletter as well as *Export Marketing for Smaller Firms*. The association is based in Cambridge, Massachusetts.

INTERNATIONAL NEWSPAPER ADVERTISING AND MARKETING EXECUTIVES (INAME) A professional association of advertising and marketing executives employed by daily newspapers. The goal of the association is to promote the use of advertising in daily newspapers, and it works to achieve this goal through the presentation of annual awards and the sponsorship of educational programs. Its *News* is published ten times per year, its *Digest,* semiannually, and its *Roster,* annually. INAME also publishes a semiannual *Sales and Idea Book.* INAME's headquarters are in Washington, D.C.

INTERTYPE CHANNEL CONFLICT A form of distribution channel conflict which occurs when middlemen of different types (e.g., specialty stores and department stores) attempt to impede the operations of one another in such a way as to create channel dissonance. See also *channel conflict.*

INTERURBIA A strip of seemingly continuous urban-suburban population centers. For example, the East Coast of the United States may be considered an interurbia—a single population center joining the cities of Washington, Baltimore, Philadelphia, New York, and Boston, and including the suburban areas surrounding each city.

INTERVIEW In marketing research, a method of gathering data in which a questionnaire is administered to a respondent. Interviews may be conducted on a one-to-one, face-to-face basis, by telephone, by mail, or by a respondent filling out a questionnaire by himself.

INTERVIEWER BIAS Distortion in the results of an interview due to the intentional or unintentional intervention of the interviewer.

INTRODUCTION See *introductory stage*

INTRODUCTORY APPROACH A technique used by a salesperson in the first few minutes of contact with a prospect. This approach features a letter of introduction, business card, or testimonial from someone known to the prospect as a means of gaining the prospect's trust and attention. See also *approach.*

INTRODUCTORY PRICE DEALING A method of pricing used to attract customers to a new product. Prices are cut temporarily during an introductory offer and raised again at the end of the introductory period. The set time period of the price cut distinguishes introductory price dealing from penetration pricing. Some competitors meet introductory price cuts in order to maintain customer loyalty to their products. Others prefer to ignore such dealing, especially if the introductory offer is neither too long nor too successful. See also *penetration pricing.*

INTRODUCTORY PRICING See *introductory price dealing*

INTRODUCTORY STAGE The beginning (or pioneering) stage in the product life cycle during which the marketing effort is directed toward introducing the product (rather than the specific brand) to the consuming public. Many products fail at this stage because they never capture the interest of the consumer. See also *fashion cycle* and *product life cycle (PLC).*

INVENTORY 1) The assets of a business other than those commonly referred to as "plant and equipment," i.e., inventory includes raw materials, semi-finished goods or work-in-progress, and finished goods to be either used internally or offered for sale. 2) A detailed, often descriptive list of goods held in stock for future sale.

INVENTORY CARRYING COSTS Those costs of doing business directly related to goods held in inventory, including warehousing, deterioration and obsolescence, theft, and insurance charges.

INVENTORY CONTROL See *stock control*

INVENTORY ECHELONING In logistics management, inventory echeloning is the practice of basing the number of inventory locations for an item on the basis of sales. In general, this means that high-volume goods will be stocked at a greater number of distribution centers within the marketing territory (including some in outlying areas), while low-volume goods will be stocked at fewer locations (perhaps even at a single, central location).

INVENTORY HOLDING COSTS See *inventory carrying costs*

INVENTORY MANAGEMENT Those activities calculated to insure that the proper stock levels are maintained at all times. Included in the inventory management function is the responsibility for the smooth flow of goods from producer to consumer. Functions include the estimation of such factors as customer demand, production capacity, lead times, etc.

INVENTORY PROFIT Profits accrued on goods held in inventory during a period when the value of the goods increased.

INVENTORY RISK The financial risk involved in carrying goods in inventory—because their value has decreased or because there is little demand for them.

INVENTORY STOCKTURN RATE See *stock turnover*

INVENTORY TRANSFER See *internal inventory transfer*

INVENTORY TURNOVER See *stock turnover*

INVERSE DEMAND A condition opposite the normal demand pattern (in which demand decreases as prices increase), inverse demand is a condition in which, as prices increase, demand also increases. A condition of inverse demand often results in prestige pricing at the retail level.

INVESTMENT OPPORTUNITY CHART A grid or matrix representation of opportunities available to a firm in the marketplace. The chart is a tool used for strategic planning.

INVOICE A bill or statement, usually itemized, which is enclosed with a shipment of merchandise or mailed later by the seller. Information generally includes quantities shipped, prices of goods, terms of sale, discount, method of shipment, and other particulars including total amount due the seller.

IRREGULAR DEMAND Variations in the demand for products or services which cannot be directly attributed to seasonal changes or fluctuations in the local or national economy.

ISOLATED STORE A free-standing building having no other retail outlets in the immediate vicinity and generally located on a highway or back street.

JIT SYSTEM See *just-in-time (JIT) system*

JOB ANALYSIS A general review of a job's requirements, the tasks involved, and the training and education required of the job holder.

JOB DESCRIPTION In any business establishment, a job description is a statement of what the employee holding that job is expected to do. It may outline specific tasks and should provide clear guidelines for the employee to follow. Job descriptions often include the kind of person who should be hired for the job, the training to be provided, and the type of motivation that should be used by the employee's supervisors.

JOB EVALUATION A process in which jobs are compared with one another in an attempt to determine their relative rank, generally on the basis of job content.

JOB INDUCTION The informal orientation of a new employee which emphasizes the responsibilities of the job and the role the new employee will play in the department. Usually performed by the department manager or other direct supervisor of the new employee. Includes expectations, hours, schedule, hourly rate, pay schedule, etc.

JOB LOT A broken lot, unbalanced assortment, or discontinued merchandise reduced in price for quick sale. Also called odd lot.

JOB SHOP A business which produces work on a special order basis. Generally the job moves through the shop (metal stamping or forging, printing, etc.) in one batch, which is completed and sent to the customer

JOBBER See *wholesaler*

JOINT COSTS In product line pricing, joint costs are those which are shared in the process of manufacturing or producing the line of products as in, for example, a line of household detergents which all share a common production process.

JOINT DEMAND The demand for industrial products which so closely relate to each other that a change in the demand for one directly affects demand for the other. Also known as complementary demand.

JOINT OWNERSHIP VENTURE A form of joint venture in which foreign and domestic investors join to create a local business. Each firm shares in the ownership and control of the new firm. Some foreign governments require joint ownership as a condition for entry into their markets. See also *joint venture.*

JOINT PROMOTIONS A marketing effort, generally widely advertised, aimed at increasing sales. The cost of the promotion is shared by the two participating companies. Joint promotions are used to introduce new products or services or to revitalize those already established. They are commonly employed to push undifferentiated products or services, e.g., airline tickets, soap, hosiery, hotels, etc.

JOINT VENTURE In international marketing, a partnership arrangement in which a domestic company shares the ownership and control of production and marketing facilities with at least one foreign partner. Some production facilities are established in the host country, which distinguishes a joint venture from exporting. A joint venture also differs from a direct investment in that a partnership is established by a citizen of the host country. There are several types of joint venture, including licensing, contract manufacturing, management contracting, and joint ownership ventures.

JUDGMENT SAMPLE A form of nonprobability sample in which researchers select subjects who they judge to be good prospects for accurate information. This form of sample selection relies on the predisposition, and hence the bias, of the researcher. In some cases, such as in award nominations, the judgment sample is desirable, since it uses experts who are thought to be especially qualified in the area of interest. See also *nonprobability sampling.*

JUDGMENTAL TECHNIQUES Forecasting techniques based on the opinions of individuals or groups of individuals. When based on the combined opinions of a group of individuals, such as customers or salespersons, the judgmental technique is said to be a consensus. When the group is a panel of experts, the Delphi technique is often used.

JUNIOR DEPARTMENT STORE Not as large as the traditional department store, the junior department store carries a relatively wide variety of merchandise in a departmentalized form of organization. Prices are often moderate and major appliances and furniture are usually not included in the merchandise offering. In many respects the junior department store is a large specialty store.

JURY OF EXECUTIVE OPINION See *expert channel* and *delphi technique*

JUST-IN-TIME (JIT) SYSTEM A control system in which inventory carrying costs are minimized by keeping just enough supplies and parts on hand at the point of production to maintain uninterrupted production. Materials are scheduled to arrive "just in time" to be used. See also *quick response* and *kanban.*

JUST NOTICEABLE DIFFERENCE

A formula developed by German scientist Ernst Weber to measure how large a change must occur to be noticed in human perception. The change, or just noticeable difference is not an absolute quantity but rather an amount relative to the intensity of the original stimulus. According to Weber's formula, the stronger the initial stimulus, the greater the secondary stimulus must be if it is to be recognized as different. The formula is used by marketers trying to determine how much of a difference must be built into a product to differentiate it from its competitors as well as in setting prices. In the latter application, the theory maintains that the more expensive an item is originally, the larger the price drop required before it is seen as a bargain by consumers.

KANBAN Variously "visible record," "card," or "sign" in Japanese, kanban has come to denote a parts-supply system in Japan and, in the U.S., a more general concept applied to vendor-carrier-retailer relations. The system aids in controlling inventory carrying costs by maintaining just enough parts or other goods to meet current demand. New parts or goods are ordered so that they arrive just as they are needed, thus the scheme is sometimed called a "just in time" inventory system. See also *just-in-time (JIT) system* and *quick response.*

KEEP-OUT PRICING See *preemptive pricing*

KEFAUVER-HARRIS DRUG AMENDMENTS TO THE FOOD AND DRUG ACT (1962) Federal legislation which required the manufacturer to test both the safety and the effectiveness of drug products before marketing them to consumers. The legislation also required that the generic name of the drug appear on the label of the product.

KEY, WILSON BRYAN See *subliminal perception*

KEY ACCOUNT MARKETING See *national account marketing*

KEY RESOURCE A vendor whose past dealings with a retailer have been excellent and from whom the retailer has consistently bought a substantial portion of its merchandise.

KICKBACK In vendor/vendee relations, the kickback is generally in the form of a money payment to the retail buyer by the vendor as compensation for the buyer's patronage.

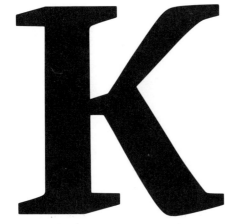

KINKED DEMAND CURVE A form of demand curve commonly found in oligopolistic markets. With few members operating in an industry, any price rise by one member results in a reduction in sales revenue as customers buy from competitors. Any price cut invites the competition to retaliate in kind. The kink in the demand curve is at the point where demand above the point is elastic and below it's inelastic.

KINKED DEMAND CURVE

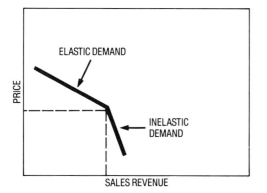

KNOCK-OFF The copying of another manufacturer's fashion design, usually at a cheaper price point.

L

LABEL A cover, wrapper, or tag, often made of paper, affixed to a product. Labels are commonly regarded as an integral part of the product package and contain a variety of descriptive matter including identification of the product and its manufacturer, its trademark, instructions for its use, its contents, size, etc.

LABOR INTENSIVE See *labor intensive industry*

LABOR INTENSIVE INDUSTRY An industry which makes greater relative use of human labor than it does of machinery and automation. Labor costs in such industries are therefore relatively high. The construction and garment industries are examples of labor intensive industries.

LAGGARD In the diffusion process, laggards are the last group of consumers to buy a product or service. They are frequently older, tradition-bound individuals of low economic and social status.

LAISSEZ FAIRE A theory in which government intervention in private economic affairs is discouraged. A laissez faire attitude is regarded as an encouragement to the free enterprise system.

LATE MAJORITY In the diffusion process, the late majority includes those consumers in the mass market who are slow to purchase new products and services. Members of this group are likely to have below average incomes, relatively little social prestige, and to be relatively unresponsive to innovation.

LATENT DEMAND A condition in the marketplace in which consumers have a desire for a product or service which is unmet, commonly because the product or service is as yet undeveloped.

LAW OF DEMAND A law stating that as the price of a product is raised the demand for this product will diminish, i.e., consumers purchase more goods at a low price than at a high price. Also known as the law of diminishing demand.

LAW OF DIMINISHING DEMAND See *law of demand*

LAW OF DIMINISHING MARGINAL UTILITY See *principle of diminishing utility*

LAW OF RETAIL GRAVITATION See *Reilly's law of retail gravitation*

L.C.L. FREIGHT RATE See *less-than-carload freight rate (L.C.L.)*

LEAD In sales, a lead is a possible new customer. A lead may be either a person or an organization, but the salesperson has not yet determined whether the lead is really interested in the product or service. Once this has been determined, the lead becomes a prospect. See also *prospect* and *qualified prospect.*

LEAD TIME 1) In physical distribution, the elapsed time between placement of an order and the arrival of the goods. Also known as order cycle time. 2) In advertising, the elapsed time between the placement of an advertisement and its appearance in the media.

LEADER PRICING A strategy in which the prices of certain items (called leaders, or loss leaders) are established at levels so low that they yield little or no profit. The objective of this practice is to increase customer traffic flow and to create the general impression of store-wide low prices.

LEADERS See *leading pricing*

LEADING SERIES See *time series*

LEARNING ADVANTAGE See *learning curve*

LEARNING CURVE A graphic representation of the fact that as production increases, unit costs decrease; i.e., when a great many items are manufactured, each individual item will be cheaper because the manufacturer has learned to reduce expenses and to increase efficiency.

LEARNING CURVE PRICING A pricing strategy in which a manufacturer reduces the price of his product as production increases and becomes more cost-efficient.

LEASE A contract or agreement for the use of equipment or the occupation of real property for a limited term at a predetermined cost to the lessee. Leases take many forms but, in general, it may be said that a lease agreement is a means of financing the use of equipment or property without the need for outright ownership on the part of the lessee. Ownership of leased equipment or property remains with the lessor.

LEASED DEPARTMENT A department or area within a store operated by an outside organization, although often not so identified to the customer. Generally the store supplies the space and those essential services such as lighting, security, etc. in return for a flat fee or for a percentage of the leased department's sales. Shoes, jewelry repair, photo services, etc. are leased departments frequently found in department or discount stores.

LEASING See *lease*

LEDGER EXPENSES See *natural classification of expenses*

LEGITIMIZATION With reference to the introduction of new products into the marketplace, legitimization refers to the process by which early triers of the product serve as examples for other consumers who may be somewhat less innovative.

LESS-THAN-CARLOAD FREIGHT RATE (L.C.L.) A shipment which does not fill a railroad freight car and thus does not qualify for full-car rates. See also *carload freight rate (C.L.)*.

LESSEE See *lease*

LESSOR See *lease*

LETTER OF CREDIT A written instrument issued by a bank to a buyer of goods which is evidence of the buyer's good credit standing. The letter of credit is presented to the seller of the goods by the buyer, the seller delivers the goods to the buyer and collects his money from the bank which issued the letter of credit which, in turn, collects from the buyer. The letter of credit is useful in international trade where the buyer has been unable to establish a line of credit with the sellers of goods.

LEVEL EXPENDITURE METHOD A method of developing media advertising schedules in which each segment of the campaign is treated equally.

LICENSING 1) An agreement between the creator of a product or line of products and a manufacturer in which the creator (licensor) gives the manufacturer (licensee) permission to use his name in the marketing of a product in return for a royalty, usually computed as a percentage of sales. 2) A form of joint venture in which a domestic manufacturer seeks entry into a foreign market by granting a license in the foreign market permission to use a manufacturing process, trademark, trade secret, etc. in exchange for a royalty or fee. The partnership thus formed allows the do-

mestic manufacturer entry to the host country market with minimal risk, since the licensee is providing the means of production. The licensee, on the other hand, gains access to a well-known product or product line.

LIFE CYCLE See *product life cycle (PLC)* and *retail life cycle*

LIFE-STYLE See *lifestyle*

LIFESTYLE A distinctive mode of behavior centered around activities, interests, opinions, attitudes, and demographic characteristics distinguishing one segment of a population from another. In this view, one's lifestyle is seen as the sum of one's interactions with one's environment. Lifestyle studies are a component of the broader behavioral concept called psychographics.

LIFESTYLE ANALYSIS See *lifestyle segmentation*

LIFESTYLE MARKETING See *lifestyle segmentation*

LIFESTYLE SEGMENTATION The division of a market into subgroups based on the way the members of each group live. Particular attention is given to the activities and interests of the members of each group.

LILIEN, GARY L. See *advisor project*

LIMITED ASSORTMENT STORE See *limited-line store*

LIMITED-FUNCTION WHOLESALER See *limited service wholesaler*

LIMITED-LINE STORE A retail outlet in some respects similar to the specialty store in that it carries a limited number of product lines but has considerable depth in the lines it carries. Limited-line stores are often known by the name of the product they sell, e.g., shoe store, furrier, bakery, flower shop, etc. Also known as limited assortment stores.

LIMITED-LINE STRATEGY A marketing strategy in which the number of products in a line is restricted.

LIMITED PROBLEM SOLVING In consumer behavior, limited problem solving is the effort taken to understand one's needs and how best to satisfy them at a particular point in time, particularly when many possible solutions are available and possible. See also *extensive problem solving*.

LIMITED-SERVICE WHOLESALER A wholesaling middleman who, like his full-service counterpart, takes title to the goods he resells, but who provides fewer services in an effort to reduce costs. Known also as a limited-function wholesaler. Included under this term are the following enterprises: drop shipper, wagon distributor, cash-and-carry wholesaler, rack jobber, mail-order wholesaler, and producer's cooperative.

LINE See *product line*

LINE CONSISTENCY Lines of products which are closely related to one another in terms of end use and production requirements, or which are distributed through the same channels are said to be line consistent.

LINE EXECUTIVE See *line manager*

LINE EXTENSION A new product added to an existing line of products, e.g., a new fragrance added to a line of perfumes. See also *brand extension*.

LINE MANAGER An executive in a firm having a line organization, i.e., a direct line of responsibility and control from top to bottom. The line manager has direct responsibility for certain operations which represent the primary mission of the organization.

LINE STRUCTURE The extension of a line of products by its manufacturer beyond the range currently produced. For example, the extension may involve products at higher and/or lower prices or products at different levels of quality.

LINEAR PROGRAMMING A mathematical technique employed in determining the allocation of resources (especially when there are a number of variables in the problem) in an effort to reach a particular objective, e.g., the maximizing of profits. The term linear is derived from the straightline algebraic formulas used in expressing the problem.

LINES OF AUTHORITY See *market division of authority*

LIQUID ASSETS Cash, money on deposit in checking and savings accounts which is not encumbered, stocks, bonds, and other securities which are readily marketable, etc.

LIQUID WEALTH See *liquid assets*

LIST PRICE The list price may be at the point of production; i.e., it may be the manufacturer's price to the distributor or retailer as represented on a list or in a catalog, but more often list price is meant to indicate the retail price suggested (and sometimes advertised) by the manufacturer before any discounts or other price reductions are made.

LOADER See *dealer loader*

LOADING As practiced by manufacturers, loading is the sale to wholesalers and retailers of more goods than they really need. Loading places the middleman in an overstocked inventory position.

LOCAL ADVERTISING Advertising sponsored by local businesses who provide products or services in the local market. When conducted by stores it is frequently called retail advertising despite the fact that some retailers are national advertisers.

LOCAL BRAND Goods marketed in a particular geographical region such as bread, beer, etc.

LOGISTICAL FUNCTION See *logistical marketing function*

LOGISTICAL MARKETING FUNCTION Any marketing function which involves the transportation and physical distribution of goods and services. Logistical marketing functions include storage, assorting, assembling, and related tasks. See also *marketing functions.*

LOGISTICS A marketing support activity primarily concerned with the flow of goods, i.e., the acquisition of supplies and materials, the distribution of finished products or the delivery of services, and the maintenance of clear channels of communication between producer and customer.

LOGO Generally one or more letters worked into some distinctive typographic or calligraphic design. Logos are often in the form of initials (representing the name of a brand or company) but the logo of the Coca-Cola Company, which is entirely written out, is probably the most famous in the world. Also known as a logotype, a signature cut, or a sig cut.

LOGOTYPE See *logo*

LONG-RANGE PLAN See *planning*

LONG-TERM PLAN See *planning*

LOSS LEADER A term used in retailing to describe an item which, in order to build store traffic, is priced so low that is does not yield a profit. Loss leaders are usually well-known high-demand products which will attract customers who will, in turn, buy other merchandise at regular prices. The term price leader is also used synonymously with loss leader, particularly in the food retailing business. See also *leader pricing.*

LOW-BALL PRICE The promotion of a product, usually by telephone, at a very low price calculated to lead a customer into a store. Upon arrival at the store the customer is informed by the salesperson that management will not allow him to sell the product at the promised price and attempts to pressure the customer into buying a more expensive item.

LOW-INVOLVEMENT GOODS Merchandise purchased on a regular basis which is low in cost and familiar to the customer. Low-involvement goods require little thought and planning on the part of the buyer.

LOWER CLASS See *social class*

LOWER LOWER CLASS See *social class*

LOWER MIDDLE CLASS See *social class*

LOWER UPPER CLASS See *social class*

MACRO ENVIRONMENT See *marketing environment*

MACRO-MARKETING See *macromarketing*

MACROMARKETING The marketing system as seen in its broadest context, i.e., how the system affects the social system (both nationally and internationally) in which it functions.

MACROSEGMENTATION A strategy employed in industrial marketing in which market potential for products or services is established by examining broad segmentation variables such as the data provided by the Bureau of the Census.

MAGNUSON-MOSS WARRANTY— FEDERAL TRADE COMMISSION IMPROVEMENT ACT, 1975 A federal consumer protection law providing for minimum disclosure standards in written warranties for manufactured products.

MAIL INTERVIEW See *interview*

MAIL ORDER ACTION LINE See *Direct Marketing Association (DMA)*

MAIL ORDER HOUSE A non-store retailing organization whose business is generated through merchandise catalogs. Customers select goods from the company's catalog and mail or telephone in their order which is subsequently filled by mail or other delivery service.

MAIL ORDER RETAILING A form of selling in which personal contact and store operations have been eliminated. The retailer contacts potential customers through the use of direct mail, catalogs, television, radio, magazines, newspapers, etc. Merchandise is described in words and pictures, customers order by mail or telephone, and orders are filled by the seller through the mail or via parcel services. See also *direct mail.*

MAIL ORDER WHOLESALER A limited service wholesaler who sells merchandise by direct mail to industrial organizations, institutions, and retailers. Orders are generated from catalogs. The wholesaler distributes to potential customers, and deliveries are made by the U.S. Postal Service or by private delivery services. Also known as catalog houses.

MAIL ORDER WHOLESALING A form of wholesaling in which personal selling has been eliminated. Mail order wholesalers send catalogs to retail firms and/or other wholesalers along with instructions on how to order goods. Mail order wholesalers often handle the merchandise of several small manufacturers who cannot afford to produce their own catalogs but who desire market exposure for their products. Many mail order wholesalers are found in the stationary and printing field.

MAIL PREFERENCE SERVICE See *Direct Marketing Association (DMA)*

MAIL SURVEY See *survey* and *questionnaire*

MAILING LIST USER AND SUPPLIER ASSOCIATION (ML/USA) An association of brokers, users, and owners of mailing lists, as well as related organizations. ML/USA seeks to promote the use of mailing lists and the respectability of the mailing list industry. The Association provides educational, legislative, and promotional services to its members. It maintains an employment assistance program, a speakers bureau, and a credit reference sharing program.

MAINTAINED MARKUP The difference between net sales and the cost of goods sold. The maintained markup figure (expressed as a percentage of net sales) does not reflect deductions for cash discounts and workroom costs, and represents the actual markup which was achieved for the selling period. See also *gross margin.*

MAINTENANCE MARKETING That form of marketing appropriate to a marketplace in a full-demand condition. Monitoring the market for changes in customer demand is of primary importance in maintenance marketing.

MAINTENANCE, REPAIR, AND OPERATING ITEMS See *supplies*

MAJOR ACCOUNT MARKETING See *national account marketing*

MAJOR EQUIPMENT See *installed equipment*

MAJORITY FALLACY The fallacy lies in the proposition that the largest segments of a market are the most profitable. Because they attract strong competition, they may, in fact, be less profitable than smaller segments in which there are fewer competitors. This concept was propounded by A.L. Kuehn and R.L. Jay in a *Harvard Business Review* article entitled "Strategy of Product Quality" (Nov.– Dec., 1962).

MAKE-BULK CENTER A central distribution point where small shipments of goods are consolidated into larger ones and then shipped to their ultimate destination.

MALL In shopping center design, the mall is composed of pedestrian walkways which may be enclosed (and thus heated and air conditioned) or open to the sky. In larger centers, the mall provides access to the anchor stores as well as the inward-facing smaller shops. See also *shopping center.*

138

MANAGED OBSOLESCENCE See *planned obsolescence*

MANAGEMENT Those activities involved in running a business or other enterprise including planning, organizing, coordinating, implementing, directing, and monitoring the program of the organization. The term management is often treated as a synonym for administration.

When used in the noun form (as in "management team") the term refers to that individual or group of individuals who are responsible for operating an organization.

MANAGEMENT BY OBJECTIVES (MBO) A management technique or style which focuses on the goals of the organization and on the contribution of each individual in attaining the stated objectives. Formulated by management consultant Peter Drucker in the 1950s, MBO involves managers at all levels in 1) setting goals, 2) implementing the plan, and 3) reviewing and appraising the results.

MANAGEMENT CONTRACTING A form of joint venture in which a domestic firm provides management expertise to a foreign company. The foreign company provides the capital investment. See also *joint venture*.

MANAGEMENT INFORMATION SYSTEM (MIS) A system of organizing, storing, manipulating, and supplying information so that it may be used effectively to support management decision-making. The system may be computerized so that the information may be processed more efficiently. However, a complete MIS involves people and procedures as well as automated machinery. The MIS system collects quantitative data as well as opinions and predictions and organizes them so that they may be stored and retrieved in an effective and timely manner. Managers at each level of the organization utilize the information relevant to their own responsibilities. When used by marketers to plan the firm's marketing strategy, the process is known as a marketing information system (MIS). See also *decision support system (DSS)* and *marketing information system (MIS)*.

MANAGERIAL APPROACH TO MARKETING An approach to the study of marketing in which managerial functions (planning, the development of strategies, supervision, etc.) are viewed as a key to understanding the marketing process.

MANAGERIAL MARKETING Marketing as it is conducted in large organizations. Involves formal planning, establishing objectives, developing strategies for their achievement, and other highly rationalized courses of action designed to reach the firm's marketing goals.

MANUFACTURED PARTS AND MATERIALS See *materials and parts*

MANUFACTURER An organization which, through the use of materials, machinery, and labor, produces finished products. In retailing, a manufacturer may also be referred to as a vendor, supplier, or resource.

MANUFACTURER WHOLESALING A practice in which a manufacturer assumes the duties commonly performed by a wholesaler or other middleman within the channel of distribution.

MANUFACTURER'S AGENT An agent middleman who represents a producer or manufacturer in what is usually an exclusive territory. The manufacturer's agent may sell the products of a number of non-competing clients simultaneously and may also carry an inventory of the products he sells. Manufacturer's agents have limited control over prices and terms of sale and act as salespersons calling on industrial customers and retailers. Sometimes called a manufacturer's representative, even though this term more accurately describes a salesperson employed by a manufacturer. Also known as a sole agent. See also *selling agent.*

MANUFACTURER'S BRANCH HOUSE See *manufacturer's branch office*

MANUFACTURER'S BRANCH OFFICE A wholesaling establishment from which a producer or manufacturer conducts sales activities and which includes warehousing or other storage facilities from which merchandise may be shipped to customers. These establishments are sometimes known as captive jobbers, distribution centers, captive wholesalers, or district offices. See also *manufacturer's sales office.*

MANUFACTURER'S BRAND Nationally advertised goods offered for sale by their producer or maker. Manufacturer's brands often carry a distinctive and widely recognized brand name or trademark. Also known as a national brand.

MANUFACTURER'S COOPERATIVE ADVERTISING See *cooperative advertising*

MANUFACTURER'S DEALER-LISTING ADS Commonly found in newspapers and magazines, this advertising promotes the product and lists the dealers who handle it.

MANUFACTURER'S REPRESENTATIVE See *manufacturer's agent*

MANUFACTURER'S SALES BRANCH See *manufacturer's branch office*

MANUFACTURER'S SALES OFFICE An establishment owned and operated by a producer or manufacturer from which sales are solicited by a permanent staff of salespeople employed by the company. Sales offices carry no inventory and thus operate like drop shippers in that they have no warehouse from which goods could be shipped to the customer. See also *manufacturer's branch office.*

MANUFACTURER'S SALESPERSON A salesperson employed by a manufacturer to sell products at all levels of the market (to industrial buyers, wholesalers, and retailers) but not to the ultimate consumer. Included are dealer-service salespeople (who call regularly on established customers), missionary salespeople (who arrange displays, demonstrate products, etc.), and detailers (who visit professionals like physicians, hospital administrators, etc. to introduce products).

MANUFACTURER'S STORE Retail outlets operated by the manufacturer of a product, e.g., automobile tires, for the purpose of selling the product and providing services to the customer. Also known as producer outlets. See also *factory outlet.*

MANUFACTURING See *manufacturer*

MARGIN See *gross margin*

MARGINAL ANALYSIS In marketing cost analysis, a method of ascertaining the point at which marginal cost and marginal revenue equal one another. Prices set on the basis of this analysis are believed to maximize profits for the organization. Sometimes referred to as analytical pricing.

Marginal analysis may also be employed in the development of a firm's sales force. In this case salespeople are added to the sales force until the profits generated by the last person hired equal the costs generated by his or her hiring.

MARGINAL COST The amount of money expended to produce one additional unit of a product or service.

MARGINAL EFFICIENCY OF CAPITAL The profit accruing to a firm generated by the last dollar it has invested.

MARGINAL PROFIT The extra profit made on the last unit sold. Marginal profit may be calculated by subtracting the marginal cost from the marginal revenue. For example, if the marginal revenue (the amount of money accruing from the sale of one additional unit of a product or service) is $10, and the marginal cost (the amount of money expended to produce that one additional unit of the product or service) is $9, the marginal profit is $1. On the other hand, if the marginal cost is higher than the marginal revenue, it may not be profitable to produce the extra unit of the product or service. For example, if the marginal cost is $11 and the marginal revenue is $10, the producer will lose $1 in producing an extra unit.

MARGINAL REVENUE The amount of money accruing from the sale of one additional unit of a product or service.

MARGINAL UTILITY The amount of satisfaction a consumer receives from the acquisition and use of one more unit of a product.

MARKDOWN A reduction from original or previous retail price, generally as a result of reduced demand for the item in question (termed a clearance markdown) or in an attempt to increase store traffic (termed a promotional markdown).

MARKDOWN RATIO In retailing, a measure of the operating efficiency of a particular department and/or entire firm. The dollar value of all markdowns and allowances is divided by net sales in each department, according to the following formula:

$$\text{Markdown \%} = \frac{\text{\$ markdowns + \$ allowances}}{\text{\$ net sales}}$$

For example, if a retailer had originally priced ten blouses at $30 each, sold four of them at the original price, marked down the remaining six blouses to $20 and sold four more of them, and gave an allowance of $5 on one of the originally priced blouses, the markdown ratio would be computed as follows:

$$\text{Markdown \%} = \frac{(\$10 \text{ markdown} \times 6) + \$5 \text{ allowance}}{(\$30 \times 4) + (\$20 \times 4)}$$

$$= \frac{\$65}{\$200}$$

$$= .325$$

The result is then multiplied by 100, which gives us a total markdown ratio of 32.5%.

MARKET 1) The physical place where goods and services are bought and sold, e.g., a farmer's market where growers sell their produce to the public. 2) The physical place where a substantial number of suppliers have established their businesses in an effort to make themselves readily available to retail buyers, e.g., the garment center in New York City where hundreds of apparel manufacturers maintain showrooms. 3) The aggregate demand for certain products or services, i.e., all the actual or potential customers who have the means to purchase the product or service and who actually have access to it should they make a decision to buy.

MARKET AGGREGATION See *undifferentiated marketing*

MARKET ANALYSIS The collection and evaluation of data on the potential markets for a firm's products and/or services in an attempt to determine which segments may offer opportunities for profitable entry and expansion. Market analysis encompasses much of what is regarded as marketing research with an emphasis on demographic, geographic, and socioeconomic market segmentation.

MARKET ANTICIPATION Efforts made, generally on the basis of market research, to guess how customers will behave in the marketplace at some time in the future.

MARKET AUDIT See *marketing audit*

MARKET-BASED PRICING See *pricing at the market*

MARKET BUILD-UP METHOD A forecasting technique in which information from a number of market segments is gathered, separately analyzed, and then added together to form a more or less complete picture of the marketing environment for the purpose of forecasting sales.

MARKET CHANNEL See *channel of distribution*

MARKET CONCENTRATION 1) A form of market segmentation in which all a firm's marketing efforts are concentrated on one segment of the market population. 2) That part of a product's sales volume (or that part of an entire industry's production) which is accounted for by a relatively small number of large companies. Such concentration may be expressed in terms of dollar volume, number of units sold, employment level, etc.

MARKET DEMAND See *demand*

MARKET DEVELOPMENT A strategy in which a firm develops new markets for its products or in which the firm develops alternative uses for its products. The objective is to increase sales.

MARKET DEVELOPMENT MANAGER See *marketing planning manager*

MARKET-DIRECTED ECONOMIC SYSTEM See *economic system*

MARKET DIVERSIFICATION See *diversification*

MARKET DIVISION OF AUTHORITY In marketing management, a form of organization in which line authority is organized so that it corresponds to the structure of the marketplace or to the way a firm's customers are segmented. This practice is prevalent in firms which market their products to two or more industries or who distribute their products through two or more channels.

MARKET ECONOMY An economic system in which, at least theoretically, free enterprise is the operating principle, i.e., one in which the forces of supply and demand are given free reign to determine the allocation of resources.

MARKET FACTOR A variable in the marketing environment which may affect demand for a product or service. For example, the number of teenagers will affect the sale of phonograph records, or high interest rates will affect the sale of new homes.

MARKET FACTOR ANALYSIS Market factors are variables in the marketing environment. When market factors can be correlated with sales trends, the resulting analysis may be used to forecast future sales. See also *direct derivation* and *correlation analysis*.

142

MARKET FACTOR INDEX When a number of market factors are taken together, analyzed, and expressed in relation to a base number, a market factor index has been created. Such an index is used in the projection of future sales trends.

MARKET FIT In product marketing, market fit refers to the degree to which a new product is suited to a company's present market, i.e., the degree to which the new product is likely to appeal to the company's existing customers.

MARKET FORECAST See *forecasting*

MARKET FUNCTIONS See *marketing functions*

MARKET GRID A device employed in market segmentation studies in which a total market is subdivided in an effort to more precisely target potential customers. The information is frequently presented in the form of a grid. See also *Boston Consulting Group Matrix.*

MARKET GROWTH See *growth stage*

MARKET GROWTH RATE The annual growth or decline of a market, either at present or as forecast. The market growth rate is most often expressed as a percentage. In the growth/share matrix, the market growth rate represents the vertical axis of the graph. See also *Boston Consulting Group Matrix.*

MARKET GROWTH STAGE See *growth stage*

MARKET INDEX See *market factor index*

MARKET INFORMATION FUNCTION One of the facilitating marketing functions. The market information function includes the collection, analysis, and distribution of the information needed by marketers in the performance of universal marketing functions. See also *facilitating marketing function.*

MARKET INTENSIFICATION See *intensive market opportunities*

MARKET INTRODUCTION See *introductory stage*

MARKET MATRIX See *market grid*

MARKET MATURITY See *maturity stage*

MARKET MEASUREMENT STUDIES See *market potential*

MARKET MINIMUM The rate of sales for a product or service which would be achieved without any demand-stimulating expenditures such as advertising or promotion.

MARKET NEWS Specific information about conditions in the marketplace having an immediate bearing on the conduct of business, e.g., news of a crop failure quickly effects commodity traders.

MARKET NICHE See *niche marketing*

MARKET OPPORTUNITY See *company marketing opportunity*

MARKET ORIENTATION See *marketing concept*

MARKET PENETRATION The extent to which a company has entered a particular market and/or the degree to which it seeks to expand its share of that market.

MARKET PENETRATION PRICING A market strategy in which goods are priced low enough to have immediate wide appeal in the marketplace. The object of market penetration pricing is to quickly capture a significant share of the market.

MARKET PERIOD In the marketing process, that period from the time a product is manufactured (or a commodity is produced) until the time it is sold. During this period costs are fixed and the amount of product does not vary. Price will be determined by current demand.

MARKET PLAN See *marketing plan*

MARKET PLANNING The process by which a firm identifies its customers and determines their needs. Market planning is a part of the marketing planning effort together with such activities as sales forecasting, sales planning, and promotion budgeting. Included in market planning are such factors as product development, quality control, packaging, shipping, pricing, advertising, sales force management, and customer service. See also *marketing planning*.

MARKET-PLUS PRICING See *pricing above the market*

MARKET POSITION ANALYSIS See *attribute mapping*

MARKET-POSITIONED WAREHOUSE A facility in which goods may be stored. The market-positioned warehouse may be owned by a manufacturer, distributor, or retailer and is used to consolidate shipments and to position products near the ultimate consumer.

MARKET POSITIONING Those efforts aimed at establishing a product or service in a particular niche or segment of the marketplace. Market positioning strategy usually includes those promotional activities which differentiate the product from competitors and which vividly establish the product's image in the minds of potential customers. Also known as positioning, product positioning, or target positioning. See also *target market* and *brand position*.

MARKET POTENTIAL Represents both the realized and unrealized total "capacity to buy" existing in a market or segment of a market. The calculation includes all the goods or services offered by all the sellers competing in the particular market over a specific period of time. See also *sales potential* and *market share*.

MARKET PRICE A price determined by supply and demand in the marketplace. Prices for farm products are almost always set in this way.

MARKET PRICING The determination of selling price for a product or service by the unrestricted forces of supply and demand. The seller has little or no control over the price his goods or services will fetch in the marketplace.

MARKET REPRESENTATIVE See *resident buyer*

MARKET RESEARCH See *marketing research*

MARKET RESEARCH FIRM See *marketing research firm*

MARKET SATURATION See *saturated market*

MARKET SEGMENT A subdivision of a population (commonly ultimate consumers), the members of which share similar identifiable characteristics, e.g., age, wealth, style, education level, marital status, sexual orientation, etc. A firm may develop different marketing programs for each segment of its target market.

MARKET SEGMENTATION The subdivision of a population (frequently ultimate consumers) into smaller parts, or demand segments, having similar characteristics. These smaller parts will, presumably, exhibit homogenous responses to various marketing programs. See also *differentiated marketing.*

MARKET SHARE That part of a total market controlled by one firm. It is expressed as the firm's sales, or the sales of a particular product or line of products, in relation to total industry sales and is commonly computed as a percentage. Also known as brand share. See also *market potential* and *sales potential.*

MARKET SHARE ANALYSIS An analysis of a firm's sales which takes into account the activities of a firm's competitors and views the company as a participant in the general marketplace. Market share analysis is a more precise measure of performance than sales volume analysis.

MARKET SHARE OBJECTIVE A benchmark which represents that portion of a market a company wishes to capture.

MARKET SKIMMING PRICING See *skimming*

MARKET STRATEGY A plan for the marketing of a product. There may be one or more strategies employed including: product differentiation (the product is carefully distinguished from its competitors), price competition (the product is marketed at a competitive price relative to competing products), market segmentation (the product is targeted for a particular customer segment) and other strategies calculated to promote and sell the product.

MARKET STRETCHING A strategy employed in marketing products which have reached the maturity stage in their life cycle. Sales are maintained at present levels or, at times, expanded through such means

as technical improvement and more effective marketing research.

MARKET TARGET See *target market*

MARKET TARGET DECISION ANALYSIS A system used to identify target markets for goods and services through an analysis of the various segments which make up the total market. Frequently the information is presented in the form of a grid to facilitate decision making.

MARKET TARGETING Those strategic decision-making activities which precede both the selection of a target market and the market positioning of a product. Market targeting enables the organization to focus its resources on the achievement of specific goals. Making a choice between targeting the total market or limiting market efforts to one or more specific segments is a significant market targeting activity. Also known as target marketing. See also *target market.*

MARKET TESTING A marketing research technique in which a new product or service is introduced, usually in a limited, carefully selected geographic area (a test market), in an effort to predict its performance in the marketplace. Market testing also provides management with the opportunity to correct production problems before a total market commitment has been made. Also called test marketing and product testing.

MARKET VALUE The prevailing price at which a product can be expected to sell in a given market. See also *value* and *price.*

MARKETBASKET PRICING A pricing strategy most commonly found in supermarkets in which some items (generally those about which the consumer is most price-conscious) are priced low to create the impression of

145

a bargain. Other less familiar items are then given a high compensating markup.

MARKETER All organizations and individuals engaged in business may be regarded as marketers in that they are all, in one way or another, selling something to somebody. In addition, many nonbusiness organizations engage in what must be regarded as marketing activities and thus must be classified as marketers.

MARKETING Broadly construed, marketing is a part of an economic process concerned with the supply of and demand for goods, services, and ideas in the society at large. It includes those activities which facilitate the exchange of goods and services as they move from production to the industrial user or ultimate consumer.

At the more narrow organizational level (both profit and non-profit), marketing involves such pre-production activities as planning and development (may also include marketing research), pricing, promotion, distribution, and follow-up services. The objective of this activity is to make a profit while satisfying some human need.

MARKETING AGAINST THE COMPETITOR A strategy in which a firm focuses its marketing efforts on the strengths and weaknesses of its competitors rather than on the wants and needs of its customers. For example, when Pepsi-Cola determined that Coca-Cola was weakest in marketing to younger consumers they focused their advertising attack on this vulnerable area.

MARKETING AND DISTRIBUTIVE EDUCATION ASSOCIATION (MDEA) An association of teachers and other educators which encourages research and promotes teacher

education in marketing and related fields such as retailing, wholesaling, and selling. It publishes *Marketing Educator's News* three times per year. MDEA is based in Reston, Virginia.

MARKETING-AS-USUAL APPROACH TO SHORTAGES An approach to actual or anticipated shortages of the raw materials required for production. When companies feel they cannot produce enough goods to meet customer demand, they may assume that such shortages are temporary and continue to produce the same quantities of their products and sell to the same customers. The firm adopting this approach continues to spend the same amount on advertising, sales force, marketing research, etc., as it did prior to the shortage. Minor changes may be made in the advertising message and prices may rise somewhat to cover cost increases, but other marketing factors remain unchanged. This approach serves to maintain the firm's profit margin as well as the good will of its customers.

MARKETING AUDIT A systematic, comprehensive evaluation of a firm's marketing, philosophy, objectives, and strategy with a view toward implementing corrective action if deemed appropriate. The audit may be applied to on-going marketing programs (a control audit) in an effort to determine their effectiveness, or to completed programs (a review audit) in an effort to evaluate their results.

MARKETING BUDGET A financial plan, often based on projected sales (or past sales), used as a basis for allocating money to cover marketing costs over a period in the future. The marketing budget includes projected costs for administration and materials, marketing research, advertising and sales promotion, and other marketing functions. In many respects, the marketing budget is a projected income statement for the particular marketing functions in question.

MARKETING CHANNEL See *channel of distribution*

MARKETING COMMUNICATION All those messages transmitted from sender to receiver which involve the buyer-seller relationship. In addition to formal promotional messages, informal nonsystematic communication such as word-of-mouth is also included.

MARKETING COMMUNICATIONS EXECUTIVES INTERNATIONAL (MCEI) An association of marketing communications executives and teachers which has its headquarters in Sea Bright, New Jersey. MCEI supports research in marketing communications and publishes *The Communicator*, its annual membership roster, and several monthly newsletters.

MARKETING COMMUNICATIONS MIX See *promotion mix*

MARKETING COMPANY ERA A stage in the evolution of marketing (from roughly the mid-1960s to the present) during which marketing departments took on dominant roles in many manufacturing organizations.

MARKETING CONCEPT A marketing management orientation in which the satisfaction of the customer's wants and needs is regarded as the primary goal of the organization, although these wants and needs may not as yet be apparent to (and, thus, not expressed by) the consumer. In essence, the marketing concept recognizes the importance of the consumer in the buying process.

Profits are generated by determin-

ing what the customer wants or may be wanting in the future and then making it, rather than by making a product and then finding a way to create demand. See also *product concept, production concept,* and *selling concept.*

MARKETING CONTROL See *control*

MARKETING CONTROLLABLES See *controllable factors*

MARKETING COOPERATIVE See *producers' cooperative*

MARKETING COST ANALYSIS An analysis of the firm's marketing operations in terms of the cost of such activities as selling, advertising, transportation, storage, delivery, etc. An effort is then made to correlate these tools with the profitability of various products, customer groups, territories, etc. The objective of the analysis is to determine the efficiency of the firm's marketing efforts. See also *contribution-margin approach to cost analysis* and *full-cost approach to cost analysis.*

MARKETING DECISION SUPPORT SYSTEM See *decision support system (DSS)*

MARKETING DEPARTMENT ERA A stage in the evolution of marketing during which the marketing department in a firm, although still subordinate to production and sales, is beginning to influence the development of the company marketing program.

MARKETING DYNAMICS Changes in a firm's marketing mix determined by changes in the external environment. Most marketing dynamics are controllable by the organization as contrasted to environmental dynamics which are largely out of the firm's control.

MARKETING ENVIRONMENT That complex of legal, political, economic, and social influences which surrounds a firm and affects its marketing activities. A firm may be seen as having two distinct marketing environments: 1) an internal, or micro-environment over which it has a degree of control, and 2) an external, or macro-environment which is largely beyond its control.

MARKETING ETHICS Those standards, values, moral principles, etc. which govern the marketer's behavior in the marketplace.

MARKETING FUNCTION ACCOUNTS See *functional account*

MARKETING FUNCTIONS Those activities which form the basis for marketing. They include product and planning development, financing, pricing, promotion (including advertising and personal selling), transportation, storage, distribution etc. Marketing research, which is sometimes regarded as a support function, may also be included. Marketing functions are also known as marketing variables and marketing instruments.

MARKETING GRID See *market grid*

MARKETING INFORMATION AND DECISION PROGRAM (MIDP) See *marketing information system (MIS)*

MARKETING INFORMATION SYSTEM (MIS) A marketing information system is a complex of persons, procedures, and equipment which, in concert, collect information relevant to marketing decision-making. It is more broadly based than marketing research in that the system gathers data from within the firm as well as externally in the marketing environment. The system provides for the evaluation of the collected data to de-

termine its usefulness to the executives responsible for planning the firm's marketing strategy. See also *decision support system (DSS)*.

MARKETING INFORMATION SYSTEM (MIS)

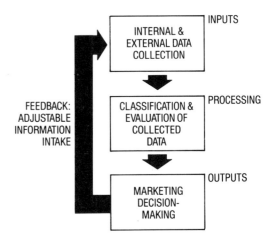

MARKETING INSTITUTIONS The organizations which make up the marketing system. Marketing institutions include manufacturers and producers, middlemen (wholesalers, retailers, etc.), and a wide variety of facilitating organizations such as trucking firms, railroads, warehouse facilities, advertising agencies, etc.

MARKETING INSTRUMENTS See *marketing functions*

MARKETING INTELLIGENCE SYSTEM The network of outside information sources through which marketing executives collect data useful in making marketing decisions.

MARKETING INTERMEDIARY See *middleman, retailer,* and *wholesaler*

MARKETING MANAGEMENT The process of planning, implementing, and directing a firm's marketing efforts with the intention of satisfying the customer and turning a profit. Among the many functions included in the marketing management process are strategy development and sales forecasting, advertising and sales promotion, analysis of market opportunities, and the establishment of the proper marketing mix.

MARKETING MANAGER That executive responsible for the firm's product planning and marketing strategy development. The marketing manager directs marketing research activities, formulates goals for the sales force, develops a sales promotion and advertising strategy, sets pricing policy, establishes budgets for particular lines, and engages in other marketing activities aimed at maximizing the firm's position in the marketplace. The marketing manager may also be known as the vice president-marketing or the director of marketing.

MARKETING MANAGER ORGANIZATION SYSTEM A company organization for product management in which a number of areas including product planning, advertising, and sales promotion report to a single manager.

MARKETING MATRIX See *market grid*

MARKETING MIDDLEMAN See *wholesaling middleman*

MARKETING MIX Those marketing variables (such as product planning, pricing, promotion, and distribution channel selection) which when blended together form a marketing strategy designed to satisfy the firm's customers.

MARKETING MIX

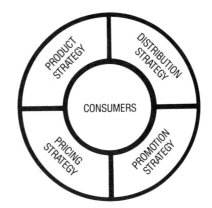

MARKETING MYOPIA A term coined by Theodore Levitt in a *Harvard Business Review* article (September–October, 1975) referring to a short-sighted, narrow view of marketing.

MARKETING OBJECTIVES That part of a marketing plan which defines the goals of the plan regarding sales volume, market share, and profit. Effective marketing objectives are clear, measurable, stated in order of their importance, and realistically attainable while remaining challenging. See also *marketing plan* and *financial objectives.*

MARKETING OPPORTUNITY ANALYSIS An analysis of the marketing environment in an effort to ascertain where changes might occur and to determine when problems might develop. Marketing opportunity analysis is commonly employed in marketing planning and strategy development, particularly with respect to the activities of competitors.

MARKETING ORGANIZATION An organizational arrangement of formal and informal relationships which

149

form a system through which marketing personnel execute a firm's marketing plans.

MARKETING ORIENTATION See *marketing concept*

MARKETING PHILOSOPHY See *marketing concept*

MARKETING PLAN The formal written document which puts the decisions reached during the marketing planning process into action. The marketing plan sets forth those activities which will carry forward the firm's marketing program and which will enable the firm to reach its ultimate goals.

MARKETING PLANNING A systematic process whose purpose is the assessment of the firm's marketing objectives and sales targets. Activities included in marketing planning are marketing research, sales forecasting, and market planning. The actual formulation of a marketing plan may be secondary to the strategic thinking carried on at the management level which ultimately leads to a consensus within the organization. Thus, while planning anticipates future market developments, it also provides management the opportunity to evaluate long-term strategy along with the tactics necessary to execute the resulting plan. See also *market planning*.

MARKETING PLANNING MANAGER That executive who, in organizations serving a number of markets, supervises the marketing research efforts as well as a number of market managers. The marketing planning manager is essentially a strategic planner. Sometimes known as a market development manager.

MARKETING POSITIONING See *market positioning*

MARKETING PROGRAM The overall plan maintained by a firm which blends all its strategic plans. The marketing program is the responsibility of the entire firm, not just one division. When the various plans are quite different, there is little concern for how they all fit together. When they are similar, however, the same sales force may have to carry out several plans. Consideration is always given to the way each plan competes for the firm's limited financial resources. See also *strategic planning*.

MARKETING RESEARCH The systematic collection of information from sources outside the business or research organization. Gathered data is subsequently analyzed to determine its usefulness in marketing decision-making.

In 1986 the American Marketing Association further elaborated on the definition: "Marketing research is the function which links the consumer, customer, and public to the marketer through information—information used to identify and define marketing opportunities and problems; generate, refine, and evaluate marketing actions; monitor marketing performance; and improve understanding of marketing as a process.

Marketing research specifies the information required to address these issues; designs the method for collecting information, manages and implements the data collection process; analyzes the results; and communicates the findings and their implications." Sometimes abbreviated MR.

MARKETING RESEARCH ASSOCIATION (MRA) An association of individuals involved in marketing research for advertising agencies, research firms, and industries. The Chicago based association maintains a job placement service and publishes a bimonthly newsletter, *Alert*, a semiannual *Journal of Data Collection,* various manuals and guidelines, and an annual *Membership Roster.*

MARKETING RESEARCH FIRM An outside firm contracted to provide marketing research to a company. There are three main types of marketing research firms: 1) syndicated service research firms which gather consumer and trade information on a regular basis and sell the data to clients for a fee (such as the reports on television audiences prepared by the A.C. Nielsen Co.); 2) custom marketing research firms which are hired to perform specific research assignments and whose reports become the property of the client; and 3) specialty-line marketing research firms which provide specialized research services to other marketing research firms and to the marketing research departments of clients (such as field interviewing services). See also *marketing research.*

MARKETING SCIENCE See *analytical marketing system*

MARKETING SCIENCE INSTITUTE (MSI) MSI is a market research center which conducts research to develop marketing information, develops testing methods, and monitors social and economic conditions which may affect the marketing climate. The Institute is supported by business. It publishes a quarterly *Newsletter,* quarterly *Research Briefs,* and books, technical reports, and working papers. The Institute is located in Cambridge, Massachusetts.

MARKETING STRATEGY The logical, comprehensive plan of action through which a firm intends to reach its objectives in the marketplace. Marketing strategy is primarily concerned with the implementation of company policy and with those marketing activities through which the company's goals are to be achieved.

MARKETING SYSTEM Marketing viewed as a system, i.e., a group of units which form a whole. Includes producers of goods and services, a number of marketing intermediaries (wholesalers, distributors, retailers, shipping organizations, advertising agencies, etc.), and finally, customers. The primary objective of the marketing system is the expeditious allocation of resources so as to efficiently meet the demands of the marketplace.

MARKETING UNCONTROLLABLES See *uncontrollable factors*

MARKETING VARIABLES See *marketing functions*

MARKETPLACE In its broadest context marketplace refers to the marketing environment. For a more restricted definition see *market.*

MARKON A term often used synonymously with markup, but certain distinctions can be made between the two. Markon is generally represented as the difference between the cost price of merchandise and its retail price expressed as a percentage of cost and added to cost to reach the final retail price. Markon may also be used to describe the total amount added to the cost of all merchandise in a department, rather than to the amount added to individual items (which is more commonly referred to as markup). Finally, markon is a term more frequently found at the manufacturing level rather than the retail level of the distribution chain. See also *markup.*

MARKUP The difference between cost price of merchandise and its retail price. Markup may be expressed in dollars or as a percentage. If stated as a percentage it may be based on either cost price or retail price. Markup is sometimes used synonymously with the term markon, but there are certain distinctions which can be made between the two. Markon is computed as follows:

$$\frac{\text{Retail price} - \text{cost price}}{\text{cost price}} = \text{markon \%}$$

$$\frac{\$20 - \$10}{\$10} = \frac{10}{10} = \frac{1}{1} = 100\%$$

Markup is computed as follows:

$$\frac{\text{Retail price} - \text{cost price}}{\text{retail price}} = \text{markup \%}$$

$$\frac{\$20 - \$10}{\$20} = \frac{10}{20} = \frac{1}{2} = 50\%$$

Markup is also a term most commonly applied to the amount added to cost price to reach a retail price for individual items, while markon more often refers to the total amount added to the cost of all the merchandise in a department. Finally, markon is a term more frequently found at the manufacturing level and markup at the merchandising/retail level of the distribution chain. See also *markon*.

MARKUP PERCENT In retailing and wholesaling, markup is generally computed as a percentage of the selling price, although some firms use cost price as the basis for comparison. The following two formulas facilitate the conversion from cost to selling price:

$$\begin{array}{l}\text{\% markup} \\ \text{on selling} \\ \text{price}\end{array} = \frac{\text{\% markup on cost}}{100\% + \text{\% markup on cost}}$$

$$\begin{array}{l}\text{\% markup} \\ \text{on cost}\end{array} = \frac{\begin{array}{l}\text{\% markup on} \\ \text{selling price}\end{array}}{100\% - \begin{array}{l}\text{\% markup} \\ \text{on selling price}\end{array}}$$

See also *markup*.

MARKUP PERCENTAGE See *markup percent*

MART See *merchandise mart*

MASLOW'S HIERARCHY A theory developed by Abraham H. Maslow which divides needs that motivate human behavior into five hierarchical levels. According to Maslow, it is only when one need level is at least partially satisfied that the need at the next level arises. The first two levels of Maslow's hierarchy are 1) the need for the basic necessities of life such as food, clothing, and shelter; and 2) the need for physical safety. Both of these levels are primarily physical in nature. The following three levels, on the other hand, are psychological. These are 3) the need for love, affection, and belonging; 4) the need to enhance one's own self-esteem or sense of personal worth; and 5) the need to become fully developed as a human being. Maslow's hierarchy provides marketers with a key to the design and marketing of products. Certain goods and services can only be successfully marketed in societies that have met the requirements of their physical needs and individuals are free to concentrate on psychological necessities. Thus, marketing to subsistence farmers using advertising messages geared to enhance one's sense of self-esteem or personal worth would be pointless. See also *motive*.

MASLOW'S HIERARCHY

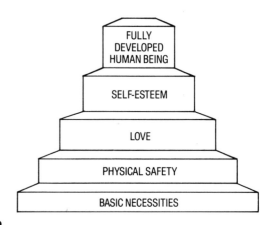

FULLY DEVELOPED HUMAN BEING

SELF-ESTEEM

LOVE

PHYSICAL SAFETY

BASIC NECESSITIES

MASS COMMUNICATIONS MEDIA See *medium*

MASS DISTRIBUTION See *intensive distribution* and *mass marketing*

MASS MARKET The mass market does not include "everyone." Each organization selling to the mass market targets a large and widely dispersed (but clearly defined) group of consumers who are its potential customers. See also *mass marketing*.

MASS MARKET THEORY See *fashion adoption process*

MASS MARKETER See *mass marketing*

MASS MARKETING A marketing strategy in which a product or service having wide appeal among the consuming public is promoted under a single marketing program and sold through such outlets as chain stores, discount stores, and supermarkets. Mass marketers do not target "everyone" as their customers but do address large numbers of consumers over broad geographic areas.

MASS MEDIA See *medium*

MASS MERCHANDISER See *mass merchandising*

MASS MERCHANDISING The retailing, on a very large scale, of goods (largely staples) at prices lower than those commonly found in department and specialty stores. Mass merchandising is characterized by: 1) an emphasis on products whose market is not highly segmented, 2) customers who are willing to sacrifice sales assistance and store services in return for lower prices, 3) high volume and a rapid stock turnover rate and, 4) a very highly competitive marketplace.

MASS PROMOTION Sales promotion activities concentrated at a particular time, e.g., the Christmas season.

MASS SELLING See *mass merchandising*

MATCHING CONCEPT In accounting, the matching of costs and revenue in an effort to relate expenses to the income they helped to produce; i.e., to determine a firm's net income for a given period, usually one year.

MATERIALS AND PARTS Materials and parts are incorporated into finished manufactured products and generally belong to one of two classes: 1) component materials including such raw materials as farm commodities, ores, and fiber and such products as lumber and cement; and 2) component parts such as electric motors, engine parts, glass windows, etc.

MATERIALS HANDLING All the activities associated with moving goods within a plant, in and out of warehousing, and to shipping points are generally referred to as materials handling.

MATERIALS MANAGEMENT Logistic activities concerned with the movement of production materials from their place of origin to the site of manufacture and with the movement of semi-finished products within the manufacturing facility.

MATERIALS REQUIREMENT PLANNING (MRP) A technique used in production management to control inventory and plan production steps. The goal of MRP is to provide the correct materials for production at the correct time, while avoiding unnecessary stockpiling. Computer programs are used to determine when materials are needed, when they should be ordered, and when they should be delivered.

MATRIX See *market grid*

MATRIX ORGANIZATION A type of business organization in which functional managers are often responsible

153

for activities such as advertising and other functions which require special expertise for all products, while product (or brand) managers are responsible for marketing their particular products, brands, or product lines. These roles may sometimes overlap and even conflict.

MATURITY STAGE That stage of the product life cycle in which demand levels off and profits begin to decline. Levels of competition have increased to the point where a shake-out is taking place in the market. See also *product life cycle (PLC)* and *retail life cycle.*

MAXIMIZING PROFIT See *rule for maximizing profit*

MBO See *management by objectives (MBO)*

MCEI See *Marketing Communications Executives International (MCEI)*

McGUIRE ACT See *Miller-Tydings Act (1937)*

MDEA See *Marketing and Distributive Education Association (MDEA)*

MEAT INSPECTION ACT (1906) Early consumer legislation which provided for the enforcement of sanitary regulation in the meat-packing industry.

MEDIA In a marketing context, generally referred to as "the media," i.e., television, radio, newspapers, magazines, direct mail material, and displays such as billboards and posters. The media are channels of communication for news, advertising, entertainment, and other messages.

MEDIA COVERAGE See *reach*

MEDIA SELECTION STRATEGY Strategy employed in choosing the appropriate advertising media. An effort is made to choose media which will effectively reach the target audience and to establish a schedule appropriate to the advertising goals.

MEDIUM A term commonly employed in marketing referring to a channel of communication (newspaper, magazine, radio, television, etc.) which carries advertising. In a broader sense, a medium may be a vehicle used to communicate, i.e., print, electronic transmission, etc.

MEETING COMPETITION See *pricing at the market*

MEGAMARKETING Defined by Philip Kotler (Kellog Graduate School of Management, Northwestern University) as "the strategically coordinated application of economic, psychological, political, and public relations skills to gain the cooperation of a number of parties in order to enter and/or operate in a given market." Kotler adds power and public relations to the four Ps of the marketing mix.

MEMBERS-ONLY OUTLET See *closed-door discount house*

MEMBERSHIP CLUB See *closed-door discount house*

MEMBERSHIP GROUP A reference group to which an individual actually belongs and with which he interacts. The group may be primary, e.g., family, neighbors, friends, co-workers, etc., or it may be secondary, e.g., voluntary associations, clubs, athletic teams, trade unions, religious organizations, etc. See also *reference group.*

MERCANTILE CREDIT Credit at the trade level, i.e., credit extended by manufacturers or wholesalers to other channel members such as retailers. Such credit avoids the need for COD shipments or for limiting business to a cash-and-carry basis.

MERCHANDISE AGENT See *broker*

MERCHANDISE ALLOWANCE See *promotional allowance*

MERCHANDISE ASSORTMENT See *product line*

MERCHANDISE BROKER See *broker*

MERCHANDISE DELIVERER See *truck wholesaler*

MERCHANDISE MART A facility in which exhibition space is rented on a permanent basis to manufacturers and wholesalers so that they may display their products to potential customers, usually distributors and retailers, not the general public. Marts are often devoted to a particular line of products, for example, apparel or furniture.

MERCHANDISING The planning involved in marketing the right merchandise at the right place at the right time in the right quantity at the right price. More specifically, it is the buying and selling of appropriate goods coupled with the accurate targeting of consumers for the ultimate purpose of making a profit, or more simply, matching the goods to market requirements.

   In retailing, merchandising includes the buying and selling of goods together with such activities as display, store layout, and various other promotional activities calculated to attract the consumer. In manufacturing, merchandising includes such promotional efforts as packaging, price deals, and advertising which will aid in selling the company's products to its middlemen.

MERCHANDISING CONGLOMERATE Corporation, or conglomerate, composed of a number of diversified retailing organizations under unified management. Stores may be of various types including department, specialty, and discount. Also known as a conglomerchant.

MERCHANDISING SALESPERSON See *missionary salesperson*

MERCHANT A middleman who takes title to the goods he buys and who, in turn, resells them. Most merchants are wholesalers or retailers and are variously known as traders, distributors, dealers, storekeepers, etc.

MERCHANT INTERMEDIARY See *wholesaling middleman*

MERCHANT MIDDLEMAN See *wholesaling middleman*

MERCHANT WHOLESALER See *wholesaler*

MESSAGE Words and symbols (in a written or oral form) which constitute an intelligible communication. In marketing, messages are frequently transmitted through the media, i.e., radio, television, newspapers, magazines, etc. See also *advertising message*.

METROPOLITAN STATISTICAL AREA (MSA) Similar to the old standard metropolitan statistical area (SMSA), the MSA is a freestanding metropolitan area which: 1) contains a city of at least 50,000 inhabitants, or 2) encompasses an urbanized area of at least 50,000 and a total metropolitan population of at least 100,000. An MSA may include, in addition to the county containing the central city, other counties which have close economic and social ties to the central city.

   Throughout the country, MSAs are composed of entire counties except in the six New England states where they consist of cities and towns. See also *Primary Metropolitan Statistical*

Area (PMSA) and *Consolidated Metropolitan Statistical Area (CMSA).*

MICRO ENVIRONMENT See *marketing environment*

MICRO-MACRO DILEMMA In economics, the realization that what is beneficial for some producers and consumers may not necessarily benefit society as a whole. See also *micromarketing* and *macromarketing.*

MICROMARKETING Marketing as seen from its narrow perspective, i.e., at the level of individual sellers and buyers.

MICROSEGMENTATION A strategy employed in industrial marketing in which market potential for products or services is established by gathering information about the characteristics of potential customers, often through the personal experience of salespeople.

MIDDLEMAN A broad term applied to individuals or firms who act as marketing intermediaries between producers and manufacturers on the one hand and the end user on the other. They may be wholesaling middlemen (which includes wholesalers, agents, and brokers) or they may be retailers. Middlemen perform a number of functions which facilitate the transfer of goods in the distribution system. See also *wholesaling middleman, wholesaler, agent middleman,* and *retailer.*

MIDDLEMAN BRAND See *distributor's brand*

MIDP See *marketing information system (MIS)*

MILKING A strategy in which a company prices an established product above the level which would ordinarily be justified by production costs and competitive conditions in the marketplace. Companies employing this strategy are cashing in on consumer brand loyalty in an effort to increase short-term profits. Sometimes called harvesting.

MILL SUPPLY HOUSE See *industrial distributor*

MILLER-TYDINGS ACT (1937) Federal legislation which permitted state governments to enact fair trade or resale price maintenance laws. The Act was declared unconstitutional by the U.S. Supreme Court in 1951, and the McGuire Act (1952) reinstated the legality of the nonsigner clause. See also *resale price maintenance (RPM).*

MILLING IN TRANSIT See *transit privileges*

MINIMUM MARKUP LAWS See *unfair trade practices acts*

MIS See *marketing information system (MIS)* and *management information system (MIS)*

MISDIRECTED MARKETING EFFORT Marketing efforts which are based upon incomplete, inconclusive, incorrect, or misleading data. Misdirected efforts are often the result of management's inability to accurately calculate marketing costs.

MISMARKETING Failed marketing efforts generally as a result of faulty information and poor decision making.

MISSION IDENTITY The company perceived by its customers in terms of its goals. Sometimes referred to as company image, mission identity is more accurately the sense of purpose which keeps a firm on track.

MISSION STATEMENT A detailed statement of the goals and objectives of an organization calculated to provide the members of the organization with a sense of direction.

MISSIONARIES See *missionary salesperson*

MISSIONARY SALESPERSON A manufacturer's representative who assists the middlemen customers of the firm (usually wholesalers and retailers) by demonstrating the manufacturer's products to salespersons and customers, arranging displays, planning advertising programs and other promotions, etc. The missionary salesperson does not usually engage directly in selling activities. In the health-care field, these sales representatives are called detailers.

MIXED BRAND STRATEGY A marketing strategy in which a manufacturer produces a number of similar products under different brand names, or in which a middleman or retailer sells products under different brand names, or in which a middleman or retailer sells products under dealer or generic names as well as under manufacturer names.

MIXED MERCHANDISING See *scrambled merchandising*

ML/USA See *Mailing List User and Supplier Association (ML/USA)*

MMIS See *multinational marketing information system (MMIS)*

MNC See *multinational corporation (MNC)*

MODEL 1) In management science, a set of variables and their interrelationships designed to represent a real system or process. Such models are developed by management scientists (also called operations researchers) in order to gain insight into the problem, control over the problem, or the ability to predict the outcome of the problem. In marketing, models are used for forecasting new product sales (where no historical data is available),

site selection, sales-call planning, media mix, and budgeting. 2) A sample, usually handmade, which serves as the prototype for a manufactured product. 3) A person who wears clothes for the purpose of displaying them.

MODEL BANK See *analytical marketing system*

MODEL STOCK See *balanced stock*

MODIFIED BREAK-EVEN ANALYSIS A form of break-even analysis in which the level of demand for a product is analyzed at various levels in an effort to determine the price-quantity mix which would maximize profits. Such analysis recognizes that profit does not necessarily increase as quantity sold increases, as increased sales are frequently the result of lowered prices.

MODIFIED REBUY An industrial buying situation in which some adjustments have been made in the specifications or price of the product to be ordered, thus making the process somewhat more complex than a straight rebuy. See also *new task buying* and *straight rebuy.*

MODIFIED STANDARDIZATION See *standardization*

MONEY AND MERCHANDISE ALLOWANCES See *allowance* and *push money (PM)*

MONEY INCOME Personal income in the form of cash (or checks)—generally from wages, salary, interest, rents, etc. Money income is calculated before deductions are made for income and Social Security taxes.

MONEY REFUND OFFER See *rebate*

MONITORING PROCEDURE See *monitoring skills*

MONITORING SKILLS The skills used by marketing managers to develop and manage a system of controls and provide feedback on the results of marketing activities. These controls may be annual-plan controls, profitability controls, and/or strategic controls. See also *allocating skills, organizing skills,* and *interacting skills.*

MONOPOLIST A business organization operating in a competition-free environment.

MONOPOLISTIC COMPETITION A condition in the marketplace characterized by 1) the presence of a relatively large number of competing firms all selling similar (if not identical) products, but in which 2) the consumer perceives the products as having significant (or at least recognizable) differences. Each firm strives for some competitive advantage (as, for example, a store strives for a more favorable location than its competition and thus carves out its own small monopoly.) Much of the competition under these market conditions is the result of the belief on the part of the consumer that they can differentiate between the various products being offered in the marketplace. Also known as imperfect competition. See also *pure monopoly.*

MONOPOLISTIC MARKET STRUCTURE See *pure monopoly*

MONOPOLISTICALLY COMPETITIVE MARKET STRUCTURE See *monopolistic competition*

MONOPOLY See *pure monopoly* and *monopolistic competition*

MONOPSONIST A buyer operating in a market in which there are no other buyers.

MONOPSONY A market condition in which there is only one buyer.

MONTAGE FORMAT A form of advertising found in the print media and on television in which a number of pictures or images are juxtaposed in such a way that an overall impression is created in the mind of the viewer.

MOTIVATION See *motive*

MOTIVATION ANALYSIS See *motivation research*

MOTIVATION RESEARCH A segment of marketing research in which the principles of behavioral science are applied to marketing problems in an attempt to explain why consumers behave in the marketplace as they do. Motivation research is primarily concerned with people's feelings and attitudes and how they affect the individual's buying behavior. Sometimes abbreviated MR.

MOTIVATIONAL NEED See *motive*

MOTIVATIONAL RESEARCH See *motivation research*

MOTIVE The inner state (or drive) that activates people toward satisfying a need or goal. Motives may be rational, aroused by appeals to reason, or emotional, aroused by appeals to feelings. Sigmund Freud, Abraham Maslow, and Frederick Herzberg each formulated theories of human motivation which have significant implications for marketers interested in analyzing consumer behavior. In brief, Freud's theory assumes that motivation is largely unconscious. Market researchers sharing this view seek to uncover customers' hidden reasons for choosing a particular product or service over others. For example, consumers may be said to avoid eating prunes because they are wrinkled and thus associated with old age in the consumer's unconscious. Maslow's theory states that human needs are arranged in a hierarchy, from the most to the least pressing, and that only when needs are met on the most pressing levels will consumers be motivated to satisfy less pressing needs. According to this theory, only when basic, physiological needs such as hunger and thirst are satisfied will the consumer be motivated to attend to his need for security, love, esteem, and self-actualization. Herzberg developed a "two factor theory" of motivation. He postulated that consumers seek to maximize "satisfiers" (i.e., characteristics of a product which contain intrinsic satisfaction) and to minimize "dissatisfiers" (characteristics of a product that are not pleasing to the consumer). According to this theory of motivation, marketers must be aware of the dissatisfiers, which may otherwise "unsell" their product. See also *motivation research* and *Maslow's hierarchy.*

MOVING AVERAGE In time series analysis, the moving average is the basis upon which predictions are made contingent upon the average outcomes of experiences over two or more recent time periods. Moving average for sales, for example, assumes that the sales figures for the next period will be the average of the sales figures for a given number of previous time periods. Thus, if a firm's cigarette sales for four previous months were 6,000, 5,000, 7,000 and 7,500 cartons, respectively, the four-month moving average would be the sum of the sales (25,500) divided by 4, or 6,375 cartons.

MR See *marketing research* and *motivation research*

MRA See *Marketing Research Association (MRA)*

MRO (MAINTENANCE, REPAIR, AND OPERATING ITEMS) See *supplies*

MRP See *materials requirement planning (MRP)*

MS See *multidimensional scaling (MS)*

MSA See *Metropolitan Statistical Area (MSA)*

MSI See *marketing science institute (MSI)*

MULTI-STEP FLOW MODEL See *multistep flow model*

MULTIBRAND STRATEGY See *multiple branding*

MULTICHANNEL MARKETING SYSTEM See *dual distribution*

MULTIDIMENSIONAL SCALING (MS) A marketing research technique in which the perceptions and attitudes of respondents are geometrically represented. The information presented in this manner is subsequently analyzed in an effort to aid managers in solving marketing problems, e.g., determining how consumers perceive a brand or product category.

MULTINATIONAL CORPORATION (MNC) A firm which conducts a significant proportion of its business in two or more countries and which almost always has a direct investment in the countries in which it operates. Multinational corporations typically perform their functions in a global context.

MULTINATIONAL MARKETING Marketing efforts in more than one foreign country which may include the operation of production and distribution facilities and the employment of local labor and management personnel.

MULTINATIONAL MARKETING INFORMATION SYSTEM (MMIS) A system which organizes and analyzes data from within the multinational corporation and from its various marketing environments and then presents the organization's managers with the information they need to make marketing decisions. The overall system generally has a separate subsystem for each country in which the corporation operates.

MULTIPLE BRANDING A marketing strategy in which a firm gives each item in a line of products a separate brand name as, for example, a large cereal manufacturer may market several dry breakfast foods under different brand names as part of an effort to reach various segments of the market and to dominate supermarket shelf space.

MULTIPLE BUYING INFLUENCE In industrial buying, a multiple buying influence is a purchase decision that is shared among several people, sometimes including top management. The influences which go into the purchase decision may include the users (workers and/or supervisors), influencers (engineering, research and development personnel, etc.), buyers (purchasing agents), deciders (those individuals in the organization who have the authority to select and approve the supplier—may be the purchasing agent or top management), and gatekeepers (people who control the flow of information within the organization).

MULTIPLE-CHANNEL SYSTEM See *dual distribution*

MULTIPLE CHANNELS See *dual distribution*

MULTIPLE CORRELATION In statistical analysis, the comparison of the effect of several independent variables on a single dependent variable. Each independent variable is carefully weighted to determine its effect.

MULTIPLE DISTRIBUTION See *dual distribution*

MULTIPLE-LINE REPRESENTATIVE A salesperson carrying the lines of several manufacturers.

MULTIPLE MARKET SEGMENTATION See *differentiated marketing*

MULTIPLE PACKAGING The packaging together of two or more items (men's underwear, cans of beer, packages of chewing gum, etc.) as a means of encouraging multiple purchases on the part of the consumer.

MULTIPLE PRICING 1) The practice of offering more than one unit at a given price, e.g., 3 for $1, with the intention of (a) creating the impression that the goods are being sold at a bargain price, thus (b) increasing the number sold per transaction. 2) The term is also applied to the practice frequently found in supermarkets of inadvertently marking an item with two or more prices.

MULTIPLE TARGET MARKET APPROACH See *differentiated marketing*

MULTIPLE-UNIT PRICING See *multiple pricing*

MULTIPLE APPROACH TO PRICING See *multistage pricing*

MULTISTAGE PRICING A planning strategy in which a broad price policy is developed by integrating a series of individual pricing decisions into a coherent price framework for the firm. A number of steps are taken in sequence beginning with the selection of a target market and ending with the formulation of a specific price.

MULTISTEP FLOW MODEL A theory of mass communication which supersedes both the hypodermic needle

160

model and the two-step flow model. The theory maintains that there are a variety of ways in which messages can flow from the mass media to the audience. In some cases, mass media may have a direct effect on its audience, as in the hypodermic needle model. In other cases, mass media messages may flow to opinion leaders and then to the general public, as in the two-step flow model. In yet other cases, however, messages may flow through a series of opinion leaders and involve more than two steps. The model also takes into account the diversified sources of information available to opinion leaders as well as the selective processes used by the audience to filter the messages they receive.

MULTIVARIABLE SEGMENTA-TION A form of market segmentation in which more than one factor (age, race, etc.) is employed to segment the population.

MYSTERY APPROACH A technique used by salespersons in the first few minutes of contact with a prospect. This approach uses a dangling statement to attract the prospect's attention. See also *approach*.

NAD See *National Advertising Division (NAD)*

NAMD See *National Association of Market Developers (NAMD)*

NAME See *National Association of Management/Marketing Educators (NAME)*

NAMLM See *National Association for Multi-Level Marketing (NAMLM)*

NARB See *National Advertising Review Board (NARB)*

NATIONAL ACCOUNT MARKETING A marketing strategy in which a firm's largest and most important national customers are given special attention in recognition of the volume of business they provide. These clients frequently are served by a specially dedicated sales force which is responsible for finding and maintaining these accounts. Also known as key account marketing and major account marketing.

NATIONAL ADVERTISING Advertising sponsored on a national or regional basis, generally by manufacturers or producers. Also known as general advertising.

NATIONAL ADVERTISING DIVISION (NAD) A division of the Council of Better Business Bureaus which serves as the investigative arm of the advertising industry's self-regulating organization, the National Advertising Review Board (NARB). The NAD initiates investigations and follows up complaints regarding deceptive advertising and renders the initial decision on the validity of the claim. NAD decisions may be appealed to NARB.

NATIONAL ADVERTISING REVIEW BOARD (NARB) An advertising industry self-regulating organization created by the Council of Better Business Bureaus and three industry trade groups in 1971. The NARB screens national advertising for deceptive practices and hears appeals of complaints brought by the public to the National Advertising Division (NAD).

NATIONAL ASSOCIATION FOR MULTI-LEVEL MARKETING (NAMLM) An association comprised of multi-level marketers and distributors as well as companies providing products and services to the industry. NAMLM promotes multi-level, or nonstore, retail sales. It provides educational services to its membership, including forums, seminars, and workshops. NAMLM publishes *Inside MLM,* and various bulletins and directories. It is based in Sacramento, California. See also *nonstore retailing.*

NATIONAL ASSOCIATION OF MANAGEMENT/MARKETING EDUCATORS (NAME) An association of college-level faculty and institutions in the fields of marketing and management, NAME encourages the combined formal classroom study of marketing and management with supervised work experience. NAME also serves as a national clearinghouse of information about marketing and management programs, compiles statistics, and provides a placement service. Its *News,* annual *Journal,* and *Membership List* constitute its primary publications.

NATIONAL ASSOCIATION OF MARKET DEVELOPERS (NAMD) An association of marketing, sales, advertising, and public relations professionals concerned with developing minority group consumer markets. The association conducts research and also maintains both a placement service and a speakers bureau. NAMD's headquarters are in Stanford, Connecticut.

NATIONAL BRAND See *manufacturer's brand*

NATIONAL MAIL ORDER ASSOCIATION (NMOA) An association of direct mail and mail order marketers based in Los Angeles, California. NMOA provides information on reports, government findings, mailing lists, and related topics of interest to its membership. It publishes a monthly magazine, *Mail Order Digest,* as well as a monthly *Washington Newsletter.*

NATIONAL TRAFFIC AND MOTOR VEHICLE SAFETY ACT (1966) Federal legislation which required manufacturers of automobiles to notify purchasers of new cars of safety defects discovered after delivery.

NATIONAL TRAFFIC AND SAFETY ACT (1958) Federal consumer legislation which made compliance with safety standards for automobiles and tires mandatory on the part of the manufacturers.

NATIONALIZATION The confiscation or expropriation of foreign property (i.e., the actual seizure of the property by a government) may be followed by nationalization, i.e., the property may be formally owned and operated by the government itself.

NATURAL ACCOUNT See *natural classification of expenses*

NATURAL CLASSIFICATION OF EXPENSES An accounting practice in which expenses are grouped into classes based on the kinds of expenses involved, e.g., rent, salaries, supplies, raw materials, taxes, interest, etc. rather than on the function of the expenditure, e.g., the costs of operating a particular department. Also known as ledger expenses or object-of-expenditure costs.

NATURAL MONOPOLY A condition in the marketplace in which, because it best serves the public, there is only one seller. Public utilities are examples of natural monopolies in which prices are regulated by a public agency.

NATURAL PRODUCTS Raw materials which occur in nature, such as fish, game, lumber, metals, minerals, oil, and coal. See also *raw materials*.

NATURAL TRADING AREA That geographic area which contains the customers who patronize a firm. Natural trading areas seldom have clearly defined boundaries—customers simply thin out as distance increases.

NEED AWARENESS The degree to which consumers may be cognizant of their needs and willing to discuss them with others. Three degrees or levels of need awareness are generally described: conscious, preconscious, and unconscious. At the conscious level of need awareness, consumers are not only aware of their needs, but also willing to discuss them with others. At the preconscious level, consumers may be aware of their needs but are reluctant or unable to discuss them with others, largely because of lack of understanding of what is actually motivating their needs. At the unconscious level, consumers are not aware of the forces that are driving them.

NEED-SATISFACTION APPROACH See *benefit approach*

NEEDS The basic motivations which cause individual consumers to make purchase decisions or take other actions. Needs may be physiological, such as the need for food, warmth, and shelter. Other needs are psychological and are concerned with an individual's self-image and relationships with others. See also *Maslow's hierarchy* and *need awareness*.

NEEDS/WANTS HIERARCHY See *Maslow's hierarchy*

NEGATIVE OPTION PLANS A form of direct marketing in which the customer (who may or may not be a member of a "club") is shipped a preannounced product at regular intervals unless he advises the seller not to ship before a predetermined date. The Book-Of-The-Month Club is a typical negative option plan. All such arrangements are regulated by the Federal Trade Commission (16 CFR 425).

NEGOTIATED BUYING See *negotiated contract*

NEGOTIATED CONTRACT A contract to buy goods or services in which the buyer and seller negotiate its specific terms. Negotiated contracts are frequently employed instead of competitive bidding when there is a sole supplier and thus no competition in the marketplace.

NEGOTIATED CONTRACT BUYING See *negotiated contract*

NEGOTIATED PRICE See *negotiated contract*

NEGOTIATED PRICING See *variable price policy*

NEIGHBORHOOD BUSINESS DISTRICT See *neighborhood shopping center*

NEIGHBORHOOD SHOPPING CENTER A small shopping center, often arranged on the strip plan, which serves its surrounding community—typically persons living within five minutes of drive time. Neighborhood centers are frequently anchored by a supermarket or variety store and may include service retailers (beauty shops, card shops, etc.). and stores selling convenience goods (drug stores, etc.). Sometimes called strip shopping centers as they usually stretch out along a well-traveled street or highway.

NET In billing, net is a term of sale which indicates that full payment for the goods contained in the invoice is due immediately. See also *1/10 net 30.*

NET COST See *cost of goods purchased*

NET COST OF DELIVERED PUR-CHASES See *cost of goods purchased*

NET COST OF PURCHASES See *cost of goods purchased*

NET INCOME See *net profit*

NET OPERATING INCOME See *net profit*

NET OPERATING PROFIT See *net profit*

NET PRESENT VALUE In accounting, a means of taking into account the value of money to be expended in an investment project. Net present value, or, as it is sometimes called, "discounted cash flow" expresses in terms of current value outlays and inflows which will occur in the future as the project is developed.

NET PROFIT Gross margin (or in manufacturing terminology, gross profit) less all the costs of running the business. Such costs include the cost of sales, operating expenses such as payroll, advertising, insurance, and (according to the American Institute of Certified Public Accountants' *Business Information Guide*) income taxes. The term net profit is frequently used synonymously with operating profit, net operating profit, net operating income, and net income.

NET SALES Sales revenue after returns, allowances, discounts, cancellations, and taxes (sales and excise) have been deducted for the accounting period. Net sales represents the actual sales dollars the company will receive.

NET WORTH In business, a synonym for owner's equity, i.e., the excess of assets over liabilities in an enterprise. In reference to an individual, one's net worth may be determined by subtracting one's total liabilities (debts, etc.) from the total of one's assets.

NEW PRODUCT A term relative to one's position in the marketplace. To customers, a product is new if it is perceived as significantly different from other available products. For manufacturers, distributors, and retailers a new product is one never before produced or sold. New products range from the truly unique and innovative to those which are merely modifications or copies of existing merchandise.

NEW PRODUCT COMMITTEE See *product planning committee*

NEW PRODUCT DEVELOPMENT The process by which an idea for a new product is carried through a series of developmental stages to final commercialization. New product development is largely concerned with determining customer needs, the technical development of a product to meet these needs, and its introduction into the marketplace.

NEW PRODUCT PLANNING PROCESS Those stages through which a product passes in the developmental process. Included are idea generation and screening, analysis and evaluation, product development and production, branding, test marketing and positioning, and finally, full scale marketing and production. To be effective the new product process must be made sensitive to the needs of the marketplace.

NEW PRODUCT PLANNING PROCESS

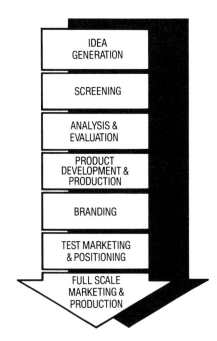

IDEA GENERATION

SCREENING

ANALYSIS & EVALUATION

PRODUCT DEVELOPMENT & PRODUCTION

BRANDING

TEST MARKETING & POSITIONING

FULL SCALE MARKETING & PRODUCTION

NEW PRODUCT SCREENING CHECKLIST A form used in the systematic evaluation of ideas for new products. Such factors as marketability and growth potential are included for consideration.

NEW TASK BUYING A form of industrial buying in which the purchasing officer must buy a new product or service. New task buying requires greater attention to detail than rebuying and often involves more than one person. See also *straight rebuy* and *modified rebuy.*

NEW TASK PURCHASE See *new task buying*

NEW UNSOUGHT GOODS Products offering new ideas and applications of which the consumer is not at all aware. The marketing of such goods requires informative promotion so that potential customers will accept and seek out the product. See also *unsought goods.*

NEWS APPROACH A technique used by a salesperson in the first few minutes of contact with a customer. The salesperson uses newspaper stories or trade journal articles as a lead-in to the presentation. The approach capitalizes on recent news events (such as a series of fires to sell fire insurance or an increase in burglaries to sell burglar alarms) to bring the message home to the prospect. See also *approach.*

NEWS RELEASE See *press release*

NICHE MARKETING A marketing strategy in which a manufacturer or supplier identifies a narrow market segment in which he believes he can successfully compete with his product or service. Products and services may be created specifically to fill these perceived niches.

NMOA See *National Mail Order Association (NMOA)*

NO DEMAND A condition in the marketplace in which there is no need or desire on the part of consumers for a product or service being offered for sale.

NO FRILLS PRODUCT See *generic product*

NOISE In a communications system, interference such as static or distortion which occurs during the transmission of a message thus reducing the effectiveness of the transmission.

NON-TITLE-TAKING AGENT MIDDLEMAN See *agent middleman*

NONADOPTERS Those persons who, at some stage in the adoption process, simply choose not to purchase a product or service.

NONBUSINESS MARKETING See *nonprofit marketing*

NONBUSINESS ORGANIZATION Although imprecise, the term nonbusiness is generally taken to mean nonprofit or not-for-profit and thus includes a very wide variety of organizations such as schools, cultural institutions, charities, fraternal organizations, health care delivery organizations, etc.

NONCOMMERCIAL ADVERTISING Advertising by nonprofit organizations to promote public interests (such as automobile safety or equal rights), encourage contributions to charities or other philanthropic causes (such as the American Red Cross), and promote political causes. The chief users of noncommercial advertising are public interest groups such as the National Organization of Women (NOW), federal and state governments, nonprofit hospitals and universities, and political parties.

NONCUMULATIVE DISCOUNT See *noncumulative quantity discount*

NONCUMULATIVE QUANTITY DISCOUNT A price reduction, usually granted on a one-time basis, based on the size of an order. Such discounts are generally made by sellers to encourage large orders.

NONDISGUISED SURVEY In marketing research, a method of gathering information in which respondents are told the real purpose of the study.

NONDURABLE GOODS Tangible products generally having a lifespan of three years or less. Most nondurable goods are consumed close to the time at which they are purchased.

NONGOODS SERVICE A category of consumer service in which no tangible product is offered for sale or rental, e.g., hairdressing, medical care, etc.

NONLIQUID ASSETS Valuable property such as real estate or jewelry which may be difficult to turn into cash quickly.

NONLIQUID WEALTH See *nonliquid assets*

NONPERSONAL COMMUNICATION CHANNELS Media that carry messages without personal contact or feedback. Nonpersonal communication channels include mass media (such as direct mail), atmospherics (environmental factors designed to stimulate sales and/or establish a particular image), and events (such as grand openings). See also *personal communication channels.*

NONPERSONAL RETAILING A form of selling in which the customer does not visit a store and in which there is no face-to-face contact between seller and buyer. There are three principal types of nonpersonal retailing: 1) catalog retailing, 2) mail order retailing, and 3) vending machine retailing.

NONPRICE COMPETITION Competition in the marketplace based on factors other than price. A firm may emphasize service, terms of sale, delivery, attractive packaging, extensive promotion, or the product's reputation in an effort to gain a competitive advantage.

NONPROBABILITY SAMPLING A method of selecting a sample for marketing research in which the judgment (and possible bias) of the researcher enters into the selection process. The three major types of nonprobability samples are the convenience sample, the judgment sample, and the quota sample. Nonprobability sampling is sometimes preferred by market researchers over probability sampling when special expertise is an important characteristic of the sample group. This sampling method may also be desirable when budget and/or time constraints are a factor. However, the results of research using nonprobability samples contain many unknowns, and such results must be regarded with caution when used to draw conclusions about the total population. See also *probability sampling*.

NONPROFIT MARKETING Conducted by organizations which operate on a not-for-profit basis. Such marketing is almost always concerned with services and ideas rather than with physical products and may include a wide variety of political, social, and religious activities. See also *nonbusiness organization*.

NONPROFIT ORGANIZATION See *nonprofit marketing* and *nonbusiness organization*

NONRECOGNITION (BRAND) See *brand nonrecognition*

NONSAMPLING ERRORS Mistakes that occur in any stage of the data collection, recording, and enumerating process, whether accidental or deliberate. This may be a miscalculation, a misinterpretation of a question or a response, falsified responses, etc. These mistakes may occur in either census or sample methods of marketing research. See also *sampling errors*.

NONSTORE RETAILING A form of retailing in which a traditional store building is not involved, i.e., in which the retailer and customer transact their business through such means as: 1) direct mail, 2) door-to-door sales, 3) in-home or party-plan selling, 4) telephone sales, 5) catalog sales, 6) interactive television, or 7) vending machines.

NONTARIFF BARRIERS Government policies and laws, other than tariffs, which restrict international trade. Nontariff barriers include local content laws (such as the Japanese restriction on U.S. paperboard which does not comply with Japanese paperboard standards), export subsidies, safety and health standards, import quotas, government purchasing rules, and border taxes. See also *tariff*.

NONTRACEABLE COMMON COSTS Those expenses in a business which cannot be assigned to a particular function, e.g., executive salaries, interest payments, etc.

NORMAL INFLATION See *inflation*

NORMS In terms useful to the marketer, norms are social rules or standards which, although not universally observed, form a basis for day-to-day behavior. Norms which influence consumer behavior and lifestyle are thus factors which the marketer must consider.

NOSE-TO-NOSE SELLING See *personal selling*

NOT-FOR-PROFIT MARKETING See *nonprofit marketing*

NOT-FOR-PROFIT ORGANIZATION See *nonbusiness organization*

NUTRITIONAL LABELING The practice of indicating on the packages of food products the nutritional value of the product (in particular, the proportion of the U.S. recommended daily allowances supplied by a specified quantity of the product) and the specific ingredients contained within the product.

OBJECT-OF-EXPENDITURE COSTS See *natural classification of expenses*

OBJECTIVE AND TASK APPROACH See *objective-task method*

OBJECTIVE-TASK METHOD A method of budgeting for promotional expenditures, including advertising, based on pre-set goals and objectives and on an analysis of the activities necessary to reach them. The promotional budget is not tied in to sales volume. Also known as the task and investment method or the building method.

OBJECTIVES The intermediate benchmarks or reference points which an organization must reach as it pursues its goals. Objectives may be regarded as forming a ladder by which an organization may achieve its mission. See also *goals, advertising objectives,* and *marketing objectives.*

OBSERVATION A marketing research technique frequently used in retailing in which primary data is collected by watching individuals, e.g., store customers, either directly or with cameras in order to record the subjects' shopping behavior and buying habits.

OBSERVATIONAL RESEARCH See *observation*

OBSOLESCENCE See *planned obsolescence*

OCR-A See *optical character recognition (OCR-A)*

ODD-CENT PRICING See *odd-line pricing*

ODD-ENDING PRICING See *odd-line pricing*

ODD-EVEN PRICING See *odd-line pricing*

ODD-LINE PRICING A method of ascribing prices ending in odd numbers, especially five, seven, or nine, to convey the impression of a lower price. For example, a retailer using odd-line pricing would charge $10.99 rather than $11.00 to convey the idea of a bargain. Also known as odd-value pricing, penny pricing, odd-cent pricing, odd-ending pricing, and odd-even pricing. See also *even-line pricing*.

ODD LOT See *job lot*

ODD-VALUE PRICING See *odd-line pricing*

OFF-PRICE MERCHANDISE Retail goods, often carrying status or premium labels, offered at lower than "regular" prices. This merchandise, which may be manufacturer's surplus in the form of end-of-season liquidations or other retailer's overstocked merchandise, is in perfect condition and is sold at prices somewhat lower than those found in traditional retail establishments. Increasingly, in-season merchandise is being made available to off-price retailers by vendors because these merchants often pay cash and seldom ask for promotional allowances, markdown money, or return privileges.

OFF-PRICE RETAILING The selling at retail of merchandise, often carrying status or premium labels, at less than "regular" prices. In contrast to discount retailing (where the discounter pays the same price for his merchandise as everyone else and sells it for less than traditional retailers) off-price retailers buy merchandise at cut-rate prices and pass the savings along to their customers. In addition, expenses are kept low by limiting advertising expenditures, turning stock over quickly, and other cost-cutting techniques. Off-price retail establishments may be independent organizations specializing in off-price merchandise, factory outlets, or closed-door discount houses.

OLIGOPOLISTIC COMPETITION A condition in the marketplace characterized by 1) the presence of a relatively small number of large competing firms who are 2) selling similar or identical products in 3) an extremely price sensitive marketing environment. Oligopolistic competition exists in such industries as chemicals, petroleum, steel, and automobiles.

OLIGOPOLISTIC MARKET STRUCTURE See *oligopolistic competition*

OLIGOPOLY See *oligopolistic competition*

ON-PACK PREMIUM A free gift or other item attached to the outside of a package. The premium acts as an incentive to purchase the merchandise offered for sale. The two items may be held together by a band of paper or tape or by plastic film. Also called a banded premium or a package band.

ONE-LEVEL CHANNEL A marketing channel in which there is only one intermediary, commonly a retailer, between the producer and the consumer.

ONE PRICE POLICY A policy in which prices are fixed and uniform for all customers buying essentially the same amounts of merchandise. Such a policy precludes bargaining or negotiation.

1/10 NET 30 In billing, 1/10 net 30 is a term of sale which means that a 1% discount is given if the invoice is paid within 10 days. If not paid within 10 days, however, the full amount of the payment is due within 30 days. See also *net*.

OPEN ACCOUNT 1) A policy under which a vendor extends interest-free credit to his customers on a short-term basis. Commonly, bills are payable in full at the end of 30 days. The practice of recording such transactions in a ledger gave rise to the popular term "on the books." 2) Any credit account in which there remains a balance to be paid.

OPEN BID An offer to perform a service or to supply goods submitted to a buyer and announced openly so that all bidders know the price submitted.

OPEN BOOK ACCOUNT See *open account*

OPEN-CODE DATING A system used on food products to include the last day on which they may be sold. Open-codes are understandable to customers and thus aid them in making judgments regarding the freshness of the merchandise.

OPEN CREDIT ACCOUNT See *open account*

OPEN DATE LABELING See *open-code dating*

OPEN DATING See *open-code dating*

OPERATING DATA See *internal data*

OPERATING PROFIT See *net profit*

OPERATING RATIOS See *financial ratios*

OPERATING STATEMENT See *profit and loss statement*

OPERATING SUPPLIES See *supplies*

OPERATIONAL BUYING MOTIVES Consumer motives based on how the product being considered for purchase functions, e.g., an automobile may be chosen for purchase on the basis of its performance. See also *motive*.

OPINION APPROACH A technique used by salespersons in the first few minutes of contact with a prospect. The salesperson shows the product to the prospect and asks for his opinion. This focuses attention on the product and directly involves the prospect in the presentation. See also *approach*.

OPINION LEADER A person whose opinions are widely respected (especially within a reference group), who is often a trend-setter, and who influences the purchase decisions of others.

OPPORTUNISTIC PRICING A strategy in which a company raises the prices for its products or services during a time of shortage in an effort to take advantage of increased demand on the part of the consumer.

OPPORTUNITY COST The cost incurred when one alternative must be chosen over another. If marketing alternative A is chosen over alternative B, then the opportunity cost of alternative A is the benefit lost by not pursuing alternative B. Another view of opportunity costs is that they may more accurately be regarded as foregone profits.

OPPORTUNITY FORECAST A form of business forecast in which an effort is made to predict future conditions in the marketplace which might present opportunities for new products, the reduction in production costs, or the avoidance of changes in the marketing environment which might prove detrimental to the organization.

OPTICAL CHARACTER RECOGNITION (OCR-A) A set of letter and number characters that may be read by the human eye as well as by machines, e.g., wands, scanners, price ticket readers, etc. OCR-A is used on price tags and labels, credit cards, bank checks, etc.

OPTIONAL PRODUCT PRICING A pricing strategy applied to products which are offered to the public with a number of options, e.g., automobiles with their nearly limitless list of optional equipment. Decisions are made regarding which items are to be included in the price of the core product and which are to be offered as options at additional cost to the buyer. Optional products may be priced to generate a profit or priced to act as enticements to purchase the core product.

ORDER CYCLE TIME See *lead time*

ORDER-GETTER A salesperson who informs and persuades existing customers to purchase goods and/or services or who actively seeks out new customers, thus generating additional business.

ORDER LEAD TIME See *lead time*

ORDER POINT See *reorder point (ROP)*

ORDER PROCESSING COSTS Those costs associated with handling merchandise, processing order forms, generating invoices and shipping bills, maintaining credit records, etc.

ORDER-TAKER A salesperson involved in the routine clerical and sales functions of taking customers' orders for goods and services. Most retail salespeople are regarded as inside order-takers as most of their customers are already inclined to make a purchase. Outside order-takers include salespeople who call on customers, note the merchandise they need, and turn in the order. Little or no creative selling is involved.

ORDER TAKING See *order-taker*

ORDERING COSTS All those costs of doing business which directly relate to the ordering of goods and services including operating expenses associated with the order and receiving departments.

ORDINARY DATING See *ordinary terms*

ORDINARY TERMS In the dating of invoices, an agreement indicating that a cash discount may be deducted if the bill is paid within the discount period. Otherwise, the full payment is due at the end of the period indicated. Both the cash discount and the net credit periods are counted from the date of the invoice, which is commonly the date of the shipment. For example, if the stated terms are 1/10 net 30, the discount period is 10 days, the end of the credit period is 30 days.

ORGANIZATION MARKETING Generally an effort on the part of non-profit organizations to sell their objectives and goals and/or to solicit contributions. Included are mutual benefit organizations (unions, fraternal organizations, political parties, etc.), service organizations (charities, schools and colleges, etc.), and government organizations (the military, police and fire departments, etc.).

ORGANIZATIONAL CONSUMER Organizational consumers include manufacturers, wholesalers and distributors, retailers, and government agencies, and non-profit organizations. They use the products they buy to make other products, to maintain the organization's operations, or to be offered for resale.

ORGANIZATIONAL INTEGRATION See *integration*

ORGANIZATIONAL OBJECTIVES See *objectives*

ORGANIZATIONAL PORTFOLIO ANALYSIS See *Boston Consulting Group Matrix*

ORGANIZATIONAL PRODUCT See *industrial goods*

ORGANIZING SKILLS The skills used by marketing managers to specify and structure the relationships among marketing personnel within the firm, both formal and informal. See also *allocating skills, monitoring skills,* and *interacting skills.*

ORIENTATION See *employee orientation*

ORIENTATION BOOKLET See *employee orientation*

ORIGINAL MARKON See *initial markup*

ORIGINAL MARKUP See *initial markup*

OSMA See *Overseas Sales and Marketing Association of America (OSMA)*

OTHER-DIRECTED A person guided primarily by those around him and whose values, goals, and ideals stem more from the opinions of others than from his own inner feelings. Other-directed people are often considered conformists by their peers. See also *inner-directed.*

OTHERS-SELF-CONCEPT See *self-image*

OTHERS-SELF-IMAGE See *self-image*

OUT-OF-STOCK See *stock-out*

OUT-OF-STOCK COST The estimated profits lost as the result of insufficient quantities of inventory on hand to meet customer demand. Customers and sales are lost through a stock-out.

OUT-OF-STOCK LOSSES See *out-of-stock cost*

OUTLET STORE See *factory outlet*

OUTSIDE ORDER-TAKER See *order-taker*

OVERALL FAMILY BRANDING See *family brand*

OVERBOUGHT An inventory position in which too much stock of a certain kind has been purchased for resale.

OVERFULL DEMAND A condition in the marketplace in which demand for a product exceeds the capacity of the suppliers to produce it.

OVERHEAD Those business costs other than direct labor (the wages of the workers actually making a product or delivering a service) and direct materials (the actual components incorporated into the product). Overhead includes the wages of support personnel, fringe benefits paid to all workers, handling and shipping expenses, etc. Unlike fixed costs, overhead expenses are directly related to production levels and sales volume. Also called burden. See also *fixed cost, variable cost, direct cost,* and *indirect cost.*

OVERRUN Production in excess of that which had been originally scheduled.

OVERSEAS SALES BRANCH In direct export, the overseas sales branch is a branch or subsidiary of the exporting firm, located in the host country. This allows the exporter greater exposure and control in the foreign market and also avoids total reliance upon a domestic-based export department employing an independent, international, marketing middleman. See also *direct export.*

OVERSTORED A condition in the marketplace in which there are more stores in an area than can operate profitably.

OVERSEAS SALES AND MARKETING ASSOCIATION OF AMERICA (OSMA) A professional association of firms engaged in export management and trading, OSMA sets professional standards and acts as a clearinghouse for international contacts. Its headquarters are in Oak Park, Illinois. OSMA publishes a monthly *Newsletter,* and an annual *Directory.*

OVERSEAS SALES SUBSIDIARY
See *overseas sales branch*

OWNED-GOODS SERVICE A service which involves existing products already owned by the customer, e.g., automobile repair service, alteration of clothing by a tailor, tree trimming, etc.

OWNER'S EQUITY See *net worth*

OWNERSHIP FLOW See *channel flows*

OWNERSHIP GROUP See *department store ownership group*

OWNERSHIP UTILITY The utility (or value or satisfaction) added to a product or service when it is in the possession of the right person at the right time. Also called possession utility.

P-AND-L STATEMENT See *profit and loss statement*

Ps OF MARKETING MIX See *four Ps of the marketing mix*

PACK PREMIUM See *on-pack premium*

PACKAGE A wrapper or container in which a product is stored and sold. In addition to protecting the product, the package also provides space for labels, instructions, and other useful information.

PACKAGE BAND See *on-pack premium*

PACKAGED ENVIRONMENT A physical entity such as a theme park, stadium, shopping mall, or cultural center which has a highly developed identity calculated to enhance the presentation of goods and services. Entertainment complexes such as Disney World are the most elaborate packaged environments, but the concept is applied on a smaller scale to such facilities as Chicago's Water Tower Place (an enclosed shopping mall).

PACKAGING Those activities relating to the design and development of a product's wrapper or container. Packages have three basic functions: 1) to protect the product from damage, 2) to make it attractive to the consumer, and 3) to carry useful information, e.g., labels listing ingredients or instructions for use.

PALLETIZATION In physical distribution, palletization is the arrangement of products on low platforms, or pallets, for efficiency of movement. Goods so arranged are moved as a unit by motorized lift trucks.

PARALLEL IMPORTS See *gray market*

PARASALESPERSON Generally sales trainees who perform one or more selling functions but leave the closing to a more experienced person.

PARTS See *fabricating parts*

PASSALONG RATE A term used with reference to the print media indicating the number of readers who may see a newspaper or magazine in addition to the initial subscriber or purchaser. Also referred to as readers per copy.

PATENT A government grant of protection to an inventor which confers exclusive rights of manufacture and sale of an invention for a fixed period of time. In order to be patentable an invention must generally be novel and useful.

PATRONAGE BUYING MOTIVE See *patronage motive*

PATRONAGE DEMAND See *patronage motive*

PATRONAGE DISCOUNT See *cumulative quantity discount*

PATRONAGE MOTIVE The reason, whether rational or emotional, for which a customer (either an individual or organization) chooses to patronize one establishment rather than another.

PAYBACK The amount of money a new product must earn (calculated as net income before depreciation but after taxes) to recover the initial investment made in its development.

PAYMENT FLOW See *channel flow*

PD See *physical distribution (PD)*

PENETRATED MARKET The total number of persons who are already customers for a product or service.

PENETRATION See *coverage*

PENETRATION PRICING A strategy in which a new product is introduced into the marketplace at a lower than usual price in an effort to rapidly penetrate the market and build sales volume. Sometimes called impact pricing, as the strategy is also calculated to increase consumer awareness of the product.

PENNY PRICING See *odd-line pricing*

PERCEIVED RISK In consumer behavior, perceived risk is the idea held by a customer that a purchase decision carries with it the risk of certain undesirable consequences; for example, that the product might not perform well, that it is not worth the price, that others may think one a fool for buying such a product, etc.

PERCEIVED-VALUE PRICING A strategy in which the price of a product or service is based upon the buyer's perception of its value rather than on the seller's cost of production.

PERCENT OF SALES METHOD OF PROMOTIONAL BUDGETING A method of computing a promotional budget in which the amount allocated is based upon a percentage of previous or projected sales.

PERCENTAGE OF SALES APPROACH TO PROMOTIONAL BUDGETING See *percent of sales method of promotional budgeting*

PERCEPTION The process by which an individual becomes aware of elements within the environment through sensory stimuli and interprets those elements in light of personal experience. Perception, therefore, involves not only receiving stimuli, but also evaluating and retaining that stimuli. In marketing, perception is important in explaining why various consumers or groups of consumers perceive products differently. The subjective, or evaluative, component of perception causes some individuals to value products differently. Marketers, therefore, attempt to differentiate their otherwise similar products through packaging, advertising, and other marketing tools. See also *selective perception* and *thresholds of perception.*

PERCEPTUAL MAPPING A marketing research tool in which a number of factors such as product attributes, customer preferences, and particular brands are plotted on a chart on the basis of computer analysis. Since various factors tend to form clusters, it is possible for marketers to distinguish between various competing brands and to spot open niches in the marketplace.

PERCEPTUAL SCREEN A mental screening mechanism employed by persons who are exposed to a large number of advertising messages. The screen makes it possible for consumers to selectively respond to advertising.

PERFECT COMPETITION A market condition so rare as to be largely theoretical, perfect competition entails: 1) so many sellers and buyers that no one party can control prices; 2) buyers and sellers who are familiar with the market and who can quickly react to changes in the supply and demand situation; 3) a product or commodity which is highly substitutable; and 4) the existence of relatively few barriers to parties entering and leaving the market. Conditions approaching perfect competition are sometimes encountered in the trade in agricultural commodities. Also known as pure competition or free competition.

PERFORMANCE ANALYSIS A method used to compare the actual performance of a marketing plan with the expectations for the plan. For example, one sales territory may be compared with another, or the sales performance of previous years may be compared with the current year. The intent of such comparative performance analysis is to improve operations, identify problem areas, and correct shortcomings.

PERFORMANCE INDEX A quantitative measure of the relationship between standards that have been set by a firm and the firm's actual performance. In a sales performance index, for example, the actual sales are divided by the expected sales (for a particular area, sales representative, or product, etc.), and multiplied by 100.

$$\text{Sales Performance Index} = \frac{\$ \text{ Actual sales}}{\text{Expected sales}} \times 100$$

PERFORMANCE MONITORING RESEARCH Research, generally in the form of interviews or questionnaires, employed to monitor a particular marketing program and to provide the marketing manager with the feedback required to evaluate the firm's marketing activities.

PERFORMANCE STANDARD A measure of performance against which actual performance may be compared.

PERIOD COST See *fixed cost*

PERIPHERAL SERVICE An additional service offered as a complement to a basic product or service offering. Peripheral services, which add to operating costs, are generally provided to enhance a firm's competitive advantage.

PERISHABILITY OF SERVICES A concept which suggests that services, by their very nature, have a limited life span, i.e., that services left unperformed cannot be stored and used at some future time.

PERSON MARKETING In an effort to cultivate the attention, interest, and preference of a target market for a person (rather than goods or services), person marketing consists of activities such as press conferences, media coverage, public appearances, etc. These activities are generally undertaken to create, maintain, or alter attitudes and/or behavior toward particular persons. Both political candidate marketing and celebrity marketing are forms of person marketing.

PERSONAL COMMUNICATION CHANNELS Any method of communication involving two or more persons communicating directly with each other. Communication may be face-to-face or may utilize telephones, television, mail, computers, etc.

PERSONAL DISPOSABLE INCOME See *disposable income*

PERSONAL EXPENDITURES See *discretionary income* and *disposable income*

PERSONAL INCOME For statistical purposes, the U.S. Bureau of the Census includes the following money income: wages and salaries, self-employment income (including losses), Social Security and Supplemental Security Income, public assistance (except noncash benefits), interest, dividends, rents, royalties, veterans' payments, unemployment compensation, workers' compensation, and both public and private income from pensions. Personal income does not include capital gains (or losses).

For the population as a whole, personal income refers to the sum of the above payments for everyone in the country.

PERSONAL INTERVIEW See *interview*

PERSONAL NEEDS The needs of the individual to achieve personal satisfaction, such as self-esteem, accomplishment, enjoyment, and relaxation. Personal needs are unrelated to the opinions and actions of others, except to the extent that they reinforce and affirm those needs. See also *Maslow's hierarchy* and *need awareness*.

PERSONAL SELLING A sales technique which frequently involves face-to-face contact between seller and customer, but which may also be conducted by telephone. Includes wholesale and contact sales in which the salesperson initiates the contact by making a call on the customer, as well as retail selling, in which the customer initiates the contact by entering a store and approaching the salesperson.

PERSONALITY The composite of characteristics that make each individual unique. An individual's personality consists of his habitual patterns of behavior, distinctive individual traits, personal identity, and individuality. Marketers are interested in linking the consumer's personality to choices made in the marketplace and gearing their marketing practices to appeal to the personality traits of target customers.

PERSUASIVE IMPACT The level of influence a form of communication has upon consumers. Television has a high degree of persuasive impact because it reaches more than one of the senses.

PERSUASIVE LABEL In packaging, a label whose chief purpose is to promote the product rather than to inform the consumer.

178

PERT See *program evaluation and review technique (PERT)*

PHANTOM FREIGHT Freight charges sometimes encountered when shipping rates are based geographically as in basing-point pricing. It is not uncommon that some customers pay rates in excess of those actually incurred by the shipper while others pay less.

PHARMACY See *drugstore*

PHONY LIST PRICE A list price designed solely to be shown to the customers as evidence that the price has been discounted from list. Customers who are unduly impressed by the size of the supposed discount may end up paying more than the actual market price. This practice is banned by the Wheeler-Lea Amendment. See also *list price.*

PHYSICAL DISTRIBUTION (PD) Although the flow of raw materials to the producer may be regarded as a part of physical distribution, the process is more commonly seen as beginning with the completed manufactured product as it enters the appropriate marketing channels and moves through various transportation and storage stages to its final consumption. See also *distribution.*

PHYSICAL DISTRIBUTION FUNCTIONS See *distribution*

PHYSICAL DISTRIBUTION MANAGEMENT Logistic activities concerned with the movement of completed products from point of manufacture to consumer.

PHYSICAL DISTRIBUTION MANAGER See *physical distribution management*

PHYSICAL FLOW See *channel flows*

PHYSICAL OBSOLESCENCE With regard to manufactured products, a broken down or worn out state generally reached through normal wear and tear.

PHYSIOLOGICAL NEEDS Those needs of individuals which are concerned with their most basic bodily requirements. Physiological needs include sleep, food, drink, and other biological needs. See also *Maslow's hierarchy* and *need awareness.*

PIG IN A PYTHON An analogy used in demographics to express the impact of a baby boom. The increased birth rate produces a bulge in the population statistics when they are graphically represented just as a pig, having been swallowed by a python, produces a bulge as it moves through the snake.

PIG IN THE PYTHON

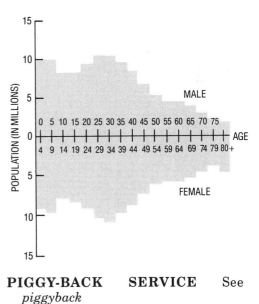

PIGGY-BACK SERVICE See *piggyback*

PIGGYBACK 1) A coordinated transportation agreement in which truck trailers are loaded directly onto railroad freight cars. Through the use of containerized freight, piggyback helps eliminate costly and time-consuming unloading and reloading of the merchandise being shipped. Also known as trailer-on-flatcar (TOFC). See also *containerization*. 2) In broadcast media advertising, a minute spot in which two distinct products of one advertiser appear in separate, back-to-back commercials rather than as part of a single message.

PILFERAGE The theft of goods (and sometimes money) in small amounts at the manufacturing, wholesaling, or retailing level of the distribution chain. The term is commonly restricted to employee theft.

PIMS See *profit impact of marketing strategies (PIMS)*

PIONEERING ADVERTISING See *primary demand advertising*

PIONEERING STAGE See *introductory stage*

PLACE See *four Ps of the marketing mix* and *place utility*

PLACE-DISTRIBUTION INTENSITY RESPONSE FUNCTION See *response function*

PLACE UTILITY The utility (added value or satisfaction) which accrues when a product or service is delivered to the right place at the proper time.

PLANNED ECONOMY See *economic system*

PLANNED FUNCTIONAL OBSOLESCENCE See *planned obsolescence*

PLANNED OBSOLESCENCE A marketing strategy in which products are deliberately changed to encourage their replacement. Planned obsolescence commonly takes one of two forms: 1) planned product obsoles-

cence, in which a product is designed to wear out quickly or is in some way functionally improved, and 2) planned style obsolescence, in which the appearance of a product is changed with the intention of creating dissatisfaction among owners of earlier models.

PLANNED PRODUCT OBSOLESCENCE See *planned obsolescence*

PLANNED PURCHASES 1) In retail planning, a method used to determine the dollar value of merchandise to be brought into stock during a given season or other period. Planning purchases help to insure having stock on hand to meet anticipated demand and are computed as follows:

$$\text{PLANNED PURCHASES} = \text{(Planned ending inventory + planned sales + planned reduction)} - \text{Beginning inventory}$$

2) In the consumer buying process, a planned purchase is one that is made before the customer enters the retail store and before the customer has had direct contact with the product.

PLANNED SHOPPING CENTER See *shopping center*

PLANNED STYLE OBSOLESCENCE See *planned obsolescence*

PLANNING The process of establishing the goals of an organization and projecting the most effective means of accomplishing them. Planning attempts to anticipate the needs of the organization both in the near and distant future. Planning may be short-range or long-range. Short-range plans are developed for those situations likely to occur month by month, weekly, or daily. They may be covered by procedures, practices, rules, etc. A firm's budget is a common form of short-range plan. Long-range plans, on the other hand, are developed for up to several years and involve the long-term goals of the organization, often expressed in a statement of purpose. The firm's objectives and policies are designed to accommodate long-range planning. See also *marketing planning, management by objectives (MBO), tactical planning* and *strategic planning.*

PLC See *product life cycle (PLC)*

PLMA See *Private Label Manufacturers Association (PLMA)*

PM See *push money (PM)*

PMA See *Produce Marketing Association (PMA)*

PMAA See *Promotion Marketing Association of America (PMAA)*

PMSA See *Primary Metropolitan Statistical Area (PMSA)*

POINT-OF-PURCHASE (POP) See *point-of-sale (POS)*

POINT-OF-PURCHASE ADVERTISING See *point-of-purchase display*

POINT-OF-PURCHASE ADVERTISING INSTITUTE (POPAI) A New York based association of producers and suppliers of point-of-purchase advertising signs and displays.

POINT-OF-PURCHASE DISPLAY In retailing, an interior display of merchandise at the register, check-out counter, or other point-of-sale designed to attract the customer's attention at a place closely associated with purchase decisions and to stimulate impulse buying. Display materials are frequently supplied by the vendor.

POINT-OF-PURCHASE PROMOTION See *point-of-purchase display*

POINT-OF-SALE (POS) In retailing, that area of the store or department where the sale is consummated, i.e.,

where the customer pays for and receives the merchandise. This is often the location of point-of-purchase displays and other promotions. Also called the point-of-purchase. See also *point-of-sale (POS) perpetual inventory control system.*

POINT-OF-SALE ADVERTISING See *point-of-purchase display*

POINT-OF-SALE DISPLAY See *point-of-purchase display*

POINT-OF-SALE (POS) PERPETUAL INVENTORY CONTROL SYSTEM In retailing, an automated system in which the store's cash registers are linked to computer processing systems. The cash register is actually a point-of-sale terminal. The register controls and records all sales (cash, charge, COD, layaway, etc.) at the point-of-sale. The terminal issues sales checks, prints transaction records, and feeds information about each transaction into the data bank of the computer. For example, in the National Cash Register (NCR) 280 Retail System, the automated equipment handles marking, checkout, and data recording functions. Merchandise is ticketed with colored bar code tags which are read with wand readers at the check-out counter. The computer accumulates sales transaction information on magnetic tape for daily input into the computer's memory bank or storage system. Also called an electronic cash register (ECR), or shortened to point-of-sale (POS) in common usage.

POINT-OF-SALE PROMOTION See *point-of-purchase display*

POINT-OF-SALE SYSTEM See *point-of-sale (POS) perpetual inventory control system*

POINT-OF-SALE TERMINAL See *point-of-sale (POS) perpetual inventory control system*

POISON PREVENTION PACKAG-ING ACT (1970) Federal legislation which required manufacturers to use safety packaging on products containing substances deemed harmful to children.

POLITICAL CANDIDATE MARKETING A form of person marketing in which activities are undertaken to create, maintain, or alter attitudes and/or behavior toward a person seeking elective office. In recent years, political candidate marketing has become a major industry and area of specialization as office seekers hire an increasing number of advertising professionals to assist in their campaigns. See also *person marketing* and *celebrity marketing*.

POLYCENTRISM A semi-decentralized form of organization found in some multinational marketing firms in which marketing efforts made outside the home country are undertaken by marketing groups located in each foreign market.

POOL CAR SERVICE See *pool car shipment*

POOL CAR SHIPMENT A mode of rail shipment in which two or more companies combine their goods in order to take advantage of carload freight rates.

POOLING A practice found in producers' cooperatives in which each member's contributions are combined with those of all other members and sold in the course of the marketing season at prevailing prices. Members are then paid an average price, less operating expenses.

POP See *point-of-sale (POS)* and *point-of-sale (POS) perpetual inventory control system*

POPAI See *Point-of-Purchase Advertising Institute (POPAI)*

POPULATION In marketing research, the entire group under observation by the researcher and about which he will draw conclusions. The terms universe and sample set are frequently used synonymously with population. See also *sampling*.

POPULATION SURVEY See *census*

PORTFOLIO ANALYSIS In strategic planning, a method of analyzing the various components of a large business organization in an effort to achieve balance much in the way an individual analyzes his investment portfolio.

PORTFOLIO MANAGEMENT See *portfolio analysis*

POS See *point-of-sale (POS)* and *point-of-sale (POS) perpetual inventory control system*

POSITIONING See *market positioning*

POSITIONING ADVERTISING A form of advertising in which a segment of the market is targeted and the product or service presented in a way which specifically appeals to that segment. Consideration may also be given to the product's position as it relates to competing products in the marketplace.

POSSESSION UTILITY See *ownership utility*

POSTADOPTION BEHAVIOR See *postpurchase behavior*

POSTAGE STAMP PRICING A method of setting uniform delivered prices throughout the national market by charging equal freight costs regardless of actual distance shipped. In this respect, it resembles letter postage. Also known as uniform geographic pricing and uniform delivered pricing.

POSTPONEMENT See *principle of postponement*

POSTPURCHASE BEHAVIOR The final stage in the consumer adoption process, postpurchase behavior includes such activities as continued evaluation of the product, the use and maintenance of the product, and the decision whether or not to repurchase the product in the future.

POSTPURCHASE DISSONANCE See *cognitive dissonance*

POWER NEED See *trio of needs*

PRAISE (OR COMPLIMENT) APPROACH A technique used by a salesperson in the first few minutes of contact with a prospect which uses honest praise or compliments to gain the prospect's attention. The salesperson may praise the prospect's furnishings, attire, reputation, etc. See also *approach.*

PREAPPROACH In the industrial/institutional selling process, the preapproach involves a preliminary investigation of a prospective customer in an effort to discover how the company conducts its business, what its needs are, and how it runs its buying operations. Such planning enables a salesperson to effectively develop a sales presentation

PRECONSCIOUS LEVEL (OF NEED AWARENESS) See *need awareness*

PREDATORY PRICE CUTTING See *predatory pricing*

PREDATORY PRICING The setting of prices at a level so low as to drive competitors out of business. Much predatory pricing is illegal under the provisions of the Clayton and Sherman Acts. Also known as put-out pricing and extinction pricing.

PREEMPTIVE MARKETING The advertising of a product or service before it is actually available in the marketplace in an effort to forestall the purchase of a competitor's product.

PREEMPTIVE PRICING A strategy in which price levels are set so low that makers of competitive products are discouraged from entering the marketplace. Also known as keep-out pricing and stay-out pricing.

PREMIUM Merchandise employed as a sales promotion device, e.g., it may be used as an incentive to encourage customers to make a purchase or to reward sales people for increased productivity. The essential appeal of premiums is that the recipient feels he is getting something for nothing.

PREMIUM (OR GIFT GIVING) APPROACH A technique used by salespersons in the first few minutes of contact with a prospect. A free gift or sample is given to the prospect who then feels obligated to hear the salesperson's presentation. The gift generally ties in with the product or service being sold. See also *approach.*

PREMIUM PRICING The setting of prices at a level above that commonly found in the marketplace in an effort to indicate that the product is of a premium quality. Similar to prestige pricing.

PRE-PRICED PRODUCT See *source marking*

PRESENT VALUE See *net present value*

PRESENTATION See *sales presentation*

PRESOLD MARKET Purchasers who exist before a product or service is available in the marketplace.

PRESS RELEASE Publicity in the form of a written communication of commercially significant news (usually of 300 words or less) distributed to the communications media. Press releases generally identify the source of the information and carry a release date.

PRESTIGE PRICING In retailing, the setting of prices at artificially high levels on certain items in an effort to attract customers who identify high prices with high quality and status. Also known as symbolic pricing.

PRICE The price of goods and services is that amount of money (or other valuable consideration such as time, goods, votes, etc.) for which they may be purchased. Asking price is a representation of the value the seller places on the product offered for sale; selling price is that amount actually exchanged when the sale is consummated and includes provision for discounts, shipping charges, credit charges, allowances, etc. See also *value* and *cost.*

PRICE AGREEMENT PLAN A central buying arrangement in which the buyer for a chain of stores arranges prices, colors, sizes, styles, and assortments of merchandise as well as the terms of shipping. The manager of the individual store can order from the pre-selected assortment as needed. Also called a catalog plan.

PRICE CEILING That maximum price level beyond which customers will no longer make purchases.

PRICE COLLUSION See *collusion*

PRICE COMPETITION A marketing strategy frequently employed as a means of gaining or maintaining a competitive advantage. Typically, a firm may reduce prices in an effort to attract new customers or as a response to the price reductions of a competitor. Some organizations, such as discount stores, engage as a matter of policy in price competition on a permanent basis.

PRICE CONTROLS Government mandated ceilings on the prices a firm may charge for its products. Firms which fail to abide by the guidelines are subject to penalties.

PRICE CROSS ELASTICITY See *cross elasticity*

PRICE CUTTING A selling strategy, usually encountered at the retail level, in which merchandise or services are offered at prices below those recommended by the vendor or at levels which are recognized by the general public to be lower than "regular retail."

PRICE-DEMAND CURVE RESPONSE FUNCTION See *response function*

PRICE-DEMAND ELASTICITY See *elasticity of demand*

PRICE-DEMAND RESPONSE FUNCTION See *response function*

PRICE DISCRIMINATION See *discriminatory pricing*

PRICE DISCRIMINATION CHAIN STORE ACT See *Robinson-Patman Act*

PRICE ELASTICITY See *elasticity*

PRICE ELASTICITY OF DEMAND See *elasticity of demand*

PRICE ELASTICITY OF SUPPLY See *elasticity of supply*

PRICE ESCALATION Advances in ultimate prices due to such factors as transportation and distribution costs, unanticipated middleman expenses, shrinkage, and, in international marketing, tariffs and other special taxes.

PRICE FIXING See *resale price maintenance (RPM)*

PRICE FLOOR The minimum price level below which a firm can no longer realize a profit.

PRICE GUARANTEE 1) An incentive offered by the vendor to the buyer (wholesaler or retailer) who buys well in advance of the season and who places a large order. The vendor promises to reimburse the retailer for any losses resulting from a decline in market price of the goods between the date of the purchase and the start of the normal selling season. 2) A promise made by a vendor to a wholesaler or retailer to reimburse the difference between the planned selling price and the actual selling price if the reseller is unable to trade the goods as planned. Also known as a price protection rebate or a vendor paid markdown.

PRICE INELASTICITY See *inelasticity*

PRICE INFLATERS Various charges added to the list price of a product which increase its true selling price. Among those devices employed are: dealer preparation charges, handling fees, credit charges, service contracts, etc.

PRICE LEADER 1) That company in any industry which, apparently without collusion, is the first to make price changes. Because the price leader is often the largest company in the industry, smaller companies tend to fall in line. 2) Price leader is also used synonymously with loss leader, particularly in the food retailing industry.

PRICE LEADERSHIP See *price leader*

PRICE LEVEL DISCOUNT A discount from list price offered on particular items to avoid reprinting the entire price list. Customers are advised that certain products carry an additional percentage discount.

PRICE LINING A retail pricing strategy in which merchandise is offered for sale at a limited number of predetermined price points. For example, a store may offer men's shirts at $18, $26, and $35 in an effort to 1) simplify the buying process, and 2) present the customer with a manageable number of choices.

PRICE MAINTENANCE See *resale price maintenance (RPM)*

PRICE-MINUS PRICING A method used to determine the price of a product or service by first estimating the price at which that product or service might achieve a particular share of the market or goal volume, and then proceeding to develop the product or service to be profitable at that price.

PRICE-ORIENTED RESPONSE FUNCTION See *response function*

PRICE PACK Products offered at a reduced price to the consumer, commonly in the form of a banded pack in which 1) two items are offered for the price of one, or 2) two products (for example, shaving cream and a razor) are sold together.

PRICE PROMOTIONS A practice found at both the wholesale and retail levels in which prices on some items are reduced for a short period to stimulate sales. These promotions may be simple price reductions or may be in the form of allowances, discounts, free goods, premiums, etc.

PRICE PROTECTION REBATE See *price guarantee*

PRICE-QUALITY ASSOCIATION A theory which holds that consumers equate high prices with high quality goods and low prices with low quality goods. See also *prestige pricing*.

185

PRICE REDUCERS Devices employed to reduce the actual selling price of a product. Includes various discounts and allowances, free service, rebates, trading stamps, etc.

PRICE RESPONSE FUNCTION See *response function*

PRICE SHADING A pricing policy in which discounts are offered by a manufacturer to wholesalers and retailers or by salespeople to the consumer. Price shading is used as a means of increasing demand for the product without changing the list or book price.

PRICE SKIMMING See *skimming*

PRICE SPACE The gap existing between price points in a product line, i.e., the distance from one price to the next. See also *price lining.*

PRICE STABILITY A condition in the marketplace in which price competition between firms is kept to a minimum, usually as the result of the price leadership provided by one or more large firms in an industry (automobiles, steel, etc.).

PRICE VARIABLE A part of the marketing mix concerned with establishing product prices. It is a variable in that it is one of the components in the mix which can be altered as conditions warrant.

PRICE WAR A fiercely competitive situation in which competing firms drastically lower their prices in an attempt to undersell each other in order to attract each other's customers. Price wars sometimes result in one or more participants being forced out of business.

PRICING Any of a variety of methods used to determine the price at which goods will be sold. These methods in-clude demand-oriented pricing, flexible rate pricing, and gross margin pricing, etc.

PRICING ABOVE THE COMPETITION See *pricing above the market*

PRICING ABOVE THE MARKET A policy of setting prices above those of the competition so as to convey an image of superior product quality or prestige and to differentiate the product in the minds of potential customers.

PRICING AT THE COMPETITIVE LEVEL See *pricing at the market*

PRICING AT THE MARKET A policy of setting prices at approximately the same level as one's competition, thus minimizing the use of price as a competitive factor.

PRICING BELOW THE COMPETITION See *pricing below the market*

PRICING BELOW THE MARKET A policy of setting prices below those of the competition in an effort to maximize the use of price as a competitive factor. This strategy may also be an alternative to expensive promotional efforts.

PRICING DECISIONS See *pricing policies*

PRICING GOALS See *pricing objectives*

PRICING OBJECTIVES Those considerations which precede the establishment of pricing policies. Pricing objectives are the comprehensive goals which the firm expects to achieve in the long run. Included may be the maximizing of sales or profits, the achievement of a predetermined return on investment, an increase in market share, maintenance of a status quo with respect to price competition, etc. See also *pricing strategy* and *pricing policies.*

PRICING POLICIES Those considerations which follow the establishment of a firm's pricing objectives. Pricing policies provide marketing decision makers with predetermined guidelines to be employed in pricing individual products or services. See also *pricing strategy* and *pricing objectives.*

PRICING STRATEGY A component of a firm's overall marketing strategy. Pricing strategy, i.e., the establishment of a realistic price framework, is crucial in determining a company's competitive position in the marketplace.

PRIMARY ADVERTISING See *primary demand advertising*

PRIMARY DATA Information generally not available at the time a problem is defined and which was collected from original sources through such techniques as observation, interviews, surveys, experiment, etc. Primary data are collected for an explicit purpose at hand.

PRIMARY DEMAND Consumer demand for a class or type of product rather than for a particular brand; e.g., the demand for jeans in general as opposed to the demand for Levi's jeans. Also known as generic demand.

PRIMARY DEMAND ADVERTISING Advertising whose objective is the development of demand for a product or service without making reference to a specific manufacturer or particular brand. This form of advertising is used primarily for innovative products in the first stages of the product life cycle. Also called pioneering advertising and primary demand stimulation.

PRIMARY DEMAND STIMULATION See *primary demand advertising*

PRIMARY GROUPS Those reference groups to which an individual belongs which exert a strong influence on his attitudes and behavior. The most significant primary groups for most individuals are the family and the peers with whom they frequently associate.

PRIMARY METROPOLITAN STATISTICAL AREA (PMSA) A metropolitan area having a population of more than 1 million and made up of two or more MSAs. PMSAs have a high degree of economic and social integration. See also *Metropolitan Statistical Area (MSA)* and *Consolidated Metropolitan Statistical Area (CMSA).*

PRIMARY NEEDS Among the basic motivations which cause individual consumers to make purchase decisions, primary needs are those which derive from basic physiological factors such as thirst, hunger, the need for shelter, etc. Primary needs are universal and neither determined nor limited by cultural factors. See also *needs, Maslow's hierarchy,* and *secondary needs.*

PRIME CONTRACTOR The business awarded the contract on a large and complex job which commonly necessitates the subcontracting of various parts of the job to other businesses.

PRINCIPLE OF DEMAND See *law of demand*

PRINCIPLE OF DIMINISHING UTILITY The utility of ownership (the satisfaction one experiences from possessing a product) decreases as the number of units increases, i.e., the more one has of something the less pleasure each added unit produces in the consumer.

PRINCIPLE OF POSTPONEMENT A theory of management which maintains that a firm should refrain from

187

changing its products and marketing mix until it becomes absolutely necessary to do so and to postpone changes in the location of its inventories until immediately prior to their sale. This strategy is intended to reduce the risks involved in the four Ps of marketing.

PRINCIPLE OF POSTPONEMENT AND SPECULATION A theory of management which combines the principle of postponement with the principle of speculation. The theory maintains that a speculative inventory will appear at each point in a channel of distribution when it costs less to move the products than the net saving that would accrue to both buyer and seller if such a movement of inventory were further postponed. See also *principle of postponement* and *principle of speculation.*

PRINCIPLE OF SPECULATION A theory of management which maintains that a firm should take the earliest possible advantage of changing the form of its products and of moving its products to market. This strategy is intended to reduce the costs of production and marketing. It stands in marked contrast to the principle of postponement.

PRIVATE BRAND Private brands, which are also known as distributor's brands, reseller brands, middleman brands, and dealer brands, are produced or manufactured by organizations which remain anonymous. The product itself may carry the name of a distributor or retailer, or it may carry a brand name owned by the seller, but the name of the producer or manufacturer remains unknown to the customer. Private brands are generally sponsored by large wholesalers, department and chain stores, cooperative chains, and consumer cooperatives. Also called store brand and

private label. See also *controlled brand.*

PRIVATE BUYING OFFICE See *resident buying office*

PRIVATE CARRIER A transportation firm (rail, truck, barge, etc.) engaged in shipping merchandise. Private carriers (unlike common carriers) are owned by the firm for which they perform the shipping function and are thus exempt from certain forms of government regulation. See also *contract carrier* and *common carrier.*

PRIVATE COSTS When calculating the cost of doing business, private costs are those actually incurred by a company—those which appear in their financial statements. Social costs are not included.

PRIVATE DISTRIBUTOR BRAND See *private brand*

PRIVATE LABEL See *private brand*

PRIVATE LABEL MANUFACTURERS ASSOCIATION (PLMA) An association of individuals and organizations involved in the manufacture and distribution of private label (store brand) products. The stated goal of the New York based association is to educate consumers about private label products.

PRIVATE OFFICE See *resident buying office*

PRIVATE WAREHOUSE A storage facility operated by the user. It has the advantage of total user control, important when items needing special treatment (such as chemicals and pharmaceuticals) are being stored or when storage volume is large and handling volume is constant. See also *public warehouse* and *contract warehouse.*

PRIZE MONEY See *push money (PM)*

188

PRIZE MONEY ALLOWANCE See *push money (PM)*

PROACTIVE SELLING A sales effort in which customers are actually pursued by a firm's sales force. See also *reactive selling.*

PROBABILITY SAMPLING In marketing research, probability sampling is a method of selecting a representative subset of the total population to study so that each member has a known and equal chance of being selected. There are three basic types of probability samples: the random sample, the stratified random sample, and the area (or cluster) sample. In each type of probability sample the members of a given group are selected through an objective process without the interference of judgments made on the part of the researcher. See also *nonprobability sampling.*

PROBLEM CHILD In the evaluation of a company's product line, the problem child is seen as a high growth product but one which commands a low market share. These products are viewed as problems because they require considerable money to increase market share. The company must decide whether to build up the product or drop it. Also known as question marks and wildcats.

PROBLEM DEFINITION The first stage in marketing research, during which a clear statement of the problem is elaborated.

PROBLEM DETECTION STUDY In determining product performance in the marketplace, a problem detection study focuses on the complaints of customers. Products may be modified or new products introduced based on the results of such a study.

PROBLEM-SOLVING APPROACH A technique used by a salesperson in the first few minutes of contact with a prospect aimed at helping the prospect solve either a specific problem known to the salesperson or a common problem assumed to affect the prospect. See also *approach.*

PROCESS MATERIALS Materials used in the production process which, unlike component parts, are not actually incorporated into the product. For example, chemicals used to degrease metal parts before they undergo further processing are regarded as process materials.

PROCESSING IN TRANSIT See *transit privileges*

PROCUREMENT See *industrial purchasing*

PRODUCE In food retailing, produce refers to fresh fruits and vegetables and the department of the store in which they are sold. This is in contrast to farm products, which are farm grown raw materials used in the manufacture of processed goods and which become part of a physical good.

PRODUCE MARKETING ASSOCIATION (PMA) An association of food producers, shippers, wholesalers, retailers, packagers, and related firms concerned with the marketing of fresh produce and floral products. The Delaware based association serves as an information center for its membership and works to improve the marketing of fresh fruits, vegetables, and flowers. PMA publishes annually a *Directory of International Trade,* the *Foodservice Directory,* the *Floral Marketing Directory and Buyers' Guide,* and the *Produce Marketing Almanac* in addition to several journals, reports, and newsletters.

PRODUCER MARKET The producer market includes a wide variety of organizations which purchase goods

189

to be 1) incorporated into other goods, 2) used to produce other goods, or 3) consumed in the day-to-day operations of the organization. The producer market is a part of the larger industrial market. See also *industrial market, government market,* and *institutional market.*

PRODUCER OUTLET See *manufacturer's store*

PRODUCERS' COOPERATIVE A limited-service wholesaling institution owned and operated by its members for the purpose of marketing agricultural products. Profits are distributed to members in the form of dividends.

PRODUCERS' COOPERATIVE MARKETING ASSOCIATION See *producers' cooperative.*

PRODUCT In addition to physical objects, the term product commonly includes services, ideas, and activities which fulfill a need for the consuming public, whether it be at the industrial/business, institutional, or retail level. In its broadest sense the term encompasses a cluster of attributes which, for example, may include the social and psychological benefits attendant to the product. In a narrower sense, products may be regarded more specifically, e.g., a particular class of products (trucks) may be manufactured in a number of forms (4-wheel drive, flat bed, etc.), and the various forms may be sold under a number of brand names (Chevrolet, GMC, etc.).

PRODUCT ADAPTATION The modification of products to meet local needs and requirements. For example, goods shipped overseas may sometimes be adapted to special conditions, e.g., different electric current, local air pollution standards, etc.

PRODUCT ADOPTION PROCESS See *adoption process*

PRODUCT ADVERTISING Advertising whose objective is the stimulation of demand for a specific product or service. It may seek an immediate response on the part of the customer, in which case it is termed direct-action advertising, or it may seek a response at some time in the future, in which case it is termed indirect-action advertising. Also known as brand advertising. See also *institutional advertising.*

PRODUCT APPROACH See *product (or exhibit) approach*

PRODUCT ASSORTMENT See *product mix*

PRODUCT ATTRIBUTES Objective characteristics of a product such as color, line, design, materials, and quality of workmanship and subjective characteristics such as the reputation of the manufacturer and brand image.

PRODUCT AUGMENTATION A strategy employed in marketing products which have reached the maturity stage in their life cycle. The life of a product may be extended by enhancing the way it is presented (more attractive packaging, etc.), by augmenting it with services (repairs, etc.), or by superficially changing it periodically as in the woman's ready-to-wear industry.

PRODUCT BREADTH See *product width*

PRODUCT BUYING MOTIVES See *motive*

PRODUCT CHARACTERISTICS See *product attributes*

190

PRODUCT CONCEPT A marketing management orientation in which the consumer is seen as primarily concerned with the acquisition of quality goods at reasonable prices. The manufacturer who adopts the product concept emphasizes product improvement and efficiency of production. See also *production concept, marketing concept,* and *selling concept.*

PRODUCT DECAY CURVE See *decay curve*

PRODUCT DELETION The withdrawal of a product from a company's line of products, generally because it is no longer profitable. Also called product pruning.

PRODUCT DEMONSTRATION See *demonstration*

PRODUCT DEPTH In terms of product mix, product depth refers to the number of items in each product line offered for sale. In retailing, assortment depth is a measure or description of the quantity of each item available in the assortment of goods. An assortment containing an item in great quantities and many sizes is said to be "deep."

PRODUCT DESIGN SIMPLIFICATION A marketing strategy in which a product's design is simplified in an effort to reduce manufacturing costs and increase profits. Generally, the consumer will perceive no difference in such a redesigned product.

PRODUCT DEVELOPMENT See *new product development*

PRODUCT DIFFERENTIATED MARKETING See *product differentiation*

PRODUCT DIFFERENTIATION A marketing strategy in which an effort is made to clearly distinguish one product from another with particular attention to features the customer might regard as superior to those of competing products. Product differentiation may be subjective, i.e., it may exist largely in terms of appearance, or it may be objective, i.e., there may be significant physical differences between products which affect quality, safety, etc.

Factors such as delivery terms, warranties, terms of credit, etc. may also be used to differentiate products from one another.

PRODUCT DIFFUSION See *diffusion process*

PRODUCT DIVERSIFICATION See *diversification*

PRODUCT DIVISION OF AUTHORITY In marketing management, a form of organization in which line authority is organized to correspond to the lines of products being manufactured. This arrangement is most common in large firms making a highly diversified line of products.

PRODUCT DRIVEN A company orientation in which products are developed and produced with little regard for the wants and needs of the customer.

PRODUCT FIT The degree to which a product meets the needs of the marketplace.

PRODUCT ITEM A particular product having enough distinctive attributes to be easily distinguished from other products in a line. For stockkeeping purposes, product items frequently are assigned a unique identifying number. See also *stock keeping unit (SKU).*

PRODUCT LIABILITY The legal responsibility of a manufacturer or seller of a product to pay damages to parties injured through the use of the product when it has proven to be defective or unsafely designed.

PRODUCT LIFE CYCLE (PLC) The product life cycle is a series of stages through which a product or service passes as it evolves in the marketplace. Four stages are readily identifiable: 1) introduction of the product, 2) its growth, i.e., the extent of demand for the product, 3) market maturity, 4) the ultimate saturation of the market by the product (or its failure to capture a market) and its eventual decline.

PRODUCT LIFE CYCLE

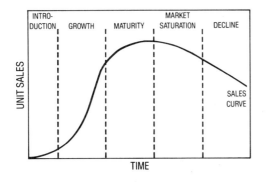

PRODUCT LINE A group of products closely related by some factor such as physical characteristic, price, end-use, etc. In retailing, various lines make up what is known as variety. Variety, in turn, is a component of the merchandise assortment.

PRODUCT LINE CONSISTENCY See *line consistency*

PRODUCT LINE MARKETING A strategy in which two or more products are marketed by a firm under a common (and frequently respected) brand name. Product line marketing enables a company to expand its prod-

uct lines and to develop coordinated advertising campaigns. See also *brand marketing.*

PRODUCT LINE PRICING A pricing strategy in which a firm's entire line of products and their interrelationships are considered when prices are set for individual products.

PRODUCT LINE PRUNING See *product deletion*

PRODUCT MANAGER An executive who functions as the head of the product team responsible for the planning and development of a particular product, product line, or brand. The product manager (or brand manager as he is sometimes called) oversees the development of a competitive strategy, coordinates all aspects of planning, and directs advertising and promotional efforts on behalf of the product. The product manager is, in many respects, the marketing manager for his particular product.

PRODUCT MANAGER SYSTEM A middle management system employed by firms marketing a relatively large number of distinct products. Each product has a manager who is totally involved in the development and marketing of the product from its conception through its commercialization. Such a system is meant to ensure that each product in the marketing mix receives adequate attention.

PRODUCT MANAGEMENT Those business activities concerned with the development of new products or brands, their introduction into the marketplace, and their management through the product life cycle. See also *product manager.*

PRODUCT MARKET A market in which vendors offer similar products which may be considered substitutes for each other. These products may be either physically or conceptually similar, and are regarded as comparable in satisfying consumer needs. For example, all luxury automobiles would be considered part of the same product market, since they may substitute for each other in satisfying customers' needs for transportation, luxury, and status. See also *generic market* and *market.*

PRODUCT/MARKET DIVERSIFICATION See *diversification*

PRODUCT MARKET EROSION Loss of market share for a product or service due to a decrease in demand. Market erosion frequently occurs as new competitive products enter the marketplace.

PRODUCT/MARKET OPPORTUNITY MATRIX A method employed in developing marketing plans in which four alternative strategies for increasing business are set forth: 1) market development (increasing sales by expanding into new markets); 2) product development (developing new products for existing markets); 3) market penetration (increasing sales of current products in existing markets); and 4) diversification (the development of new products for new markets).

PRODUCT MIX The aggregate of products offered for sale by a firm. The product mix may be measured in breadth (i.e., the number of product lines carried), or in depth (i.e., the assortment of sizes, types, colors, and styles within each product line). The consistency of a company's product mix depends on how the various lines relate to one another in terms of distribution requirements, ultimate end use, etc.

PRODUCT MIX DEPTH See *product depth*

PRODUCT MIX WIDTH See *product width*

PRODUCT OBSOLESCENCE See *planned obsolescence*

PRODUCT (OR EXHIBIT) APPROACH A technique used by a salesperson in the first few minutes of contact with a prospect. In this approach the item to be sold is handed to the prospect for his own inspection. The prospect is then asked for an opinion of the product. See also *approach.*

PRODUCT ORIENTATION See *production concept*

PRODUCT PLANNING See *new product planning process*

PRODUCT PLANNING COMMITTEE A group of executives drawn from various areas of management whose primary responsibility is the evaluation of new product ideas. Although, for the most part, concerned with idea generation and screening, a product planning committee may guide the product further down the line through the developmental stages of marketing. Once this stage has been reached the committee may be disbanded or continue to meet on a part-time basis. See also *venture team.*

PRODUCT PORTFOLIO CONCEPT A strategic marketing tool in which a firm views the products it produces as part of a larger product mix and then treats the various product mixes (or divisions within the company) as though they were parts of a stock portfolio. These units are evaluated in terms of profitability and are either given support or are sold off just as stocks with a poor return on investment are sold off. The portfolio approach to marketing management is somewhat limited in that it takes a short-run view of product performance.

PRODUCT POSITIONING See *market positioning*

PRODUCT PRUNING See *product deletion*

PRODUCT QUALITY See *quality*

PRODUCT-QUALITY RESPONSE FUNCTION See *response function*

PRODUCT RECALL The call back of products because of defects, imperfections, or other shortcomings. Agencies such as the Consumer Products Safety Commission or the Federal Trade Commission may compel a producer to recall a product when it violates safety or other regulations.

PRODUCT REPOSITIONING See *repositioning*

PRODUCT SCREENING A stage in the new product planning process during which product proposals which are deemed unsuitable are weeded out and dropped from further consideration.

PRODUCT SEGMENTATION In industrial marketing, the subdivision of a market on the basis of product specifications which meet the requirements of the purchaser.

PRODUCT TESTING See *market testing*

PRODUCT VARIABLES Those aspects of a product which are subject to change such as color, size, price, operating cost, reliability, availability, brand name, packaging, etc. Product variables are marketing mix variables in that they are controllable by the organization. They are unlike variables in the marketing environment which are largely out of the control of the firm.

PRODUCT VARIANT See *product item*

PRODUCT WARRANTY See *warranty*

PRODUCT WIDTH In terms of product mix, product width (or breadth) refers to the number of product lines offered for sale. In retailing, assortment width refers to the number of different categories or classifications available in a store or department without reference to the quantity available in any one style. An assortment is said to be wide (or broad) when a large variety of different items is available within a classification.

PRODUCTION ACCESSORIES See *accessory equipment*

PRODUCTION BUDGET See *budget*

PRODUCTION CONCEPT A marketing management organization in which the desires of the consumer are seen as secondary to the efficient production of high quality products which may be sold at competitive prices. The production concept is commonly held in traditional manufacturing organizations where a good product is believed to assure success in the marketplace. See also *product concept, marketing concept,* and *selling concept.*

PRODUCTION ERA OF MARKETING A stage in the evolution of marketing (during the Industrial Revolution) characterized by a high level of competition. Manufacturers concentrated their efforts on producing goods and moving them to their customers as efficiently as possible. Little consideration was given to the wants and needs of the consumer.

PRODUCTION FIT In product marketing, production fit refers to the degree of compatibility of a new product with the firm's existing machinery of production.

PRODUCTION ORIENTATION See *production concept*

PRODUCTIVITY As a marketing concept, a measurement of the efficiency of a producer, generally expressed in terms of the number of man hours expended per unit of production. The concept may also be applied to such factors as capital or land.

PRODUCTS MANAGER See *product manager*

PROFESSIONAL ADVERTISING 1) Advertising by professionals, such as lawyers, physicians, dentists, etc. 2) Advertising by manufacturers or distributors of products whose success in the marketplace depends on the acceptance and approval of professionals. The message is directed to the professional in the hope that he will recommend or specify the particular product. For example, physicians are encouraged to prescribe particular drugs, engineers to specify particular building materials, etc.

PROFESSIONAL PRICING A pricing strategy employed by professionals (lawyers, architects, etc.) in which services are rendered for a flat, predetermined fee rather than calculated on an hourly basis.

PROFIT Although profit may be regarded in a general sense as the abstract goal of a business or profession, in its marketing context it is generally taken to mean total revenue less all costs and expenses. Profit is commonly qualified by another term such as gross or net, thus making the concept more precise.

PROFIT AND LOSS STATEMENT An accounting statement of net profit (or net loss) based on the firm's revenues less expenses and losses for a specific period of time. Also called an income statement, operating statement, or statement of operations.

PROFIT IMPACT OF MARKETING STRATEGIES (PIMS) An ongoing study initiated by the Marketing Science Institute in 1971 whose basic aim was to relate the profit performance of a number of large companies to the marketing variables they encountered while conducting their business and to assess how these variables affected their marketing strategies.

PROFIT MAXIMIZATION The realization of the highest attainable profit in a business enterprise. Profit maximization is a primary goal when a firm sets pricing strategy.

PROFIT MAXIMIZATION OBJECTIVE A firm's stated desire to make as much profit as it can. Since this is considered somewhat socially undesirable and firms openly espousing profit maximization may be viewed as failing to operate in the public interest, it is more common among small firms operating away from public scrutiny. However, if the increase in profits is viewed as deriving from increased efficiency and/or better service to customers, both business and consumers may be seen to benefit from this objective. The profit maximization objective may be stated as a rapid return on investment, or "all the traffic will bear." See also *profit maximization.*

PROFIT-ORIENTED AUDIT An evaluation of a marketing plan in terms of the expenses and revenues generated by that plan. See also *marketing audit.*

PROFIT RESPONSE FUNCTION See *response function*

195

PROFIT TARGET ANALYSIS A method used to calculate the volume of sales needed to pay for all costs (both fixed and variable) of operation and return a predetermined profit. Similar to a break-even analysis, except that fixed costs include a predetermined level of profit. That level of profit represents a targeted return on investment, often required by the firm's management. See also *break-even analysis.*

PROGRAM EVALUATION AND REVIEW TECHNIQUE (PERT) An analytical process which breaks large projects down into component parts and uses probabilities to estimate the time needed to complete each part. The technique is similar to the critical path method (CPM).

PROJECT DESIGN See *research design*

PROJECTIVE TECHNIQUE A technique employed in marketing research in which a respondent is asked to perform a task, e.g., a sentence completion or word association test, in the belief that he will reveal certain attitudes which motivate his behavior. The assumption is that respondents will not or cannot answer certain questions because of social pressure (the answer is not acceptable), or because the answer lies buried in the unconscious, or because the respondent simply cannot find the words to express it.

PROMOTION See *sales promotion*

PROMOTION-ADVERTISING RESPONSE FUNCTION See *response function*

PROMOTION BLEND See *promotion mix*

PROMOTION COMMUNICATIONS MIX See *promotion mix*

PROMOTION MARKETING ASSOCIATION OF AMERICA (PMAA) A New York based association of promotion service companies, sales incentive organizations, and related businesses. PMAA's membership also includes manufacturers of premium merchandise, consultants, and advertising agencies as associate members. The association studies and promotes premium usage and co-sponsors both the New York Premium Show and the National Premium Show.

PROMOTION MIX The selected combination of advertising, publicity, sales promotion, and personal selling used to communicate with, inform, and sell goods to the consumer. The elements may be varied to arrive at the most effective and cost-effective program.

PROMOTION MIX

PROMOTION OBJECTIVES See *advertising objectives*

PROMOTION PLANNING Those activities which lead to the development of a firm's comprehensive promotional plan including the formulation of objectives, budgeting, and the development of an appropriate promotional mix.

PROMOTION RESPONSE FUNC-TION See *response function*

PROMOTION VARIABLE See *promotion mix*

PROMOTIONAL ALLOWANCE A price reduction granted a buyer by a seller of a product or service in compensation for the buyer's special promotional efforts on the part of the product. Promotional allowances are usually calculated as a percentage of the final invoice price. Sometimes called a merchandise allowance. See also *cooperative advertising.*

PROMOTIONAL DEPARTMENT STORE A discount store which, due to its size and merchandise mix (both hard and soft lines), approximates a department store. Promotional department stores operate at lower gross margins than traditional department stores because of their relatively low-rent locations, lack of amenities, and minimal service. They are, however, often as profitable as other types of stores in their price class. Also called full-line discount stores.

PROMOTIONAL DISCOUNT See *promotional allowance*

PROMOTIONAL FIT In product marketing, promotional fit refers to the degree of compatibility of a new product with the firm's established promotional and advertising programs.

PROMOTIONAL MARKDOWN See *markdown*

PROMOTIONAL MIX See *promotion mix*

PROMOTIONAL PRICE A reduced price offered on a temporary basis to promote specific merchandise.

PROMOTIONAL PROGRAM See *sales promotion*

PROMOTIONAL QUADRANGLE See *four Ps of the marketing mix*

PROSPECT In sales, a prospect is a potential customer, whether a person or an organization, who can benefit from the product or service being sold, or who may want or need the product or service. See also *lead* and *qualified prospect.*

PROSPECTING That step in the personal selling process involving the discovery of potential customers.

PROSPERITY See *business cycle*

PROTECTION IN TRANSIT In shipping, the function performed by a product's package, i.e., protection from damage.

PRUNING See *product deletion*

PSYCHIC INCOME Non-money recompense such as job satisfaction, desirable location of employment, etc. which may be counted on as part of an individual's total income.

PSYCHOGRAPHIC MARKET SEGMENTATION See *psychographic segmentation*

PSYCHOGRAPHIC SEGMENTATION The division of a market into subgroups based on such sociopsychological determinants as personality, lifestyle, attitudes, and self-concept. Psychographic segmentation facilitates the targeting of potential customers.

PSYCHOGRAPHICS The results of a research procedure through which consumer behavior is explained, at least in part, by the study of such variables as personality, lifestyle, attitudes, and self-concept with a view of predicting consumer response to products, stores, advertising, etc.

PSYCHOLOGICAL BUYING MOTIVE Consumer motives which have

their roots in social or psychological needs. Products such as expensive automobiles and jewelry are frequently purchased to satisfy psychological needs, which are the time motivating factors. See also *motive*.

PSYCHOLOGICAL DISCOUNTING The use of deceptive prices in the promotion of products or services. The illusion created is that the current selling price is a substantial reduction from a previous price, i.e., the reference price, even though there was never any intention of changing the reference price. Also called superficial discounting or was-is pricing.

PSYCHOLOGICAL OBSOLESCENCE See *planned obsolescence*

PSYCHOLOGICAL PRICING A pricing strategy most commonly found in retailing in which an effort is made to generate an emotional response on the part of the consumer through one of a number of tactics. See *leader pricing, odd-line pricing, even-line pricing, prestige pricing,* and *customary price* for examples of psychological pricing.

PUBLIC 1) With reference to a business organization, the public refers to all those persons external to the organization who in some way affect its operations. They may be consumers, middlemen, government agencies, stockholders, or any other segment of the population which affects marketing strategies. 2) A corporation is said to be public when it issues and sells shares in the stock market. Also called "publicly held."

PUBLIC HEALTH SMOKING ACT (1970) Federal consumer legislation which banned cigarette advertising on radio and television and required a warning to be printed on all cigarette packaging and print advertisements.

PUBLIC POLICY ENVIRONMENT That part of the total marketing environment which is directly influenced by activities of the government. Includes laws which regulate trade, regulations of various administrative agencies, public policy decisions affecting marketing activities, etc.

PUBLIC RELATIONS Activities aimed at enhancing the public image of an organization, individual, or product, etc. Public relations includes the dissemination of information intended to generate good will on behalf of the organization and to identify its activities with the public interest.

PUBLIC RELATIONS ADVERTISING See *institutional advertising*

PUBLIC SERVICE ADVERTISING Advertising designed to serve the general public on a nonprofit basis. Such advertising is generally meant to inform the public or to encourage or discourage certain behavior, e.g., campaigns against drunk driving. Not a synonym for institutional advertising.

PUBLIC WAREHOUSE An independently owned storage facility serving a variety of users. The public warehouseman does not own or take title to the goods stored. The user of the facility is charged on the basis of cost per unit and the storage arrangements are made on a month-to-month basis. Other services such as receiving, packing, and invoicing may be available at additional cost. See also *private warehouse* and *contract warehouse*.

PUBLICITY Unpaid, nonpersonal public notice in the print or electronic media (usually in the form of news stories) which may stimulate the sales of a product or service, or enhance the reputation of a person. A firm may attempt to plant favorable stories in the media via news releases which convey commercially significant information about the company, its products, or its role in the community.

PUBLICITY PLAN A company's overall plan for nonpaid, nonpersonal promotional activities. Includes the objectives, rationale, evaluation of the program, and the media used. See also *publicity*.

PUBLICLY HELD See *public*

PUFFERY A slightly exaggerated advertising or public relations claim, sometimes regarded as "artistic license," as to the benefits to be derived from a product or service. Intended to put the product or service in the best possible light and to generate additional sales. The line between puffery and deceptive advertising is not always clear and distinct.

PULL STRATEGY A marketing distribution strategy in which a firm's promotional efforts are directed toward the ultimate user in an effort to create strong consumer demand. The consumer then asks his dealer for the advertised product which, in turn, tends to pull the goods through the channel of distribution from the producer to the ultimate consumer. Sometimes known as pull-through marketing. See also *push strategy*.

PULL-THROUGH MARKETING See *pull strategy*

PULLING STRATEGY See *pull strategy*

PULSING In advertising, pulsing is a strategy designed to build customer awareness. Marketers using this strategy expend advertising money and effort in periodic spurts or waves.

PURCHASE ACT In general the act of buying a product or service. More specifically, in the consumer adoption process the purchase act follows the evaluation and trial stages of the process.

PURCHASE BEHAVIOR See *consumer behavior*

PURCHASE DECISION PROCESS See *adoption process*

PURCHASE DISCOUNT See *cash discount*

PURCHASER The person who actually buys a product or service. The purchaser may be a buyer at the industrial level or a customer at the consumer level.

PURCHASING See *industrial purchasing*

PURCHASING AGENT A professional buyer employed by governmental, industrial, or institutional organizations charged with the responsibility for procuring equipment and supplies for use in the organization.

PURCHASING COOPERATIVE See *consumer cooperative*

PURCHASING POWER See *buying power*

PURE COMPETITION See *perfect competition*

PURE FOOD AND DRUG ACT (1906) See *Food and Drug Administration (FDA)* and *Federal Food and Drug Act (1906)*

PURE MARKET-DIRECTED ECONOMY See *economic system*

PURE MONOPOLY A market condition in which there is a single seller of a product or a single provider of a service and thus no competition.

PURELY COMPETITIVE MARKET STRUCTURE See *perfect competition*

PUSH MARKETING STRATEGY See *push strategy*

PUSH MONEY (PM) Bonus money paid as an incentive to push specially designated products. Push money is generally paid by a manufacturer to the salespersons employed by wholesalers and retailers and may also take the form of prizes such as appliances and vacation trips. Also called prize money.

PUSH MONEY ALLOWANCE See *push money (PM)*

PUSH OR PULL DISTRIBUTION STRATEGY See *pull strategy* and *push strategy*

PUSH STRATEGY A marketing distribution strategy in which a firm's promotional efforts are directed toward members of the channel of distribution, e.g., wholesalers, distributors, and retailers who are motivated (i.e., pushed) through such devices as ad-

vertising allowances and discounts to stock and sell the firm's products. See also *pull strategy.*

PUSH STRATEGY/PULL STRATEGY

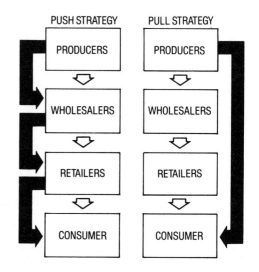

PUSHING STRATEGY See *push strategy*

PUT-OUT PRICING See *predatory pricing*

200

QUALIFIED PROSPECT In sales, a qualified prospect is a potential customer, whether a person or an organization, who not only is known to want, need, or potentially benefit from the product or service being sold, but who has the authority to make the purchase and the financial ability to pay for it. See also *lead* and *prospect*.

QUALIFYING DIMENSIONS The needs and preferences of the customer which are relevant to a product market and which help determine whether an individual or firm is a potential customer for a particular class of products, without determining which brand or specific product type the customer will select. Such factors as sufficient income to purchase the product, suitability of the product to meeting the customer's needs, and ability of the customer to use the product are qualifying dimensions. See also *determining dimensions*.

QUALITY Although essentially a relative term (it may be expressed as high, low, first-class, poor, etc.) quality most commonly refers to a degree of excellence or fineness—often in conformance to a preestablished standard.

QUALITY CONTROL An activity which includes the monitoring of products as they are produced in an effort to measure their quality, the comparison of the product to an established standard, and all subsequent efforts to maintain that standard.

In a narrower sense, quality control is sometimes used in reference to product inspection activities or is applied to the department having the responsibility for quality assurance.

QUALITY CREEP In new product development, the constant improvement of a product to the point where it is simply better than it needs to be to satisfy its target customers.

QUALITY RESPONSE FUNCTION See *response function*

QUANTITY DISCOUNT A reduction in price offered by the seller of goods as an inducement to the buyer to purchase large quantities.

QUANTITY PRICE DISCOUNT See *quantity discount*

QUESTION APPROACH A technique used by a salesperson in the first few minutes of contact with a prospect. In this approach, the salesperson gives the prospect an interesting fact about the product or service phrased as a question. This question is intended to stimulate the prospect's participation in the sales presentation. See also *approach*.

QUESTION MARK See *problem child*

QUESTIONNAIRE A data-gathering instrument (usually a printed form) used to collect information from respondents. Generally one of three methods is employed: 1) personal interview, 2) telephone interview, or 3) mail survey.

QUESTIONNAIRE METHOD See *survey*

QUICK RESPONSE A strategy in which a manufacturer or service industry makes an effort to supply its customers with products or services in the precise quantities required at exactly the right time. In the U.S. quick response operations are sometimes found in the soft goods industry where an attempt is made to shorten the cycle time in the textile maker/apparel manufacturer/retailer pipeline. See also *kanban* and *just-in-time (JIT) system*.

QUOTA A predetermined part or share of a total. In marketing, quota may mean a number of things, e.g., it may refer to a goal or objective (as in quotas for sales by staff), it may be used to mean a guideline (as in employment quotas for minority workers), or it may mean a share or maximum number (as in import quotas for particular products). See also *trade quota*.

QUOTA BONUS PLAN For salespeople, a compensation plan in which a base salary is paid without regard to productivity, but which also includes a bonus when a fixed quota of sales is exceeded.

QUOTA SAMPLE A type of nonprobability sample in which the interviewers are given specific numbers of subjects to find and interview in each of several categories. Participants are selected on the basis of characteristics thought pertinent to the study. For example, a researcher may be told to find twenty women between thirty-five and forty years old, half of whom are employed and half of whom are homemakers. See also *nonprobability sampling*.

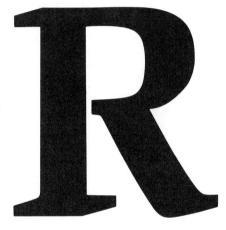

RACHET EFFECT See *ratchet effect*

RACK JOBBER A limited-service wholesaler who sells specialized merchandise, e.g., books, pantyhose, records, sunglasses, etc. to supermarkets, drugstores, and other self-service retailers. The store provides the counter or floor space and the jobber sets up racks, stores merchandise, marks prices, and maintains stock levels through periodic calls. The rack jobber is a consignment wholesaler in that he is paid only for goods actually sold by the retailer who, in turn, keeps a percentage of the profit. Also known as service merchandisers.

RAIL-TRAILER SHIPMENT See *piggyback*

RANDOM ERROR In sampling, a mistake, generally statistical, due to blind chance. A certain amount of random error is present in all samples.

RANDOM SAMPLE See *random sampling*

RANDOM SAMPLING In marketing research, a method of selecting a representative subset of the total population in which each member of the population has a known and equal chance of being included in the sample group. The members are selected on an objective basis, such as every tenth name on a list. Random sampling is one form of probability sampling.

RAPID INFLATION See *inflation*

RAPID RETURN ON INVESTMENT See *profit maximization objective* and *return on investment (ROI)*

RATCHET EFFECT An economic condition which sometimes accompanies inflation in which prices continue to advance despite a reduction in demand. The term ratchet refers to the toothed wheel equipped with a device called a pawl which allows motion in one direction only.

RATIONAL BUYING MOTIVE Any factor affecting a consumer's decision to buy merchandise or services which is based on logic, reason, and careful thought. See also *motive* and *emotional buying motive.*

RAW MATERIALS Materials in their unprocessed natural state (e.g., iron ore), or in a semi-finished state (e.g., pig iron), used in the production of other goods. Raw materials may be produced (such as cotton, grain, and livestock), or they may be extracted (such as lumber, ore, or fish).

REACH The number of readers or viewers who are exposed to a medium, e.g., radio, television, magazines, newspapers, at least once in a given period of time. Reach is a term commonly used in advertising to describe the breadth of coverage of a single advertisement, a series of advertisements, or an entire advertising campaign. Also known as media coverage.

REACTIVE SELLING A sales effort in which customers are allowed to take the initiative in seeking out a vendor. See also *proactive selling.*

READERS PER COPY See *passalong rate*

REAL INCOME Income (whether that of an individual, group, or country) expressed in terms of purchasing power rather than dollars. Real income is a useful concept when incomes are compared over time and price levels have changed, e.g., price increases between 1970 and 1980 reduced the value of dollar increases in salaries during that period by about half.

REBATE A reduction in price granted the buyer of goods (wholesaler, retailer, or consumer) by the manufacturer or producer of the goods for the purpose of encouraging sales. The rebate is generally made as a cash refund sent to the buyer after the transaction has been completed at the regular price. Also known as a money refund offer.

RECALL TEST See *aided recall* and *unaided recall*

RECEIPT OF GOODS DATING An invoice agreement specifying that the discount period allowed by the seller to the buyer does not begin until the goods are actually received by the buyer.

RECEIVER In communications, the recipient of a message.

RECESSION See *business cycle*

RECIPROCAL BUYING See *reciprocity*

RECIPROCITY An arrangement commonly found in industrial purchasing in which two organizations buy each other's products. Simple reciprocity (sometimes called innocent reciprocity) in which there is no effort on the part of one firm to dominate another, may degenerate into coercive reciprocity if one firm attempts to force a subordinate firm to purchase its products.

RECOVERY See *business cycle*

REDUCED-PRICE PACK A package conspicuously marked with a price lower than regular retail.

REFERENCE GROUP Those persons from whom an individual derives his values, standards, tastes, etc. and on whom the individual molds his attitudes and behavior; i.e., a group that forms a basis of comparison for the individual. A person need not belong to a group nor have direct contact with it for it to serve as a reference group. In fact, certain groups exert a negative influence in that an individual, in an attempt to avoid identification with the group, avoids certain kinds of behavior. See also *membership group, dissociative group,* and *aspirational group.*

REFERRAL APPROACH A technique used by a salesperson in the first few minutes of contact with a prospect. In this approach, the salesperson mentions the name of someone known to the prospect who has referred the salesperson to him as someone who might be interested in the good or service being sold. See also *approach.*

REFERRAL LEAD See *chain prospecting*

REFERRAL SAMPLE A form of nonprobability sample in which the research is done in waves, i.e., the first stage of the research uncovers other organizations or individuals who may be sampled in a second wave. Also called a snowball sample.

REFUND OFFER See *rebate*

REFUSAL-TO-SELL The right of a seller to refuse to sell merchandise to another party, e.g., a wholesaler or retailer, because that party fails to meet his standards or qualifications.

REGIOCENTRISM A decentralized form of organization, found in some multinational marketing firms, in which the marketing effort centers around regions rather than individual countries, on the one hand, or the entire world market, on the other. Such regions may be comprised of countries that possess any or all of the following criteria: 1) are contiguous to each other; 2) share a common lan-

guage; 3) are at similar levels of economic development; and/or 4) belong to the same economic community. See also *geocentrism.*

REGIONAL COOPERATION GROUPS An association of two or more countries cooperating in one or more joint ventures. Each country contributes to the financing of the project and agrees to buy a percentage of the project's output.

REGIONAL SHOPPING CENTER The largest of the shopping centers, usually anchored by one or more full-line department stores and complemented by as many as 150 or more smaller retail stores and related businesses. Most regional centers have a gross leasable area of 400,000 square feet or more—centers having over 750,000 square feet are regarded as super-regionals and are generally anchored by three or more department stores. Most regional centers need a surrounding population of at least 150,000 to operate profitably. Their radius of attraction is in the 10–15 mile range. See also *shopping center.*

REGRESSION STAGE See *fashion cycle*

REGRESSION ANALYSIS In causal research, regression analysis is the attempt to project the future levels of one unknown variable, such as sales, on the basis of forecasts for one or more known variables, such as disposable personal income. Variables are selected on the basis of whether a relationship between them has been observed in the past.

REGRESSION STAGE See *fashion cycle*

REGROUPING ACTIVITIES See *sorting process*

REGULARLY UNSOUGHT GOODS Products that are regularly needed by consumers, but which they will not extend themselves to find. For example, gravestones, insurance, and encyclopedias are all regularly unsought goods. This class of goods requires extensive promotion. See also *unsought goods.*

REILLY'S LAW OF RETAIL GRAVITATION A theory concerning the relative pull of two competing shopping areas on potential customers residing between them. Proposes that customers will be drawn from the intermediate town at, or close to, the point of equal probability, approximately in direct proportion to the populations of the two shopping areas and in direct proportion to the squares of the distance between the town and the two shopping areas.

REINFORCEMENT In the learning process, reinforcement is the presentation of a reward or satisfaction of a need following a particular response. The reward, or reinforcer, reduces the tension of the original drive and strengthens the relationship between the cue and the response. This results in an increase of that behavior, so that a similar response may be given the next time the drive occurs. Repeated reinforcement may lead to the development of a habit, thus making the decision-making process routine for the individual. For example, an individual experiencing thirst (a drive) may encounter a billboard advertising a particular brand of soft drink (a cue) while driving along the highway. If the individual's response is to purchase that brand of soft drink, and if the beverage satisfies the initial drive, reinforcement will occur. In the future, the individual may find it quicker to satisfy the same need with the same soft drink, and may be said to have developed a liking for the product. If, on the other hand, the beverage failed to satisfy the individual's thirst, the experience is unsatisfactory, and the individual may be said to have developed a dislike for the product. See also *reinforcement advertising.*

REINFORCEMENT ADVERTISING Advertising which assures the purchaser of a product that he has made a wise choice and informs him on ways in which he may derive the most satisfaction from his choice.

REINFORCER See *reinforcement*

REJECTION See *brand rejection*

RELATIVE ADVANTAGE In new product development, relative advantage is the degree to which the product is viewed by potential customers to be superior to all the products available for sale in the marketplace.

RELATIVE MARKET SHARE The share of the market held by a firm or product as compared to the market shares of competitors.

RELEVANT MARKET In strategic planning, a market selected as best corresponding to a firm's own purposes. The relevant market offers opportunities for the firm to obtain its objectives given its available resources. The relevant market selected should be bigger than the firm's current market, thus allowing for expansion. It should not, however, be so large that the firm would be unable to become a significant competitor in the new market. For example, a small manufacturer of children's clothing that distributes its goods locally may have the production and/or marketing capability to expand to a national market. However, worldwide distribution may be considerably beyond the company's grasp. See also *market* and *strategic planning.*

RELIABILITY In marketing research, reliability is the accuracy with which data portrays reality, particularly when a sample group is studied in order to make generalizations about a total population. See also *sampling*.

REMARKETING A strategy aimed at reviving demand for a product which has been in a state of decline. For example, space heaters for use in the home were remarketed as the cost of heating oil increased.

REMERCHANDISING A strategy to improve the salability of a product while leaving the product itself unchanged. Changes are made instead in the accompanying services (such as standardization of product quality, improvement of product service, and the provision of promotional guarantees). Packaging may also be modified in design, cost, and size of package. Branding, the broadening of price points, and an increase in the variety of styles offered may also be used to increase the market share of the product.

REMINDER ADVERTISING A form of competitive advertising calculated to keep a product, service, industry, viewpoint, etc. in the public eye. It reinforces previous promotional efforts and, in the case of products, is generally used at the maturity stage in the product life cycle. Sometimes called retentive advertising.

RENTED GOODS SERVICE 1) A category of consumer service in which a product is rented or leased for a specified period, e.g., automobile rentals. 2) In retailing, a service firm or department in a store renting products at a fee to customers for their temporary use, e.g., the rental of rug shampooing equipment by supermarkets.

REORDER POINT (ROP) The pre-established minimum inventory levels at which additional orders should be placed for a particular item so as to avoid going into an out-of-stock position. Also known as threshold-point ordering.

REPOSITIONING A marketing strategy designed to increase the consumption of an already existing product by changing its target market. For example, the product may be repositioned to appeal to a larger or faster-growing market segment. Brands, too, may require repositioning. Shifting customer preferences and/or a competitor's incursions into the brand's original market may leave a company's brand with diminished demand and a smaller share of the market. In order to capture a new target market and increase sales, a company will select a new group of consumers to whom it gears its advertising and other promotional activities. As with the original selection of a target market, the new target group is selected on the basis of the number of potential customers in the group, their average purchase rate of similar products, the quality and quantity of competitors in the segment, and the pricing structure of the brands in the new segment. See also *market positioning*.

RESALE PRICE MAINTENANCE (RPM) 1) A trade practice in which manufacturers or suppliers attempt to control the price at which their products will be sold at subsequent steps of distribution. Interstate price maintenance agreements, which were most commonly imposed on retailers, have been terminated by the *Consumer Goods Pricing Act* of 1975. Also known as fair trade, vertical price fixing, and retail price maintenance. 2) Resale price maintenance is also used to describe the laws enacted by some states to control the minimum price at which specific products may be sold at retail, e.g., milk.

207

RESEARCH DESIGN The formal model or plan for the conduct of a research study. The research design usually states the hypothesis to be tested, the research method to be employed, and the manner in which the collected data is to be analyzed.

RESELLER BRAND See *private brand*

RESELLER MARKET Those marketing intermediaries such as wholesalers, distributors, and retailers who buy finished goods for the purpose of reselling them. Resellers generally do not significantly alter the goods they sell nor do they incorporate them into other products.

RESERVE STOCK A supply of merchandise kept in inventory to avoid going into an out-of-stock condition. Also called "safety stock."

RESIDENT BUYER A market representative employed in a resident buying office which, in turn, acts as an agent for its clients and member stores. The resident buyer is often a specialist, buying in a particular segment of the market. Once the merchandise has been purchased the resident buyer, unlike the store buyer, has no further merchandising responsibilities, i.e., he or she does not have to resell the merchandise as does the retailer.

RESIDENT BUYING OFFICE A purchasing agent located in a national or international market center whose representatives shop the market daily in order to provide their clients or member stores with information and to select and buy merchandise for them. Buying offices are either independent (the salaried office and the commision buying office) or store-owned (the private office, the cooperative office, and the corporate office).

The resident buyer-client relationship is most commonly found in the apparel industry.

RESOURCE See *vendor*

RESOURCES See *tangible resources* and *intangible resources*

RESPONSE 1) In communications, the response to a message is the reaction on the part of the receiver. 2) In consumer behavior, the individual reaction to environmental cues.

RESPONSE FUNCTION A mathematical and/or graphic representation of ways in which a firm's target market is expected to react to changes in particular marketing variables. The response function is usually plotted as a curve, showing how sales and profits will vary at different levels of marketing expenditures, changes in prices, changes in promotional mixes, changes in the level of quality, etc. A response function may be plotted for each of the 4 Ps of the marketing mix, or for the marketing mix as a whole. The response functions for each of the 4 Ps are as follows: 1) A product-quality response function demonstrates how a product's quality and the features it contains will influence sales. Since, however, additional quality and features will also increase production costs, the profit response function may reach a high point and then decline. The best level for product quality, therefore, will be the high point achieved prior to the decline. Also called quality response function. 2) The place-distribution intensity response function illustrates the desired degree of market exposure, which may range from exclusive distribution to intensive distribution. Since sales may level off as the extreme end of intensive distribution is approached and most outlets already carry the product, the response function shows that little increase in sales can be expected from the last few marginal outlets. Also called distribution intensity response function. 3) A promotion-advertising response function shows the increase in sales that would follow from advertising. Although, through personal selling and other promotional efforts, some sales would occur with absolutely no advertising, sales will increase with additional advertising up to a certain point as demonstrated on the curve. Where sales begin to level off, and perhaps even decline, additional advertising becomes undesirable. Also called advertising response function and promotion response function. 4) A price-demand response function shows the impact of price level variations on sales and the quantity of goods sold. Ultimately, the price-demand response function illustrates that it is not possible to expand total dollar sales indefinitely through price cutting. Also called price-demand curve response function, price-oriented response function, and price response function. The response function for the total marketing mix would be the result of all the mix ingredients. Marketing planning involves selecting the best response function based on the firm's own resources and objectives.

RESPONSIBILITY In organizations, responsibility defines the job to be done by an individual, including the measurement of the individual's performance. The responsibilities of any given job are generally defined in the job description, as is the degree of power or authority associated with that position.

RESTRAINT OF TRADE An act or agreement which is calculated to limit the free exercise of commercial competition. Restraint of trade often takes the form of monopolies, attempts by one or more parties to control prices or levels of production, or other restraints on free trade to the detriment of the public.

RETAIL ADVERTISING See *local advertising*

RETAIL CATALOG SHOWROOM See *catalog showroom*

RETAIL COOPERATIVE A voluntary association of independent retailers who jointly own and operate their own wholesale facilities and/or who act together as a buying club in order to achieve the economies of large scale purchasing. The member stores often display a common emblem or logo and carry, in addition to nationally recognized brands, their own distributor brands. Also known as a retailer-owned cooperative, retailer-sponsored cooperative, and a retailer's cooperative chain. See also *voluntary chain* and *consumer cooperative*.

RETAIL COOPERATIVE CHAIN See *retail cooperative*

RETAIL DEAL See *deal*

RETAIL LIFE CYCLE A theory which attempts to describe the evolution of a retail store from its inception to its decline. The theory maintains that a retail establishment passes through four identifiable stages: 1) innovation, 2) accelerated development, 3) maturity, and 4) decline. In the innovation stage, the store (or type of store) is new and must be introduced to customers in hopes that it will attract a following. If the store or concept catches on, it enters a period of rapid growth (accelerated development) in which other retailers imitate or adopt the store's concept and seek to attract the same target customers. The store itself may experience rapid growth in sales and popularity. As competitors enter the market by using the same or similar strategies, the market eventually approaches saturation, and growth slows. The store enters the maturity stage. Once growth has significantly decreased or even ceased, the decline stage follows. This is comparable to the product life cycle. See also *product life cycle (PLC)* and *wheel of retailing theory.*

RETAIL MARKETING A concept in which sales goals are set on the basis of market potential with increased attention to the behavior of the consumer. While merchandising has lines and departments as its point of focus, i.e., what is selling, retail marketing is more concerned with who is buying what and the underlying reasons for this behavior.

RETAIL PRICE INDEX See *Consumer Price Index (CPI)*

RETAIL PRICE MAINTENANCE See *resale price maintenance*

RETAIL SALE See *retail transaction*

RETAIL-SPONSORED COOPERATIVE See *retail cooperative*

RETAIL STORE See *store*

RETAIL TRADING AREA See *trading area*

RETAIL TRANSACTION A sale made to an ultimate consumer. Such sales are retail transactions regardless of how the outlet describes itself, e.g., a wholesaler making sales to the ultimate consumer is engaged in a retail transaction.

RETAILER A merchant intermediary (either an individual or a firm) engaged in selling goods or services to the ultimate consumer. The term is sometimes restricted to enterprises which generate one half of their total income from such sales.

RETAILER COUPON A coupon, usually of the "cents-off" variety, distributed by a retailer through advertisements. Since the objective of the promotion is to build customer traffic the coupon is redeemable only in the store running the promotion. See also *coupon.*

RETAILER-OWNED COOPERATIVE See *retail cooperative*

RETAILER-SPONSORED COOPERATIVE See *retail cooperative*

RETAILER'S COOPERATIVE CHAIN See *retail cooperative*

RETAILING That business activity concerned with the selling of goods and/or services to the ultimate consumer for his personal or household use. Retailing activities are commonly conducted in stores, but telephone and mail-order sales, automatic merchandising, in-home selling, and street vending are all forms of retailing and represent the final step in the marketing process.

RETAILING COOPERATIVE See *retail cooperative*

RETAILING CYCLE See *retail life cycle*

RETAILING MIX A retail store's particular combination of controllable variables that give it its distinct image and position in the marketplace. These variables include product, price, promotions, place, operating policy, buying, human resources, service, etc. See also *marketing mix.*

RETAILING MIX

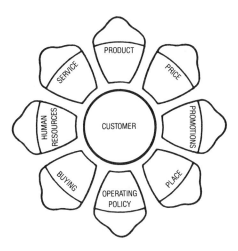

RETENTIVE ADVERTISING See *reminder advertising*

RETURN See *returns*

RETURN ON ASSETS (ROA) A measure of the profitability of a business which compares the net profit (after taxes) to the assets of the business used to generate that net profit.

$$ROA = \frac{\text{Net profit}}{\text{Assets used}}$$

The result is then multiplied by 100. See also *return on investment (ROI)*.

RETURN ON INVESTMENT (ROI) A measure of the profitability of a business which compares the net profit to the amount of money needed to operate the business and, by extension, create that profit.

$$ROI = \frac{\text{Net profit}}{\text{Amount of investment}}$$

See also *return on assets (ROA)*.

RETURN ON INVESTMENT PRICE A selling price which will generate a predetermined margin of profit which represents a desired return on investment.

RETURNS Goods bought or sent back to the vendor by the customer. The vendor may exchange the merchandise for the customer, give a cash refund, or credit the customer's account. The term applies equally to goods returned by consumers to retail establishments and to goods returned by retailers to manufacturers or wholesalers. Returns are generated by such factors as delay in delivery, defective goods, customer dissatisfaction, etc.

REVALUATION An increase in the value of a nation's currency, undertaken by the government of that nation, in relation to other currencies or to gold. A revaluation is designed to bring a nation's currency more into line with other currencies so as to facilitate international trade. See also *devaluation.*

REVENUE A term lacking a single precise definition, revenue is generally taken to mean either 1) the total income derived from the sale of a firm's products or services together with earnings derived from interest, rents, etc.; or 2) the gross intake of a unit of government from such sources as taxes, duties, fines, etc.

REVENUE-ORIENTED AUDIT An evaluation of a marketing plan in terms of the program's ability to generate sales of the product. See also *marketing audit.*

REVERSE DISTRIBUTION See *backward channel*

REVIEW AUDIT See *marketing audit*

REVOLVING CREDIT A regular 30-day charge account which may be paid in full or in monthly installments. If paid in full within 30 days of the date of the statement, there is no finance charge. When installment payments are made, a finance charge is assessed on the balance at the time of the next billing. The customer may continue to add new purchases to the account until the credit limit is reached.

RIBBON DEVELOPMENT See *strip shopping center*

RISK AVERSION PRICING A pricing strategy aimed at the elimination (or at least the reduction) of risk and uncertainty in the marketing environment through the careful analysis of all available marketing intelligence. The basis of the strategy is the development of clearly stated price policies aimed at maximizing profits.

RISK REDUCTION In the consumers buying process, risk reduction is the customer's attempt to solve a problem and make a purchase while cutting down on the uncertainties associated with the product or service. Marketers assist in reducing the customer's sense of risk by providing information about their products and services, explaining the uses and functions of their products and services, and otherwise assisting the customer in making an acceptable choice. Since the customer's sense of risk tends to be greatest when purchasing complex, high-priced goods, marketers of such items are more likely to provide such ancillary services as training, installation, and consultation. In the purchase of home computers, for example, most customers are dealing with a highly complex and high-priced item of which they have little or no prior knowledge or experience. Trained sales personnel, training sessions, support services, warranties, etc. help to reassure the customer by reducing the risk involved in the purchase.

RISK TAKING One of the facilitating marketing functions. Risk taking includes handling the uncertainties that are part of the marketing process and exposing oneself and one's firm to the chance of loss or failure. See also *facilitating marketing functions.*

ROA See *return on assets (ROA)*

ROBINSON-PATMAN ACT A revision of Section 2 of the Clayton Act, the Robinson-Patman Act was, at the time of its passage in 1936, commonly called "The Price Discrimination Chain Store Act."

The act prohibits vendors from providing "extraordinary" quantity discounts to large volume retailers, thus affording some protection to small businesses by limiting the large retailer's buying strength and price advantages. The Act forbids a manufacturer engaging in interstate commerce from selling to similar customers at different prices if both sales involve products of the same quality and grade and if the resultant price difference serves to substantially lessen competition or create a monopoly. Certain quantity discounts are allowed, as are different prices for private vs. national brands, even if the only difference between them is the label. The Act is administered by the Federal Trade Commission.

ROG DATING See *receipt of good dating*

ROI See *return on investment (ROI)*

ROLE The rights, duties, actions, and activities, appropriate to a person who occupies a particular position in a group or in society at large.

ROLL OUT The extension of the physical distribution and promotion of a product to a wider geographical area. Thus a firm marketing its products regionally may seek a national market. The firm is then said to have "rolled out" to a national distribution.

ROP See *reorder point (ROP)*

ROUTINE CONSUMER DECISION MAKING In consumer behavior, decisions which require little deliberation and planning because of the routine nature of the purchase. Goods involved are generally low-cost and carry no perceived risk to the consumer.

ROUTINE ORDER TAKING See *order-taker*

ROUTINIZED RESPONSE BEHAVIOR See *routine consumer decision making*

RPM See *resale price maintenance (RPM)*

RULE FOR MAXIMIZING PROFIT A method to calculate a firm's optimum output so that the marginal cost is just less than equal to the marginal revenue. Total cost and total revenue may also be used to calculate the optimum output. See also *profit maximization.*

RUNAWAY INFLATION See *inflation*

S-CURVE EFFECT A graphic representation of the decline in sales which follows the withdrawal of advertising support for a product.

SAFETY NEEDS Those of an individual's needs which are concerned with basic protection and physical well-being. Safety needs include health, food, medicine, exercise, etc. See also *needs* and *Maslow's hierarchy*.

SAFETY STOCK See *reserve stock*

SALARIED BUYING OFFICE See *resident buying office*

SALARIED OFFICE See *resident buying office*

SALARY PLAN See *straight salary*

SALARY PLUS COMMISSION See *commission*

SALES ADMINISTRATION See *sales management*

SALES AGENT See *selling agent*

SALES ANALYSIS The actual examination of a firm's sales results, generally in terms of territory, product classification, type of customer, cost of sales, order size, or other measure. A primary objective of sales analysis is to detect marketing problems before they become acute and to facilitate the marketing management function.

SALES AND MARKETING EXECUTIVES INTERNATIONAL (SMEI) An association of executives in sales, marketing management, and related fields. The association promotes research in the fields of selling and sales management. It sponsors a Sales Management Institute as well as various workshops, career education programs, clinics, and seminars. SMEI also offers a Graduate School of Sales Management and Marketing at Syracuse University in New York. With affiliates in 49 countries, SMEI

also seeks to facilitate foreign trade through the international exchange of marketing information. The association publishes *Marketing Times,* a bimonthly journal and an *Annual Report and Directory.* SMEI is based in Cleveland, Ohio.

SALES APPROACH See *approach*

SALES BRANCH See *manufacturer's branch office*

SALES BUDGET See *budget* and *sales expense budget*

SALES COMPENSATION Money paid to salespeople. May be in the form of straight commission, salary, or a combination of the two.

SALES CONCEPT See *selling concept*

SALES CONTEST A manufacturer or dealer sponsored competition in which superior sales efforts are rewarded with prizes. Competitors may be members of the producer's sales force or may be employed by other marketing intermediaries.

SALES-DECAY CONSTANT See *advertising sales-response and decay model*

SALES ERA OF MARKETING A stage in the evolution of marketing (following the production era) during which the roles of advertising and the sales force were expanded in an effort to create consumer demand for products. No genuine effort was made to determine the consumer's needs before goods were produced.

SALES EXCEPTION REPORTING A form of sales analysis in which products are reported as slow-selling and fast-selling. Used by managers to evaluate the accuracy of sales forecasts.

SALES EXPENSE BUDGET A budget which allocates expenditures

relating to personal selling activities. Included are salaries, commissions, incentives, and expense account charges as well as the cost of managing the sales operation. Such activities as sales meetings are also included. See also *budget.*

SALES FINANCE COMPANY 1) An institution which finances inventories, thus assisting the marketer with the financing function. Floor planning is one method used by sales finance companies. See also *financing function* and *floor plan financing.* 2) In retailing, a sales finance company is a financial institution which takes over a retailer's "paper" at a discount rate. The finance company buys retail installment contracts at somewhat less than their full value and assumes responsibility for collections.

SALES FORCE A term generally applied to a firm's field sales organization, i.e., those salespersons and their immediate supervisors who have direct contact with customers and who perform the selling function.

SALES FORCE COMPOSITE A build-up, or bottom-up, approach to sales forecasting in which the firm's sales force estimates potential sales in their individual territories. This information is added together to form a comprehensive sales forecast for the company.

SALES FORCE FORECASTING SURVEY See *sales force composite*

SALES FORCE INDOCTRINATION The initial phase of sales training which covers knowledge of the company, its products, policies, and promotional support. Indoctrination also may encompass knowledge of the marketing environment and the competition. Finally, sales force indoctrination covers fundamental selling skills, and the principles of time and territory management (where applicable). See also *sales training*.

SALES FORCE MANAGEMENT See *sales management*

SALES FORECASTING An attempt, on the basis of subjective and/or statistical methods of research, to predict the market response to a product or group of products or to predict the performance of an entire division or company. This predictive effort results in a sales forecast which provides the firm with a reliable guide for planning and efficient production.

SALES INDOCTRINATION See *sales force indoctrination*

SALES MANAGEMENT Those management efforts directed toward the development of a sales force (recruiting, selecting, and training) and its maintenance (planning, supervision, and motivation) which, taken together, will provide the firm with salespersons who are able to achieve the dollar volume necessary for profitable operation.

SALES MANAGEMENT DEVELOPMENT TRAINING That stage in sales training in which sales personnel are taught to perfect their selling skills and prepare to become sales managers. Sales management development training focuses on developing administrative, decision-making, and leadership skills. See also *sales training*.

SALES MANAGEMENT TRAINING See *sales management development training*

SALES MANAGER A line marketing executive responsible for directing sales force activity. Principal duties fall into six major areas: recruitment, selection, training, planning, supervision, and motivation. The sales manager may set levels of compensation for the members of his sales force and, in some organizations, may also have such broad responsibilities as planning and developing advertising and sales promotion programs, developing positive customer relations, etc. See also *advertising sales manager* and *department manager.*

SALES OBJECTIVES A clear statement of the tasks to be performed by the salespeople in a firm. Objectives may be expressed in terms of total sales in dollars or units, as increases over past results, or in number of sales calls completed, etc. See also *sales quota.*

SALES OFFICE See *manufacturer's sales office*

SALES-ORIENTED OBJECTIVE See *sales quota*

SALES-ORIENTED ORGANIZATION See *selling concept*

SALES PERFORMANCE INDEX See *performance index*

SALES POTENTIAL A measure of the total amount of goods or services a particular firm might reasonably be expected to sell in the marketplace over a specified time period and to a particular market segment. See also *market share* and *market potential.*

SALES PRESENTATION That stage in the selling process during which the salesperson presents the product, service or idea, explains its benefits, and attempts to convince the prospect to accept the promises being made and to make a purchase.

SALES PROMOTION Short-term non-recurrent efforts to increase buying response on the part of the consumers or to intensify sales efforts by the firm's sales force or resellers in the distribution channel. When directed at the sales force, the promotions may take the form of sales contests, bonuses, incentive gifts, prizes, etc. When directed at resellers (i.e., middlemen and retailers), the effort often takes the form of buying allowances, free goods, cooperative advertising money, push money, sales contests, etc. Sales promotion at the retail level is commonly taken to include advertising, visual merchandising (display), public relations (including publicity), special events, and the selling efforts of the store's sales people. Specific incentives such as coupons, trading stamps, price-off deals, demonstrations, samples, premiums, etc. may also be offered to the ultimate consumer as a stimulus to purchase.

SALES PROMOTION MANAGER The individual within a firm responsible for filling the gaps between the sales and advertising managers and handling the firm's diversified sales promotion activities. In some organizations, sales promotion managers are responsible to the sales manager, while in others they are responsible to the marketing manager.

SALES PROMOTION PROGRAM See *sales promotion*

SALES QUOTA A performance standard in the form of a specific goal or objective set by management for its sales staff. It may be applied to individuals, departments, divisions, or other marketing units. The sales quota is set for a specific time period and may be based on a percentage of total sales, the number of customers serviced, the number of units sold, etc.

SALES REPRESENTATIVE Generally applied to a salesperson who sells a manufacturer's product in a particular territory. Sometimes called manufacturer's representatives, these salespeople may sell to industrial customers, wholesalers and retailers, or,

in some cases, to the ultimate consumer.

SALES-RESPONSE AND DECAY MODEL See *advertising sales-response and decay model*

SALES-RESPONSE CONSTANT See *advertising sales-response and decay model*

SALES-RESULTS TEST An effort to measure the impact on sales of a particular advertisement or advertising campaign.

SALES REVENUE The total income derived from sales for a given period.

SALES STAFF See *sales force*

SALES TERRITORY A geographical area assigned to a salesperson (or group of salespeople) in which they have the responsibility for selling the firm's products.

SALES TRAINEE See *sales training*

SALES TRAINING A company's systematic program of training sales personnel. The objective of such a program is to increase sales and reduce costs by maximizing the effectiveness and efficiency of the sales force. The company must first identify and analyze its needs and objectives. This allows priorities to be established and specific programs to be set in motion. The company must also determine the type of learning required, the specific training time allowed, and the training methods to be employed. Each of these elements varies considerably from company to company, depending on the nature of the product or service being sold and related factors. In most companies, training and development includes initial indoctrination and training of sales employees (or trainees), advanced training on an ongoing basis, and management development training (for potential sales managers). Trainers may be drawn from sales management, staff training personnel, experienced salespeople, or outside specialists. Training may take place within the firm itself, in the field, or at outside locations (such as college campuses, hotel seminars, etc.).

SALES VOLUME ANALYSIS A technique employed to evaluate an organization's performance in the marketplace. Sales volume analysis simply measures the target market's reaction to the firm's offerings.

SALES WAVES TEST A technique employed in market testing in which a product is placed in a consumer's home on a trial basis and made available for purchase. Over a period of time, it is believed, repurchase activity on the part of the selected consumers will approximate the actual usage which might be expected should the product be introduced into the marketplace.

SALESMANSHIP See *personal selling*

SALESPERSON A broad term which includes a variety of order-takers, sales employees at both the wholesale and retail levels of the market, manufacturer's representatives and sales engineers, missionary salespeople, and detailers, etc.

SAMPLE See *sampling*

SAMPLE FRAME In sampling, that part of the target population which is actually studied. See also *sampling.*

SAMPLE SET See *population*

SAMPLE SIZE The number of people, companies, or other units surveyed in marketing research.

SAMPLING 1) In marketing research, sampling is the process of selecting a representative subset of a total population for obtaining data useful in the study of the whole population. The subset is known as the sample. Inferences about the characteristics of the population as a whole are drawn from the characteristics of the sample. The total population is known as a universe. The study of the characteristics and attitudes of the sample are meant to decrease the time and costs involved in studying the total universe, and may actually be more accurate. All marketing research samples fall into one of two major classes: probability samples and nonprobability samples. Probability samples are those that are selected randomly, so that each member of the total population has an equal and quantifiable chance of being selected. In nonprobability samples, the judgment of the researcher enters into the selection process. See also *nonprobability sampling, probability sampling, random sampling,* and *stratified sampling.* 2) In sales promotion, sampling is the distribution of a product to a consumer free of charge in an effort to encourage trial use of the product and bolster consumer demand. Samples may be placed with channel intermediaries, or given directly to end users, as is often done in direct mail marketing.

SAMPLING BUYING In industrial buying, the practice of purchasing a product after examining a portion of the potential shipment for quality. This kind of buying is often used in grain markets.

SAMPLING ERRORS Mistakes (or errors) in the marketing research sample itself, causing it to be unrepresentative of the universe from which it is drawn. See also *nonsampling errors.*

SAMPLING PLAN The design of marketing research which specifies the composition of the sampling unit, sample size, and sampling procedure (probability or nonprobability). See also *sampling*.

SAMPLING PRINCIPLE The concept that if a small number of units (otherwise known as the sample) is chosen at random from the total population or universe being studied, the sample will tend to have the same characteristics, and in the same proportion, as the universe. See also *sampling*.

SAMPLING PROCEDURE The process of selecting the respondents to be studied and interviewed in marketing research. This may be done through probability samples or nonprobability samples.

SAMPLING UNIT The segment of the total population that is to be sampled in marketing research.

SATISFIER See *motive*

SATURATED MARKET A condition in the marketplace in which there is a greater supply of a particular product than there is demand. A firm's product can gain market share only at the expense of another product.

SBD See *secondary business district (SBD)*

SBU See *strategic business unit (SBU)*

SCIENTIFIC MARKETING See *analytical marketing system*

SCIENTIFIC METHOD A research approach applicable to both the sciences and the social sciences, of which marketing research is a part. The scientific method consists of four stages: 1) observation, 2) developing a hypothesis or series of hypotheses, 3) predicting an outcome or future, and 4) testing the hypothesis or hypotheses. In marketing research, the scientific method is usually applied as follows: 1) definition of the problem, 2) situation analysis, 3) informal investigation, and 4) formal research. See also *marketing research*.

SCRAMBLED MERCHANDISING In retailing, the practice of offering merchandise for sale which is not usually associated with a particular kind of store, e.g., the sale of many non-food items in supermarkets. In scrambled merchandising, the lines added to the merchandise mix will generally be fast sellers which carry a high margin of profit.

SCREENING STAGE In new product development, the stage at which new ideas are evaluated to determine which ones may offer opportunities for development by the firm.

SEALED BID An offer to perform a service or to supply goods submitted to a buyer in a sealed envelope to be opened at a specified future time. Under this system competitive bids are not revealed publicly. Sealed bids are commonly required in government purchasing in an effort to get the lowest possible price.

SEALED BID PRICING A pricing strategy in which a firm sets the prices for its products on the basis of what it anticipates its competitors will bid.

SEASONAL DATING A method of dating invoices in which the manufacturer extends more liberal terms of credit to the retailer in order to sell goods well in advance of a particular season. See also *dating*.

SEASONAL DEMAND Consumer demand which is directly related to the season of the year or to special holidays such as Thanksgiving and Christmas.

SEASONAL DISCOUNT A reduction in price offered by a manufacturer to middlemen and retailers as an incentive to place their orders in advance of the normal buying period. Early orders enable manufacturers to even out their production schedules.

SEASONAL GOODS See *seasonal merchandise*

SEASONAL MERCHANDISE Goods closely identified with a particular season or holiday, e.g., Christmas decorations, bathing suits, antifreeze, etc. Seasonal merchandise commonly has a short sales life.

SECONDARY BUSINESS DISTRICT (SBD) An unplanned urban shopping area which often contains one or more supermarkets, a variety store, a small department store, and a number of small service stores. Secondary business districts are often found at the intersection of two main streets.

SECONDARY DATA Information collected prior to the time a particular problem is defined. Secondary data may be internal to the organization (company files, etc.) or external (collected by such agencies as the U.S. Bureau of the Census or private sector marketing research firms).

SECONDARY INFORMATION See *secondary data*

SECONDARY NEEDS Among the basic motivations which cause individual consumers to make purchase decisions, secondary needs are those which result from the particular culture or environment in which the individual lives, rather than from basic physiological factors such as thirst, hunger, and shelter. Secondary needs would include, therefore, the need for status, self-advancement, individual fulfillment, and other culturally determined factors. See also *needs, Maslow's hierarchy,* and *primary needs.*

SECONDARY SHOPPING DISTRICT See *secondary business district (SBD)*

SEGMENTATION See *market segmentation*

SEGMENTATION DESCRIPTORS In market segmentation studies, the descriptors are the individual units of analysis within each segment. For example, if the segment is a demographic characteristic such as race, the descriptors would be white, black, oriental, etc.

SEGMENTATION PRICING A strategy in which prices are set at different levels for different segments of the population. This legal form of price discrimination is commonly found in the airline industry (where different classes of service are provided for different segments of the traveling public) and in other industries where costs do not decline greatly when consumption or use declines.

SEGMENTATION VARIABLE A segmentation variable is a factor or characteristic which is attributable to a group and which makes it possible to differentiate that group from the total market. Residence, sex, and age are among the variables which are commonly used for this purpose.

SEGMENTER A marketing firm which employs either the single target market approach or the multiple target market approach (also called differentiated marketing) when developing a marketing strategy. See also *market segmentation* and *differentiated marketing.*

SELECTIVE ADVERTISING See *competitive advertising*

SELECTIVE DEMAND The market demand for a particular brand of merchandise as opposed to demand for the total class of products. For example, demand for Levi's jeans as opposed to demand for jeans in general. See also *primary demand.*

SELECTIVE DISTORTION See *selective perception*

220

SELECTIVE DISTRIBUTION A marketing strategy standing between exclusive distribution on the one hand and intensive distribution on the other. Manufacturers engaging in selective distribution restrict the number of middlemen and retailers who resell their product in a particular area in order to better control both the degree of exposure and the cost of distributing the product. Also called selective selling.

SELECTIVE EXPOSURE See *selective perception*

SELECTIVE PERCEPTION The ability of individuals to filter out certain sensory data, or stimuli, while retaining others. Marketers have learned that consumers tend to notice only a portion of the stimuli to which they are exposed (selective exposure), to selectively interpret the information they do receive (selective distortion), and remember only those perceptions that seem relevant to their own lives or current needs (selective retention). Consumers are also more likely to perceive stimuli they anticipate and those that show a major change in price, quality, or design. Marketers have devised various methods of overcoming selective perception, such as increasing the frequency with which advertising messages are repeated, creating unusual and attention-grabbing ads, varying the format of the ads run for any given product, etc. Some marketers have also experimented with the use of subliminal perception to reach consumers below the level of their conscious perception. See *perception, subliminal perception,* and *thresholds of perception.*

SELECTIVE RETENTION See *selective perception*

SELECTIVE SELLING See *selective distribution*

SELF-CONCEPT See *self-image*

SELF-IMAGE The mental picture an individual has of himself and the way he imagines others perceive him. Self-image, also called self-concept, includes characteristics, traits, possessions, role, behavior, etc., but emphasis is on the way these things are perceived rather than on the things themselves. An individual's ideal self, or ideal self-image, is the person the individual would like to be, or the end to which the individual is striving. An individual's others-self-concept is the way the individual thinks others perceive him. The problem for the marketer is to determine which concept of self will prompt the purchase of the product or service and how best to appeal to that concept. See also *motivation research.*

SELF-LIQUIDATING PREMIUM A consumer premium which is offered for sale in conjunction with the purchase of another product. It is self-liquidating in that its sale price is usually the premium's cost price to the firm running the promotion.

SELF-SELECTION A form of retail selling in which the customer is required to select the item he wants from the array of merchandise available on the selling floor and to then take the item to a salesperson who will complete the transaction. Cash registers are usually placed strategically around the store rather than concentrated at the exit as they are in self-service outlets. See also *self-service.*

SELF-SERVICE A form of retail selling in which merchandise is displayed so that the customer can make a selection without the aid of a salesperson. The customer then takes his purchases to a checkout point (usually near the exit of the store) where a cashier completes the transaction.

SELF-SERVICE RETAILING See *self-service*

SELLER CONCENTRATION The number of sellers in a single industry. The more sellers, the less likely it is that one firm can influence price.

SELLER'S MARKET An economic situation in which there is a shortage of goods and services so that demand exceeds supply. This situation favors sellers and gives them considerable power in the marketplace. It also tends to push prices upward. A company may create a seller's market intentionally by keeping production low so that prices and apparent desirability of the product remain high.

SELLING In a general sense, selling is simply the offering of goods or services for sale—thus, to be "in sales" is to be a professional salesperson. In a more restricted sense, selling may be regarded as a marketing function whose object is to arouse demand for a product on the part of potential customers. This may be a creative endeavor which includes advertising and other forms of promotion or it may be more mundane, e.g., the order-taking which so often passes for selling at the retail level.

SELLING AGAINST THE BRAND One is selling against the brand when artificially high prices are maintained on certain categories of merchandise in an effort to increase sales on some other merchandise. This tactic is sometimes employed by retailers in an effort to sell private label merchandise at the expense of manufacturer's brands.

SELLING AGENT An agent middleman who sells all the products of his client manufacturer under a contrac-

tual agreement, but who does not take title to the merchandise. He may also provide his client with market information for the extensive territory he covers. The selling agent has considerable authority with regard to prices, credit, delivery dates, and other terms of sale, and, in fact, is virtually in charge of the selling activities of the firm. See also *manufacturer's agent.*

SELLING CONCEPT A marketing management orientation in which persistent personal selling coupled with an aggressive advertising campaign is seen as the most effective way to build sales. Organizations influenced by the selling concept view high sales levels as meaning high profits and believe that customer demand can be generated for nearly any product if sufficient effort is expended.

SELLING EXPENSE BUDGET See *sales expense budget*

SELLING FORMULA APPROACH A technique used by salespersons, both in taking orders and receiving them, which combines the canned presentation with the benefit approach. The salesperson uses a prepared outline to take the customer through a series of logical steps building to a close. During the course of the presentation, however, the salesperson involves the customer in a discussion to help clarify the customer's needs. The salesperson demonstrates how the product will satisfy these specific needs and only then goes on to close the sale using one of several possible prepared closings. See also *canned presentation, approach* and *benefit approach.*

SELLING FUNCTION See *selling*

SELLING INTERMEDIARIES See *reseller market*

SELLING, PERSONAL See *personal selling*

SELLING PRICE The actual price the customer pays at the time the transaction is completed.

SELLING PROCESS A series of steps taken by a salesperson engaged in selling activities. These include prospecting, the preapproach and approach, the sales presentation, and finally the closing. Follow-up activities are sometimes included as a part of the selling process.

SELLING PROCESS

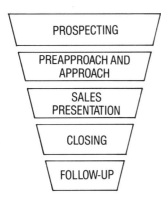

SELLING UP See *trading up*

SEMANTIC DIFFERENTIAL SCALE A technique used by marketers to determine and measure consumer attitudes. The scale consists of opposite pairs of words separated by a line divided into seven parts. Respondents check the space that most nearly describes their attitude. Thus a check in the fourth (or center) space indicates a neutral attitude and a check in the extreme position on either side indicates a strongly held point of view. After the test is completed, a researcher connects the checks to get a composite picture of the attitudes indicated.

SEMI-INTEGRATED ORGANIZA- TION See *retail cooperative*

SEMIMANUFACTURED GOODS Products which have required manufacturing (plate glass, insulation, textile fabrics, etc.) but which will be incorporated into another product.

SENDER In communications, the party transmitting a message. Also known as the source or the communicator.

SENSORY APPEAL Promotional efforts which appeal to the senses (sight, hearing, touch, taste, or smell) and are calculated to influence consumer behavior.

SERIES DISCOUNT A series discount is generally granted by manufacturers to retail stores. It is a price reduction taken on a base price which has already been reduced by a preceding discount. Several consecutive reductions are given, e.g., 35%, 5%, and 3.5%, each time on the new, lower base price. Also called a chain discount.

SERVED MARKET See *target market*

SERVICE See *services* and *customer services*

SERVICE APPROACH A technique used by a salesperson in the first few minutes of contact with a prospect. The salesperson promises to relieve the prospect of some work or responsibility through the product or service being sold. See also *approach*.

SERVICE BUSINESS Business organizations that sell services rather than tangible products.

SERVICE MARK A word, symbol, sign, design, or slogan which identifies a particular service. There is no significant difference between a trademark and a service mark.

SERVICE MERCHANDISER See *rack jobber*

SERVICE POSITIONING A market positioning strategy in which a service rather than a tangible product is established in the marketplace.

SERVICE SALESPERSON A salesperson concerned with such matters as delivery and installation and whose responsibilities generally begin after the sale has been consummated.

SERVICE WHOLESALER See *full-service wholesaler*

SERVICES Although services may sometimes be included in broad marketing definitions of the term product they are for the most part separately identifiable intangible activities or benefits. Services are just as real as physical products and may, in fact, be closely tied to the sale of a product (for example, service contracts on appliances), but they are essentially different in that services do not entail the permanent ownership of any tangible object on the part of the buyer.

Services may be offered for sale (for example, carpet cleaning) or may be provided free (for example, repair services under warranty).

At the retail level, services are activities which benefit the consumer and which are provided by the retailer to attract customers. Such services as layaway, personal shopping service, gift wrap, delivery, etc. may be free or may carry a charge. See also *customer services.*

SERVICES CONCEPT See *bundle of services concept*

SERVICES MARKETING Those activities which facilitate the sale or delivery of a service. Included are those services offered for profit by private concerns, those provided by government agencies, and those furnished by non-profit organizations. See also *marketing* and *services.*

SETTLEMENT DISCOUNT See *cash discount*

SHAPING In learning theory, a process in which a series of rewards or reinforcements are employed in an effort to form (or shape) an individual's behavior patterns.

SHARE OF AUDIENCE See *audience share*

SHARE OF THE MARKET See *market share*

SHARED SERVICES Common carriers, a combined captive sales force, or public warehousing are among those services which may be shared by two or more marketers at the same time. These services may be provided by one of the cooperating firms or by a third party.

SHERMAN ANTITRUST ACT (1890) Federal legislation intended to limit the growth of monopolies and the unlawful restraint of trade. There are two main provisions: 1) all contracts in restraint of trade are illegal, and 2) all attempts to monopolize any part of trade among the several states is a misdemeanor. This act is the basis for all U.S. antitrust activity, its major contribution being to turn restraint of trade into a federal offense.

SHIFTING LOYALS See *brand insistence*

SHOCK APPROACH A technique used by a salesperson in the first few minutes of contact with a prospect in which the salesperson uses a mild form of shock to gain the interest of the prospect. For example, an insurance salesperson may use the possibility of the death of a spouse as a shock to stimulate a prospect's interest in life insurance. See also *approach.*

SHOPKEEPER See *merchant* and *retailer*

SHOPLIFTING The act of stealing merchandise in a store by a person posing as a customer. One of several forms of retail crime classified as external theft.

SHOPPING CENTER A cluster of stores and related facilities (community rooms, restaurants, automobile service areas, parking lots, etc.) which have been planned and developed to serve a particular trading area. Shopping centers are managed as a unit and the component stores generally observe uniform operating hours. They are located on convenient access roads and are surrounded by large parking lots. Most centers include one or more large anchor magnet store designed to attract customers. The largest shopping centers are called regionals; the smaller centers are called community or neighborhood shopping centers.

SHOPPING GOODS Merchandise purchased by the consumer only after considerable effort has been made to comparison shop. Shopping goods are often expensive products, e.g., automobiles and major appliances, in which price and quality comparisons are of primary importance. They may also be products in which appearance or style comparisons are of greater significance, e.g., clothing.

SHOPPING ITEMS See *shopping goods*

SHOPPING GOODS STORES Most large department stores, discount stores, and supermarkets may be regarded as shopping goods stores, i.e., stores which have such breadth of assortment in their merchandise offerings that the customer may compare prices, styles, and quality.

SHOPPING PRODUCTS See *shopping goods*

SHOPPING STORE See *shopping goods stores*

SHORT-RANGE PLAN See *planning*

SHORT-TERM PLAN See *planning*

SHORTAGE ADVERTISING Advertising which is run when a product or service is in short supply as a result of an interruption in production, especially strong demand, etc. The sponsor, instead of simply promoting the product or service, attempts to educate the public, or to influence it in some other way.

SHRINKAGE The difference between book inventory and actual physical inventory; i.e., the difference between what one is supposed to have and what is actually on hand. At the retail level most shrinkage can be attributed to customer shoplifting and employee pilferage.

SIC See *standard industrial classification (SIC)*

SIG CUT See *logo*

SIGNAL In communication, a signal is the actual transmission of the message from the encoder to the decoder. The strength of the message is contingent upon a number of factors, such as the frequency with which the signal is transmitted, the skill with which the signal is designed, the media by which the signal is transmitted, the ability of the signal to compete with all other signals for the decoder's attention, and the degree to which a common pool of experiences (or frame of reference) is shared by the decoder and the encoder.

SIGNATURE CUT See *logo*

SIMPLE RANDOM SAMPLE See *random sampling*

SIMPLE RECIPROCITY See *reciprocity*

SIMULATION A marketing decision making technique in which complex conditions in the marketplace are examined and analyzed by means of a model. The model is commonly created through the use of a computer and the resulting simulation takes the place of the real world in problem-solving activities.

SINGLE-LINE RETAILER See *limited-line store*

SINGLE-LINE STORE See *limited-line store*

SINGLE-LINE WHOLESALER See *general line wholesaler*

SINGLE PRODUCT STRATEGY A manufacturing strategy in which a decision is made to produce a single product or a single product with a limited number of options.

SINGLE TARGET MARKET APPROACH A method of market segmentation in which one homogeneous group is selected as the target market and one marketing mix is used to market the product. See also *market segmentation.*

SINGLE-VARIABLE SEGMENTATION The least complex form of market segmentation in which only a single factor, e.g., age of the individual, is used to segment the population.

SITUATION ANALYSIS The stage in marketing research in which the central issue or situation is thoroughly investigated to more clearly define the problem and to develop a hypothesis which might lead to a solution.

SKIM PRICING See *skimming*

SKIM-THE-CREAM PRICING See *skimming*

SKIMMING A pricing policy in which products are introduced into the marketplace at a relatively high price with the intention of selling as much as possible before competition drives the price down. Market segments are targeted, or skimmed, from top to bottom. Also known as step pricing and creaming.

SKINNERIAN PSYCHOLOGY See *behavioral engineering*

SKU See *stock keeping unit (SKU)*

SLICE-OF-LIFE FORMAT A form of advertising (mainly television) in which a small segment of a lifelike experience is dramatized in order to spotlight a product. Typically, in the course of the commercial, a problem is stated and then a solution is found in which the product plays a leading role.

SMALL ORDER PROBLEM Orders for merchandise which are so small that the transaction does not yield a profit.

SMEI See *Sales and Marketing Executives International (SMEI)*

SMSA See *Metropolitan Statistical Area (MSA)*

SNOWBALL SAMPLE See *referral sample*

SNOWBALLING METHOD A method of developing media advertising schedules in which the climax of a campaign is regarded as most significant and thus allocated the largest share of the budget. Also known as the crescendo method.

SOCIAL CHANNEL A personal communications channel consisting of neighbors, friends, family members, and associates talking to potential customers. Also known as word-of-mouth influence.

SOCIAL CLASS A relatively distinct and homogeneous division of a society, composed of individuals who share similar values, interests, and behavioral characteristics. Social classes also show distinct product and brand preferences and differ in the type and amount of media exposure they receive. The six social classes commonly recognized in American society are the upper upper class, the lower upper class, the upper middle class, the lower middle class, the upper lower class, and the lower lower class. The upper upper class is comprised of the social elite who generally have inherited wealth and whose families have been prominent in American society. The lower upper class includes persons who have earned exceptional wealth or income through their own business or professional ability. These individuals generally come from the middle classes. The upper middle class is comprised of individuals who are primarily concerned with career, and although they possess neither great wealth nor elevated family status, are highly motivated to better themselves and their children. They tend to be professionals, independent business owners, or corporate managers. Lower middle class individuals are primarily white-collar workers, such as office workers and owners of small businesses, grey-collar workers, such as uniformed civil servants, and higher-level blue-collar workers, such as plumbers and factory foremen. The upper lower class tends to be the largest social class and includes most of the blue-collar working class of skilled and semi-skilled factory workers. Finally, the lower lower class are those individuals within the society that are poorly educated, unskilled laborers who are often unemployed and may require public assistance just to survive.

SOCIAL COSTS When calculating the cost of doing business social costs are those incurred by society in the form of damage to the environment, increases in illness, etc. Social costs are viewed in much the same way as private costs in determining the total costs of a business.

SOCIAL ELITE See *social class*

SOCIAL MARKETING The application of marketing strategies, concepts, and techniques to the promotion of social ideas or programs. The effort may be designed to propagate a particular idea (e.g., that freedom and democracy are synonymous), to encourage a particular form of behavior (e.g., one should vote in an election), or to support a particular non-profit organization (e.g., The League of Women Voters). See also *societal marketing concept.*

SOCIAL PROFITS The benefits which accrue from the operations of non-profit organizations, e.g., health care, police protection, education, etc.

SOCIAL RESPONSIBILITY A concept embodying the notion that business has an obligation to society to operate in the public interest.

SOCIAL ROLE See *role*

SOCIALISM See *economic system*

SOCIALIZATION See *consumer socialization*

SOCIETAL FORCES In the marketing context, societal forces are social pressures and influences which affect the operation of the marketplace. They include changes in demographics, alteration of lifestyles, modification of expectations, etc.

SOCIETAL MARKETING CONCEPT A marketing management orientation in which the interests of society at large are taken into consideration when new products and services are planned. Primary among these concepts are the conservation of resources and the preservation of the environment.

Societal marketing may be adopted as a strategy for one of two reasons: 1) a company may feel that socially responsible behavior attracts customers and avoids government regulation, or 2) a company may act responsibly for the simple reason that it is the proper thing to do.

SOCIOECONOMIC SEGMENTATION A method of market segmentation based on such factors as age, income, occupation, education, sex, marital status, social class, stage in the family life cycle, etc. Usually, several of these factors will be used in combination to help identify potential buyers of specific brands or products. The same socioeconomic factors may be used to identify and describe radio, television, and print media audiences. This correlation enables marketers to use socioeconomic segmentation to find appropriate advertising media for their products and to reach a target segment effectively. See also *market segmentation.*

SOFT CORE LOYALS See *brand insistence*

SOFT GOODS Merchandise made from textile fabrics, e.g., apparel, piece goods, towels, sheets, etc. Sometimes known by older term "dry goods."

SOFT SELL See *humorous sell*

SOLE AGENT See *manufacturer's agent*

SORTING See *grading*

SORTING ACTIVITIES See *sorting process*

SORTING OUT See *grading* and *allocation*

SORTING PROCESS The combined processes of assembling, allocation, grading, and assorting in the channel of distribution. The sorting process serves to bring homogeneous groups of products together for economical handling and shipping early in the distribution process and, later, to break the inventories down into increasingly smaller quantities on their way to the ultimate consumer. Also called regrouping activities. See also *discrepancy of quantity* and *discrepancy of assortment,* both of which are overcome by the sorting process.

SORTING THEORY See *sorting process*

SOURCE See *sender*

SOURCE EFFECT In the marketing communication process, source effect refers to the impact the reputation of a sender has upon the credibility of the message. Sources of information (individuals, publications, etc.) which have a high degree of prestige will convey a message with a high degree of credibility.

SOURCE MARKING The price marking of merchandise (generally destined for retail sale) at the point of production. Products so marked are said to be pre-priced.

SPAN OF CONTROL The number of people that one supervisor will be able to deal with effectively. The concept is based on both personal limits and the demands of various supervisory assignments. The span of control varies inversely with the level of difficulty of the supervisory task.

SPECIAL EVENT PRICING A form of promotional pricing in which a sale is advertised, often in connection with some event such as a holiday. The objective of special event pricing is to bring inventories into line with demand or to raise cash.

228

SPECIAL PROJECT TEAM See *venture team*

SPECIALIZATION See *differentiated marketing*

SPECIALTY ADVERTISING See *advertising specialties*

SPECIALTY CHAIN A retailing firm operating a chain of small stores frequently located in shopping centers or in high-traffic urban shopping areas. Specialty chains are characterized by a lack of advertising (the shopping center in its entirety is the magnet which draws customers), an emphasis on high markup merchandise like women's apparel, limited assortments, high turnover rates, and few amenities such as store credit and delivery service. Specialty chains are particularly adept at precisely targeting a market segment and quickly reacting to shoppers' desires.

SPECIALTY DISCOUNT STORE A store (often a unit in a chain organization) which carries a single product category and sells at below regular retail prices.

SPECIALTY GOODS Merchandise well known to the consumer because of its high quality, brand identification, uniqueness, or other specific characteristic. Shoppers will often make a special effort to find this merchandise and are unlikely to accept substitutes. Price is seldom the deciding factor in the purchase of specialty goods.

SPECIALTY ITEMS See *specialty goods*

SPECIALTY-LINE MARKETING RESEARCH FIRM See *marketing research firm*

SPECIALTY-LINE WHOLESALER See *specialty wholesaler*

SPECIALTY PRODUCTS See *specialty goods*

SPECIALTY RETAILER See *specialty store*

SPECIALTY SHOP See *boutique*

SPECIALTY STORE A retail enterprise carrying a product mix narrower than a department store and broader than a single-line store. The specialty store has a clearly defined market segment as its target, i.e., buyers who seek a wide variety of unique merchandise. Specialty stores generally offer wide assortments within their product lines, trained salespeople, credit, delivery services, and other amenities.

SPECIALTY STRIP SHOPPING CENTER Stores in the straight line configuration of the common strip shopping center, but with a tenant mix narrowly defined around a particular product classification, e.g., restaurants and food-related establishments. These shopping centers are often near a major mall and tend to attract affluent customers.

SPECIALTY WHOLESALER A highly specialized full-service wholesaler, or middleman, who carries a narrow range of products which are offered to carefully targeted customers. Services provided are similar to those offered by general merchandise wholesalers. The specialty wholesaler may deal in a single product, e.g., frozen foods, while his general merchandise counterpart would carry a complete line of groceries.

SPECIFICATIONS Exact descriptions of goods. Specifications are commonly used when purchasing is carried on by bidding.

SPECULATION The purchase of a product or other property in anticipation of an increase in price at the time of resale. Most speculation is on a relatively short-term basis.

SPECULATION PRINCIPLE See *principle of speculation*

STABILIZING PRICES See *status quo pricing*

STAFF EXECUTIVE See *staff manager*

STAFF MANAGER An executive in a firm's staff organization, i.e., in that part of the firm responsible for providing line managers with special services and support activities.

STAGFLATION An economic condition characterized by inflation (rising prices) on the one hand and stagnation (little economic growth) on the other. Stagflation is often accompanied by high levels of unemployment.

STAKE In distribution channel relationships, a stake is the degree of dependency one channel member has on another for its success or survival. For example, if a channel member sells 75% of its products to a single customer within the channel, it has a high stake in its relationship to that customer. See also *channel of distribution.*

STANDARD INDUSTRIAL CLASSIFICATION (SIC) A scheme developed by the U.S. Office of Management and Budget for classifying business establishments by the type of economic activity in which they are engaged. Established in the 1930s, the SIC code is updated every fifteen years. Categories for goods producing industries tend to be broken down in detail while service businesses tend to be lumped together in general categories.

STANDARD INDUSTRIAL CLASSIFICATION (SIC)

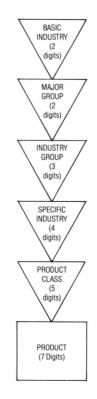

STANDARD METROPOLITAN STATISTICAL AREA See *Metropolitan Statistical Area (MSA)*

STANDARDIZATION The process of insuring that the basic qualities of a product are consistent with previously established criteria. In international marketing this is an important element of a marketing strategy, since standardization provides the benefits of product cost savings, broader product recognition, facility of planning and control, and permits marketing campaigns to extend across national boundaries. In short, standardization is the transference of all elements of the marketing mix from one country to another. When cultural, economic, and/or legal differences make complete standardization untenable, marketers may utilize a modified standardization approach, in which one or more elements of the marketing mix are changed. For example, an identical product may be marketed worldwide, but the advertising campaigns for that product may vary from culture to culture, and different consumers may even be targeted in different countries. See also *marketing mix.*

STANDARDIZE To make or bring to an established or uniform size, weight, quality level, etc. Some products may be standardized in conformance with specifications recognized on an industry-wide basis. See also *grading.*

STANDBY COST See *fixed cost*

STAPLE Generally, merchandise offered at retail which the consumer buys on a regular basis, e.g., sugar, flour, basic clothing such as underwear, gas and oil, etc.

STAR In the evaluation of a company's product line, a star is seen as having a high growth rate and a generally substantial share of the market. However, stars require considerable cash to finance their continued growth.

STARTLING-STATEMENT AP-PROACH A technique used by a salesperson in the first few minutes of contact with a prospect. A startling statement of facts known about the prospect's needs or problems is used to attract attention to the sales presentation. See also *approach.*

STATEMENT OF OPERATIONS See *profit and loss statement*

STATEMENT OF PROFIT AND LOSS See *profit and loss statement*

STATEMENT OF PURPOSE See *planning*

STATISTICAL BANK See *analytical marketing system*

STATISTICAL RANDOM ERROR See *random error*

STATUS A condition, rank, or standing, especially high rank or standing. Status may derive from family of birth, education, nature of employment, place of residence, etc. Certain goods and services may bestow a measure of status on the individual. These vary within reference groups.

STATUS QUO OBJECTIVES See *status quo pricing*

STATUS QUO PRICING A strategy in which prices are maintained at the level charged in the mature stage of the product life cycle. This practice tends to avoid price wars with competitors.

STATUS SYMBOL A possession, practice, etc. which tends to bestow a certain social rank, especially high social rank. These symbols include mannerisms, style of dress, and possessions such as expensive automobiles. Different products have different values as status symbols. This symbolic quality adds a social and psychological element to the utilitarian virtues of the product or service.

STAY-OUT PRICING See *preemptive pricing*

STEP PRICING See *skimming*

STIMULUS Some aspect of the environment (for example, advertising) which provokes feelings or incites activity on the part of an individual.

STIMULUS-RESPONSE MODEL A technique used in the study of consumer behavior in which people are seen to respond to a stimulus in a predictable way, but which does not attempt to explain why they do so. Researchers using this model seek to establish relationships between consumer characteristics (such as demographics), stimuli (such as products), and responses (such as consumer buying behavior). For example, researchers may seek to predict how high school educated consumers will respond to a new diet soft drink. They use the stimulus-response model to establish a correlation between educational level, the diet soft drink, and consumer buying behavior. See also *behaviorism.*

STIMULUS-RESPONSE THEORY OF LEARNING See *behaviorism*

STOCK CONTROL The activity of regulating inventory levels so that stock-on-hand is properly balanced between market demand on the one hand and production capacity on the other.

STOCK KEEPING UNIT (SKU) In retail inventory control and identification systems, the stock keeping unit represents the smallest unit for which sales and stock records are kept. See also *product item.*

STOCK-OUT An out-of-stock condition with regard to a particular item, i.e., insufficient quantity was ordered to meet demand.

STOCK SPOTTING In warehousing, a practice by which manufactured goods or other commodities are warehoused near the customer rather than at the point of production in an effort to reduce delivery time and transportation costs.

STOCK TURNOVER A financial ratio commonly calculated for one year which is determined by dividing net sales (in dollars) by average inventory at selling prices (in dollars). Stock turnover rate is the number of times the average inventory has been sold and replaced in a given period. Also called inventory turnover.

$$\text{Stock turnover} = \frac{\$\text{Net sales}}{\$\text{Average inventory at selling price}}$$

STOCKTURN RATE See *stock turnover*

STORAGE An intermediate stage in the distribution chain which is usually accomplished in warehouses and involves the holding of goods until demand meets supply. Storage activities (which include receiving, sorting, assembling, and shipping) may be accomplished at the manufacturer-production level, or later in the chain by wholesalers or retailers.

STORAGE WAREHOUSE See *warehouse*

STORE A retail business establishment which regularly offers products and services for sale to the ultimate consumer, i.e., to customers who will use the product themselves, not resell it. Stores commonly buy, store, and promote the merchandise they sell. Some wholesale businesses give the outward appearance of being retail stores but, in fact, restrict their customers to members of the trade. See also types of stores, i.e., *department store, specialty store,* etc.

STORE AUDIT A data collection method employed in retailing to track the performance of particular brands or products in a specific time frame. Store audits commonly conform to the following formula.

Inventory on hand + new purchases (less returns) = stock available for sale − present inventory = consumer sales.

STORE BRAND See *private brand*

STORE IMAGE The store as perceived by the customer. Factors which contribute to store image are store location, price ranges, merchandise, architecture, color schemes, advertising, sales people, etc.

STORE-OWNED BUYING OFFICE See *resident buying office*

STORE OWNERSHIP GROUP See *department store ownership group*

STORE SERVICES See *services*

STOREKEEPER See *merchant* and *retailer*

STORING See *storage*

STORYLINE FORMAT A form of advertising in which a story unfolds which features the product or in some way relates its history to some present day useful purpose.

STRAIGHT COMMISSION For salespeople, straight commission payment means that they receive a fixed percentage of their total sales as their sole compensation. See also *commission*.

STRAIGHT EXTENSION STRATEGY A strategy employed in international trade in which a company exports the same products that it manufactures for the domestic market. No attempt is made to alter them to meet the requirements of foreign markets.

STRAIGHT REBUY In industrial buying the straight rebuy situation is one in which the buyer reorders a product which needs no modification. It is generally a routine transaction which has been repeated on numerous occasions. See also *new task buying* and *modified rebuy*.

STRAIGHT SALARY A method of payment in which an individual is paid on a fixed rate basis and at regular intervals, independent of productivity considerations.

STRATEGIC BUSINESS UNIT (SBU) Within a large business organization a strategic business unit (a term first used at General Electric) may be a division, a line of products, or an individual product. Strategic business units are strong enough to stand by themselves in the marketplace and are generally treated as separate profit centers by the parent organization.

STRATEGIC MARKETING A marketing posture in which an effort is made to make a company more customer oriented by forging a stronger link between marketing functions and strategic planning functions. Generally, marketing activities such as marketing research and new product development are given a larger share of the organizations budget.

STRATEGIC MARKETING PLANNING See *strategic planning*

STRATEGIC OPPORTUNITY MATRIX See *product/market opportunity matrix*

STRATEGIC PLANNING Long-range business planning in which the organization's capabilities, resources, goals, and abilities are matched with existing or projected opportunities in the marketplace. See also *tactical planning*.

STRATEGIC WINDOW In market planning, that particular period of time during which a firm's competencies best match up with the requirements of the marketplace.

STRATEGY In a marketing context, strategy refers to the long-range plan of action calculated to achieve the objectives of the organization.

STRATIFIED RANDOM SAMPLE See *stratified sampling*

STRATIFIED SAMPLING A two-stage method of probability sampling in which the units of a population are first divided into groups according to a common characteristic or attribute relevant to the study, such as age, sex, or educational level. Particular members of each group are then randomly selected for study. Researchers often choose stratified sampling over other methods when the total population to be investigated is composed of several heterogeneous subgroups. See also *probability sampling.*

STRIP SHOPPING CENTER A shopping center configuration in which the stores are arranged in a straight line along a street or highway. The line of stores is usually set back enough to allow for a covered pedestrian walkway and for automobile parking between the street and the row of shops.

STRIPPED-DOWN PRICE A product, frequently an automobile, may be advertised at a particularly low price. Once at the showroom the customer discovers that the car offered at the low price is stripped-down, i.e., is lacking in many of the amenities most consumers desire in a new car.

STRONG INFLATION See *inflation*

STRUCTURAL APPROACH TO ATTITUDE See *cognitive component, conative component,* and *effective component*

STRUCTURED QUESTIONNAIRE A questionnaire in which all the questions are precisely sequenced to elicit a particular type of response from the subject. The interviewer adheres to the formula, and does not depart from the wording and arrangement of the questions. The questions are arranged in a logical order with difficult or personal questions reserved for the end of the interview so that the subject does not become defensive. See also *questionnaire* and *unstructured questionnaire.*

STYLE 1) Style is that quality which distinguishes an object from all others, or as *Women's Wear Daily's* John Fairchild expressed it, "style is an expression of individualism mixed with charisma." 2) In the apparel industry, a style refers to a particular design.

STYLE MODIFICATION The changing of a product (mainly in terms of appearance) in an effort to 1) create a new image for the product, or 2) to differentiate it from other brands.

STYLE OBSOLESCENCE See *planned obsolescence*

SUBCULTURE A clearly distinguishable subgroup existing within a larger surrounding culture. Subcultures may be based on such factors as age or race or upon a form of distinctive behavior. In a marketing context subcultures may be used as a basis for market segmentation.

SUBLIMINAL PERCEPTION The level at which individuals receive sensory stimuli without consciously being aware of having picked up any messages. Marketers have experimented with subliminal perception by hiding messages in print ads, magazines, and TV commercials. Fear of the brainwashing implications of subliminal perception have made its practice controversial, and even illegal in certain areas. Wilson Bryan Key's still popular *Subliminal Seduction* (1974) alerted the public to the dangers of the practice.

SUBLIMINAL SEDUCTION See *subliminal perception*

SUBOPTIMIZATION A condition in an organization in which at least one component is operating at a level lower than its very best.

SUBSIDIARY A separate company which is a part of a larger business organization, which controls the smaller company but does not necessarily wholly own it.

SUBSTANTIATION To establish proof of a claim as, for example, the submission of data in support of an advertising claim.

SUBSTITUTE METHOD OF FORE-CASTING In forecasting the potential sales of new products, the substitute method may be used to predict the upper limit on potential sales of the new product. Researchers examine and analyze the sales of products which the new one may displace. The resultant figures must then be modified to include customer preferences at various price points and the availability of other substitutes in the marketplace. The substitute method may be used to forecast new product sales in both the consumer and the industrial markets.

SUBSTITUTES Goods or services that may be used interchangeably, thus offering a choice to the customer. The greater the number of acceptable substitutes available, the greater will be the elasticity of demand. Soft drinks, for example, have many substitutes and thus will have an elastic demand curve. On the other hand, a product having few or no acceptable substitutes (such as salt) will tend to have an inelastic demand curve.

SUGGESTION SELLING A sales technique in which the salesperson recommends to the customer related merchandise, such as seasonal items, thus encouraging additional purchases.

SUNK COSTS Costs, generally developmental, which have been incurred and are unrecoverable.

SUPER-REGIONAL SHOPPING CENTER See *regional shopping center*

SUPER-STORE See *superstore*

SUPER WAREHOUSE A store at least twice the size of the typical supermarket operating on a high-volume, low-overhead basis. The super warehouse is a hybrid, being partly a no-frills warehouse outlet, but, at the same time, stocking much of the merchandise found in a traditional supermarket. Goods are often displayed in cartons and the customer is expected to pack and carry his own groceries.

SUPERAGENCY See *integrated marketing*

SUPERETTE A grocery store in which much of the merchandise is arranged for self-service, but in which counter service is still available. Superettes stand between supermarkets and convenience stores.

SUPERFICIAL DISCOUNTING See *psychological discounting*

SUPERMARKET A large retail store specializing in groceries, produce, meat, dairy products, and a wide variety of non-food items. Supermarkets operate on a self-service basis with customers paying at a central checkout. These stores are characterized by high unit volume, low unit prices and a broad assortment of merchandise.

SUPERSTORE A large retail establishment combining many of the features of the supermarket with those of the discount store. Superstores often have 25,000 to 30,000 square feet of floor space and carry food and non-food general merchandise in a ratio of approximately 70% to 30%. These stores carry from 3 to 4 times the number of products found in the conventional supermarket out of which the superstore evolved. Superstores are geared to meet all the routine needs of the customer in one stop.

SUPERVISION OF SALESFORCE See *sales management*

SUPPLIER See *vendor* and *manufacturer*

SUPPLIES Business or industrial goods treated as expense items which are not incorporated into a finished product. Most supplies fit into one of three categories: 1) maintenance items such as cleaning materials and paint; 2) repair items such as glass and pipe; and 3) operating items such as paper and fuel. The three categories are sometimes known by the acronym MRO.

SUPPLY CURVE A schedule, generally represented as a graph, depicting the relationship between the quantity of goods entering the market and the price being offered for the goods. High prices commonly draw more goods into the market so that the supply curve slants upward. Also called a supply schedule.

SUPPLY HOUSE See *industrial distributor*

SUPPLY SCHEDULE See *supply curve*

SUPPORT SALESPEOPLE A salesperson generally not directly involved in order-getting, i.e., is more concerned with the technical details of the product being offered for sale. Detailers and technical salespeople as well as parasalespeople (trainees, etc.) are all employed in a support role.

SUPPORT SERVICE See *supportive service*

SUPPORTING ACTIVITIES See *supportive service*

SUPPORTING SALESPEOPLE See *support salespeople*

SUPPORTIVE SERVICE In marketing, any auxiliary benefit or service which makes the product more attractive to the customer. Supportive services contribute to the firm's overall marketing effort. For example, the extension of credit is a supportive service which facilitates the selling process. Warranties, guarantees, installation, and initial free service contracts are also supportive services which may encourage customers to select one product over another. Also known as supporting activities. See also *services.*

SURPLUS STORE A store which sells, along with other goods of nongovernmental origin, merchandise which has been declared surplus by an agency of the U.S. Government, e.g., clothing and equipment no longer of use to the armed forces.

SURVEY A method of gathering primary data from a sample of the population using such techniques as face-to-face and telephone interviews and mail surveys (self-administered questionnaires). The survey method is commonly used to determine the knowledge, attitudes, and beliefs of particular segments of the population.

SURVEY APPROACH (SALES) A technique used by salespersons in the first few minutes of contact with a prospect in which the salesperson asks the prospect a number of survey-like questions. This approach is designed to ascertain the prospect's familiarity with the product or service. Questions may range from the simple and straightforward to the specific and technical. The method serves to qualify prospects as well as to lead into the presentation. See also *approach.*

SURVEY METHOD See *survey*

SWAP MARKET A meeting place where people gather to exchange goods, generally personal or household articles for which they no longer have a need. Early swap markets did not involve the exchange of money, but soon evolved into more conventional retail operations like the flea market.

SWEEPSTAKE A sales promotion device in which the participant competes for prizes by simply entering his name. A drawing is held at some future date and winners are determined by pure chance as names are drawn at random. A sweepstake requires no skill of the participant and has no fixed, predictable odds. See also *game* and *contest.*

SWITCHER See *brand switcher*

SYMBIOTIC MARKETING A strategy in which two or more firms enter into a venture jointly, e.g., the marketing of European automobiles in the U.S. through already established dealerships for American cars.

SYMBOLIC PRICING See *prestige pricing*

SYNDICATED SERVICE RESEARCH FIRM See *marketing research firm*

SYNERGISM In the context of a marketing system, synergism refers to the cooperative interaction of the various parts of the system so that its total effect is greater than the total of the effects of the parts taken independently, i.e, the whole is greater than the sum of its parts.

SYSTEM SELLING In personal selling, a team effort built around a master salesperson and a team of less experienced salespeople. The technique is calculated to overwhelm the prospect and to systematically answer his objections.

SYSTEMS APPROACH A concept in which the various components of the marketing environment are viewed as interrelated and interdependent making up a rational system. The systems approach may also refer to a form of company organization in which the firm's various functions are integrated to facilitate the marketing effort.

SYSTEMS CONTRACTING See *systems selling*

SYSTEMS SELLING A form of selling found primarily in industrial markets in which products, supplies, and services are sold in combination in an effort to meet the needs of the customer on a continuing basis. For example, a firm may sell a materials handling system which includes transporters together with an array of packaging materials used for shipping.

SYSTEMS THEORY See *systems approach*

237

T

TACTIC In marketing context, a tactic is a specific, generally short-term, course of action taken to execute a strategic plan.

TACTICAL PLANNING Short-term business planning, particularly when focused on the implementation of the organization's long-term strategic goals. See *strategic planning*

TANGIBLE PRODUCT See *product*

TANGIBLE RESOURCES With reference to a business organization, tangible resources include the firm's physical plant and equipment, cash reserves, raw materials, etc.

TARGET AUDIENCE See *audience*

TARGET MARKET That particular subdivision, or segment, of a total potential market selected by a company as the target of its marketing efforts. Choice of a target market is usually based on some common characteristic possessed by the market segment, e.g., sex, education level, income, etc. Also known as market target or served market. See also *market positioning* and *market targeting*.

TARGET MARKETING See *target market*

TARGET POPULATION In sampling, that part of the population at large from which a sample is selected.

TARGET POSITIONING See *market positioning*

TARGET PRICING A pricing strategy in which the selling price of a product is determined by adding a sum to the fixed cost of the product to achieve a predetermined profit margin.

TARGET PROFIT PRICING See *target pricing*

TARGET RETURN PRICING See *target pricing*

TARGETED RETURN ON INVEST-MENT See *profit target analysis*

TARIFF A tax levied against imported products. The actual amount of the tax is referred to as the duty or customs duty. There are two forms of tariff: 1) revenue tariffs which raise money, and 2) protective tariffs which are meant to protect domestic producers or manufacturers by excluding foreign competitors to raise the price of the imported goods to a competitive level.

TARIFFS The rates charged by shippers (rail, truck, air freight, barge) for their services.

More specifically, under the Interstate Commerce Act or Civil Aeronautics Act, tariffs are those schedules containing all interstate rates, charges, and regulations for shipping between different points. Once published, such tariffs have the force of law as long as they are in effect.

TASK AND INVESTMENT METHOD See *objective-task method*

TASK FORCE In new product development, a group drawn from a number of functional departments within the firm which is responsible for seeing that the development of the new product is given coordinated and sufficient support. Members of a task force generally perform these duties in addition to their regular assignments.

TASK METHOD See *objective-task method*

TEASER CAMPAIGN See *campaign plan*

TECHNICAL MARKETING SOCIETY OF AMERICA (TMSA) An international association of professionals interested and involved in the marketing of technical products and services in the aerospace and technology industries. TMSA provides technical marketing education and disseminates information. The association also sponsors conferences, conducts seminars for the exchange of technical information, and sets industry standards. It maintains both a library and a placement service. TMSA publishes a bimonthly journal, *Aerospace Marketing Research,* a bimonthly *Newsletter,* and *Abstracts of Seminar Presentations.* The association is based in Long Beach, California.

TECHNICAL SALESPERSON An industrial salesperson whose principal duties are those of the technical consultant. Technical salespeople, who often possess special knowledge and skills, are commonly called upon to provide assistance to purchasers of complex equipment such as computers.

TECHNICAL SPECIALIST See *technical salesperson*

TECHNOLOGICAL BASE See *technological environment*

TECHNOLOGICAL ENVIRONMENT The manner in which technical skills and equipment are converted into output in the particular economy in which a marketer conducts business. These skills and equipment form the economy's technical base. Modern economies make greater use of the technological base than do tradition-bound societies, thus utilizing labor more productively. Research and development (R&D), an important component of technological advancement, leads to breakthroughs which affect the way businesses produce and market their goods. In recent years, these technological improvements tend to indicate greater use of computer technology.

As new developments occur, a marketer's use of (or failure to use) each technological improvement can affect the competitive position of the firm.

TECHNOLOGICAL FORCES Those technical developments in a society which influence the way people live and which determine what they desire and which, in turn, affect the activities of marketers who supply these wants and needs.

TECHNOLOGICAL OBSOLESCENCES See *planned obsolescence*

TELEMARKETING A term commonly employed to describe two distinct forms of marketing: 1) Sales of products and services via the telephone in what AT&T calls the "marriage of telecommunications technology and direct marketing techniques." Telemarketing is conducted at both the industrial and consumer levels of the marketplace. 2) Sales of products and services via an interactive system or two-way television, i.e., electronic in-home or in-office systems which employ cable television, telephone lines, data banks, etc. See also *electronic direct marketing*.

TELEPHONE INTERVIEW See *interview*

TELEPHONE MARKETING See *telemarketing*

TELEPHONE RETAILING Selling by telephone at the retail level, i.e., to the ultimate consumer. It may be employed to canvass potential customers or customers may be encouraged by other advertising, e.g., print, radio, or television, to call by telephone to place an order. See also *telemarketing* and *teleshopping*.

TELEPHONE SELLING See *telephone retailing*

TELESHOPPING The use of the telephone by customers to order merchandise or services they have seen in print advertising, heard about on the radio, or seen on television. Teleshopping is frequently facilitated through the use of toll-free numbers for inbound calls. See also *telemarketing* and *telephone retailing*.

TENANT MIX See *balanced tenancy*

TERMS-OF-PAYMENT DISCOUNT See *ordinary terms*

TERMS OF PURCHASE See *terms of sale*

TERMS OF SALE The conditions governing a sale as set forth by the seller. Terms include amount of discount (if any), payment period, date of delivery, point of transfer of title to the merchandise, allocation of transportation costs, and any other specific obligations and conditions.

TEST MARKETING See *market testing*

TESTIMONIAL See *celebrity testimonial*

THEORY OF CONSUMER EFFICIENCY A theory of retail institutional change in which consumer cost saving efforts (with regard to price, transportation costs, time expended, physical effort) are viewed as influencing the development of new retail organizations. For example, the growth of shopping centers may be attributed to consumers' desire for time efficient shopping.

THIRD WORLD DISTRIBUTION A term used by manufacturers to refer to such nontraditional retail institutions as discounters, promotional department stores, and off-price merchants.

THREE LEVEL CHANNEL A marketing channel in which there are three levels of distribution between the manufacturer/producer and the ultimate consumer. For example, there may be an agent or broker, a wholesaler or distributor, and a retailer acting as intermediaries.

THRESHOLD EXPENDITURE LEVEL The minimum dollar expenditure required for a firm to be in a market and obtain sales. After this minimum level, small increases in expenditures may lead to large increases in sales up until the point at which additional expenditures lead to fewer and finally no sales increases, with an actual decline in profits.

THRESHOLDS OF PERCEPTION The points at which individuals no longer consciously sense stimuli. See also *perception* and *just noticeable difference.*

THRESHOLD-POINT ORDERING See *reorder point (ROP)*

TIE-IN PRODUCTS Products sold together as a package either literally (as razor and shaving cream may be packaged together) or as a deal (as cosmetic products are frequently sold, the purchase of one being contingent on the purchase of another). Some tie-in arrangements (for example, camera film being tied-in with film processing by the same company) have been found to be in restraint of trade and thus illegal.

TIE-IN SALES See *tie-in products*

TIME SERIES Historical records of past economic and/or sales behavior, used in time series analysis to predict future trends. For example, time series may show the sales of a particular product in a particular country for the past fifteen year period. The rate of growth or decline in this market may

be analyzed and predictions made about future sales. A related time series that changes in the same direction as the series under study but consistently precedes that change is called a leading series. The leading series is watched particularly closely as an indicator of future trends. See also *time series analysis.*

TIME SERIES ANALYSIS A sales forecasting technique in which the analysis is based on the firm's performance over past time. An effort is made to discover patterns of activity which can be used to forecast sales volume in the future.

TIME UTILITY The utility (or value or satisfaction) added to a product when it is available at the precise time the customer wants it.

TITLE FLOW See *channel flows*

TMSA See *Technical Marketing Society of America (TMSA)*

T.O. MAN The turn-over man, or closer, is a master salesperson who is responsible for bringing the sales process to a conclusion, or closing the sale.

TOFC (TRAILER-ON-FLATCAR) See *piggyback*

TON-MILE A transportation term meaning the movement of one ton of goods one mile.

TOP DOWN See *top-down planning*

TOP-DOWN PLANNING A managerial system in which planning is conducted by top management.

TOTAL COST APPROACH In the management of physical distribution, the total cost approach is a planning tool that attempts to take into account possible variations in transportation, inventory, and order-processing costs by showing the hypothetical results of alternative strategies. The approach considers all distribution costs in total and emphasizes trading off certain types of costs for others, with the ultimate goal being the determination of the lowest possible cost. In order to accomplish this, planners must identify transportation, warehousing, inventory control, and order entry and processing costs which may occur. The implication of this approach is that it is easier to control distribution costs by looking at the total picture than by trying to make piecemeal reductions.

TOTAL COST CONCEPT See *total cost approach*

TOTAL COSTS The sum of a firm's fixed and variable expenses.

TOTAL MARKET APPROACH See *undifferentiated marketing*

TOTAL PHYSICAL DISTRIBUTION CONCEPT A management strategy in which all distribution functions in an organization are fully integrated, generally accomplished by making the distribution department the equal of the marketing and production departments. The objective of the total physical distribution concept is to minimize distribution costs while maintaining adequate customer service.

TOTAL PRODUCT CONCEPT A marketing concept in which all the services and benefits which may accompany a product are considered as a package with the product itself. For example, a new automobile brings with it transportation, but also a warranty, a sense of pride, and other benefits. Sometimes referred to as the generic product because consumers are seen as shopping not just for products but for a cluster of benefits which include the product itself.

TOTAL PRODUCT CONCEPT

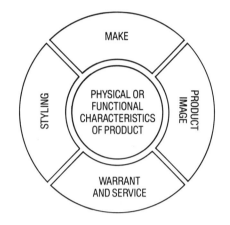

TOTAL VERTICAL INTEGRATION See *vertical integration*

TRACEABLE COMMON COSTS Those expenses in a business which can be assigned to a particular activity despite the fact they they are not immediately apparent. For example, the costs related to production space in a plant may be determined by calculating the square footage given over to that activity and then subtracting that amount from the plant's total (the costs for which are known).

TRADE ADVERTISING Advertising by the producers of products or the providers of services directed to customers other than the ultimate consumer, i.e., wholesalers, distributors, middlemen, retailers, etc. The objective is to widen the distribution of the product or service.

TRADE AREA See *trading area*

TRADE ASSOCIATION A nonprofit voluntary organization of businesses having common interests. The association sponsors research, promotes educational programs, attempts to form public opinion and to influence the passage of legislation which might affect members.

TRADE AUDIT See *store audit*

TRADE BALANCE See *balance of trade*

TRADE CHANNEL See *channel of distribution*

TRADE CREDIT Credit offered by manufacturers and wholesalers to their customers on a short-term basis.

TRADE DEFICIT A condition in international trade in which the value of a country's imports is in excess of the value of it's exports.

TRADE DISCOUNT A reduction in price granted by manufacturers to middlemen (including, at times, retailers) to compensate them for performing some marketing functions which would ordinarily have been the responsibility of the producer. These functions may include storage of merchandise, transportation, processing, selling, etc. Trade discounts are calculated independently of quantity discounts and are not dependent on the terms of sale stated on the invoice. Also known as a functional discount. See also *allowance, promotional allowance,* and *discount.*

TRADE EXHIBIT See *trade show*

TRADE FAIR See *trade show*

TRADE-IN ALLOWANCE A price reduction granted by a seller to a customer in the form of a credit for traded-in equipment. The list price is unaffected but the buyer pays less as a result of the allowance.

TRADE INDUSTRY In industrial marketing, trade industries are made up of organizations like wholesalers and retailers who, for the most part, purchase for resale to others or for use in conducting their business.

TRADE MART See *merchandise mart*

TRADE NAME A name used to designate a particular business organization, i.e., the firm together with its reputation and accrued goodwill. Trade names may or may not be exclusive. The term trade name is not applied to individual products which often carry the firm's trademark. Sometimes known as the commercial name. See also *brand name, trademark,* and *brand.*

TRADE-OFF ANALYSIS See *conjoint measurement*

TRADE PROMOTION See *trade sales promotion*

TRADE QUOTA In international trade, a quota which imposes a specific limit on the amount of goods which may be imported into a country.

TRADE SALES PROMOTION Short-term non-recurrent effort whose object is an increased buying response on the part of wholesalers and retailers. These efforts commonly take the form of buying allowances, free goods, cooperative advertising money, push money, sales contests, etc.

TRADE SALESPERSON A salesperson whose primary responsibility is promotional, i.e., helping customers to promote the company's products at the wholesale or retail level by setting up displays, stocking shelves, providing demonstrations, etc. Trade salespeople write orders, but are, for the most part, concerned with maintaining good relations with established cutomers.

TRADE SELLING See *trade salesperson*

TRADE SHOW A gathering of manufacturers or wholesalers in a particular industry (housewares, food, electronics, etc.) for the purpose of exhibiting their wares. Trade shows are commonly held in exhibition centers or hotels and give buyers (at the retail level) an opportunity to see many lines of merchandise in one place and to form an opinion as to what is available in the market.

TRADE SURPLUS A condition in international trade in which the value of a country's exports is in excess of the value of its imports.

TRADEMARK A word, symbol, sign, or design (or any combination of these elements) which identifies a particular product or service. Certain trademarks are registered with the U.S. Patent and Trademark Office and are thus afforded added protection from infringement by competitors.

Some controversy surrounds the use of trademarks which, properly, should be used as adjectives, not as verbs or nouns. For example, the Xerox Corporation insists that while a "Xerox photocopy" (used as a proper adjective) is correct, "to xerox" (verb use) or a "xerox" (noun use) are unacceptable as they are generic uses and thus threaten the validity of the trademark. See also *brand, brand name, brand mark, trade name,* and *service mark.*

TRADER See *merchant*

TRADING ACROSS A practice in which a firm (such as a store), in an effort to broaden its customer base or to reposition itself in the marketplace, alters its marketing strategy in a way calculated to appeal to a new market segment. In trading across, the firm is seeking to attract a customer on the same economic level as the original segment, but whose lifestyle, demographics, or psychographics are somewhat different. See also *trading down* and *trading up.*

TRADING AREA In a general sense a firm's trading area is that geographic zone containing the people who are likely to purchase the firm's goods or services. The term is most commonly applied to retailing where it refers to that area from which a store or shopping center attracts most of its customers.

TRADING COMPANY Companies organized to do business in foreign countries (or, for example, in Japan where they operate within the country), the trading company is involved in all aspects of buying, accumulating, transporting, distributing, and selling goods.

TRADING DOWN A practice in which a firm (most commonly a store), in an effort to broaden its customer base or to reposition itself in the marketplace, alters its marketing strategy. Generally it would reduce prices and/or lower the quality level of its products. It may also promote itself in a way calculated to appeal to customers of a lower socioeconomic level.

TRADING STAMPS Printed stamps given to customers by retailers as a continuity premium for shopping in the store. Stamps are pasted into books and redeemed for merchandise offered by the trading stamp company or for their value in cash. Trading stamps are regarded as a form of nonprice competition.

TRADING UP 1) A practice in which a firm (frequently a store), in an effort to attract customers of a higher socioeconomic level, alters its marketing strategy. Goods of higher quality may be produced or offered for sale at generally higher prices than before and the firm may promote itself in a manner calculated to attract more affluent customers. 2) A salesperson is said to be trading up (or selling up) when he or she encourages the customers to buy more expensive merchandise.

244

TRADITIONAL CHANNEL SYSTEM See *conventional channel*

TRADITIONAL DEPARTMENT STORE See *department store*

TRAFFIC AND MOTOR VEHICLE SAFETY ACT (1966) See *National Traffic and Motor Vehicle Safety Act (1966)*

TRAFFIC AND SAFETY ACT (1958) See *National Traffic and Safety Act (1958)*

TRAFFIC MANAGEMENT In a narrow industrial sense traffic management means buying transportation service for the purpose of shipping goods. This includes such functions as the determination of freight charges, application of tariff regulations, freight consolidation, etc. In a broader marketing sense, traffic management is concerned with the transportation and warehousing of goods in the distribution chain. Efficiency of movement and cost reduction are primary goals of traffic managers.

TRAILER-ON-FLATCAR (TOFC) See *piggyback*

TRANSACTION An individual act of reciprocal giving and receiving (involving either money or barter) in the exchange process. A transaction nearly always involves the transfer of ownership of some product or the transfer of the use of some service from one party to another. See also *exchange.*

TRANSACTION PRICE See *selling price*

TRANSACTIONAL FLOW See *channel flows*

TRANSACTIONAL FUNCTION See *transactional marketing function*

TRANSACTIONAL MARKETING FUNCTION Any marketing function which involves the transfer of ownership of either goods or services between parties. Transactional marketing functions include buying, selling, risk assumption, and related tasks. They overlap somewhat with facilitating marketing functions. See also *marketing functions.*

TRANSFER PRICE Intracompany charges made for goods transferred from one division to another or for goods shipped to foreign subsidiaries.

TRANSIT PRIVILEGES In transportation, the privilege offered a shipper by a shipping company (usually a railroad) of unloading goods in transit for future processing (e.g., wheat to be milled into flour) then reloaded and delivered to their destination without incurring additional charges. Also known as processing in transit or milling in transit.

TRANSIT TIME The period of time a carrier (railroad, trucker, etc.) has possession of a shipment.

TRANSLOADING In transportation, a practice in rail shipping in which less than carload lots of goods are combined into one carload and shipped to a point nearest the majority of a firm's customers. At that point the various lots are unloaded and reloaded onto freight cars headed for the specific destination of each lot. This practice allows shippers of relatively small lots of goods to take advantage of the railroad's carload rates for at least part of the trip.

TRANSLOADING PRIVILEGE See *transloading*

TRANSNATIONAL COMPANY See *multinational corporation (MNC)*

TRANSPORTATION A part of the physical distribution function concerned with the physical movement of goods from point of manufacture to consumption point.

TRANSPORTATION MANAGE-MENT See *traffic management*

TRAVELING EXPORT SALES REPRESENTATIVE See *export sales representative*

TRAVELING SALES REPRESENTATIVE See *traveling salesperson*

TRAVELING SALESPERSON A firm's traveling representative who covers a particular region or territory soliciting orders for the firm's products. Also called a commercial traveler or traveling sales representative.

TREND ANALYSIS See *trend extension*

TREND EXTENSION A method of forecasting sales for existing products. Since such products have a record of previous sales data, market forecasters simply project past sales performance into the future.

TREND PROJECTION See *time series analysis*

TREND-SETTER See *opinion leader*

TRIAL SAMPLING In sales promotion, the encouraging of product trial by the consumer through the giving of free samples.

TRICKLE-DOWN THEORY See *fashion adoption process*

TRIO OF NEEDS Three of the basic motivations which cause individual consumers to make purchase decisions are known as the trio of needs. These are the needs for power, affiliation, and achievement. The achievement need is the drive for personal accomplishment; the affiliation need is the drive for belonging to a particular group; the power need is an individual's desire to control his environment. They are sometimes considered to be independent of the five levels of need identified by Maslow, although a case can be made for including them in Maslow's hierarchy. See also *Maslow's hierarchy* and *needs*.

TRIPARTITE VIEW OF ATTITUDE See *affective component, cognitive component,* and *conative component*

TRUCK JOBBER See *truck wholesaler*

TRUCK WHOLESALER A limited-service wholesaler who operates his business from a truck from which he sells and delivers merchandise and collects payment. Truck wholesalers carry a limited line of goods, e.g., bread or dairy products, and generally serve retail outlets, industrial facilities, or institutions. Known also as truck jobbers, wagon distributors, and merchandise deliverers.

TRUTH-IN-LENDING ACT (1968) See *Consumer Credit Protection Act (1968)*

TRUTH-IN-PACKAGING ACT (1966) See *Fair Packaging and Labeling Act (1966)*

TURNKEY OPERATION A business arrangement involving a buyer, a prime contractor, a number of subcontractors, and a product. The prime contractor pulls all the sub-contractors together, manufactures the product and, finally, delivers it to the buyer. Thus it is said that the buyer, to achieve his needs, simply turns a key and it is accomplished.

TURN-OVER MAN See *T.O. man*

TURNOVER See *stock turnover*

TWO-FACTOR THEORY See *motive*

TWO-LEVEL CHANNEL A marketing channel in which there are two levels of distribution between the manufacturer/producer and the ultimate consumer. For example, there may be a wholesaler or distributor and a retailer acting as intermediaries.

TWO-STEP FLOW MODEL A theory of mass communication which held that both mass media and opinion leaders influenced behavior. In this two-step process, information was seen to flow from the mass media to the opinion leaders who then influenced the general population. The theory has now been superseded by the multistep flow model. See also *hypodermic needle model* and *multistep flow model.*

TYING AGREEMENT An agreement in which a manufacturer requires a dealer or middleman to purchase certain goods in order to purchase certain other goods, or in which the manufacturer requires that the dealer not sell competing goods. In return, the dealer may be granted exclusive rights to sales of the manufacturer's products in a specified territory.

TYING CLAUSE See *tying agreement*

TYING CONTRACT See *tying agreement*

U

UCC See *uniform commercial code (UCC)*

ULTIMATE CONSUMER The ultimate consumer is the end user—the person buying goods or services for personal use or for use in the home. In retailing, the term is commonly taken to mean the store's customers. Also known as the final consumer.

UMBRELLA MARK See *family brand*

UMBRELLA PRICING A strategy in which a large firm maintains the prices of its products at a level higher than necessary in an effort to protect smaller competitors from ruinous competition. Umbrella pricing is the opposite of predatory pricing.

UNAIDED RECALL A method of testing a consumer's ability to remember an advertisement and, hence, a means of determining the ad's effectiveness. Subjects are asked to identify advertisements they have recently seen or heard but are given no stimulus to aid their memory, i.e., they are not shown the actual ads and are not given any other hints or clues.

UNAIDED RECALL TEST See *unaided recall*

UNBUNDLING PRICES A pricing policy in which customers (usually at retail) are permitted to choose certain services on an optimal basis. Prices are unbundled in the sense that a single price is no longer quoted for a product/service package.

UNCHANGING LIST PRICE List prices that remain the same for extended periods of time, despite the fact that both add-ons and discounts may affect the actual selling price of the goods. See also *list price*.

UNCONSCIOUS LEVEL (OF NEED AWARENESS) See *need awareness*

UNCONTROLLABLE FACTORS
Those elements in the marketing environment which are out of the control of the organization, e.g., shifts in the economy, government regulations, international politics, etc.

UNDIFFERENTIATED MARKETING A marketing strategy in which one or more products are offered for sale to the total market, i.e., no attempt is made to address individual market segments. Undifferentiated marketing, which is usually applied to staple products (gasoline, sugar, salt, etc.), focuses on those characteristics which are common to large numbers of customers. It is a simpler and cheaper strategy to execute than differentiated marketing. Also known as the total market approach or as market aggregation.

UNDUPLICATED MEDIA AUDIENCE See *reach*

UNFAIR PRACTICES ACTS See *unfair trade practices acts*

UNFAIR TRADE PRACTICES ACTS
State laws intended to discourage predatory pricing by wholesalers and retailers. In general the acts prohibit the reselling of goods for less than their purchase price (except in the case of legitimate clearance sale merchandise) and, in addition, may require a minimum markup of, for example, 6%. In some states these laws apply to all products, in others, to certain categories of products, e.g., alcoholic beverages, groceries, etc. Also known as minimum markup laws.

UNIFORM COMMERCIAL CODE (UCC) A uniform set of statutory laws (adopted in its entirety by 49 states between 1953 and 1969, and partially adopted by the state of Louisiana), designed to facilitate commercial transactions for firms doing business in more than one state. The Uniform Commercial Code covers sales, contracts, warranties, physical transfer of goods, financing, bills of lading provided by transport carriers to shippers, etc. Any disputes which arise concerning matters covered by the UCC are decided by the courts of the state in which the alleged offenses occurred. The UCC was developed jointly by the National Council of Commissioners on Uniform State Laws and the American Law Institute.

UNIFORM DELIVERED PRICING
See *postage stamp pricing*

UNIFORM GEOGRAPHIC PRICING
See *postage stamp pricing*

UNIFORM PRICING CODE See *universal product code (UPC)*

UNIQUE SELLING PROPOSITION (USP) The unique selling proposition was the brainchild of Rosser Reeves, co-founder of the Ted Bates advertising agency. He explained the concept in his 1961 book *Reality in Advertising*. Essentially, Reeves advocated using research to verify the truthfulness of advertising claims and to then launch hard-hitting campaigns based on the unique properties of the product. The unique selling proposition is a promise made in a highly competitive and convincing manner which positions the product clearly in the minds of the consumer.

UNIT CONTRIBUTION See *contribution*

UNIT PRICING The practice of pricing merchandise (groceries, meats, etc.) relative to a common denominator such as price per pound, price per quart, price per dozen, etc. The label displaying unit pricing will also display the price for the package as a whole.

UNIT TRAIN Trains which carry a single cargo, such as bulk grain, nonstop between two points.

UNITARY ELASTICITY See *elasticity of demand*

UNITIZING The consolidations of a number of boxes or packages into one load, frequently stacked on a pallet to facilitate movement.

UNIVERSAL BAR CODE See *universal product code*

UNIVERSAL FUNCTIONS OF MARKETING See *marketing functions*

UNIVERSAL MARKETING FUNCTIONS See *marketing functions*

UNIVERSAL PRODUCT CODE (UPC) Adopted by the food industry in 1973, the UPC is a classification system in which each product (and each size, flavor, color, etc.) is assigned a ten-digit number. The numbers are premarked on the package by the manufacture in the form of a bar code (thick and thin vertical lines) over the ten corresponding Arabic numerals. The bar code is readable by an optical scanner at the checkout counter and the information it contains is transmitted to a computer. It is the computer which contains the prices, not the UPC, and it is the computer which controls the cash register.

UNIVERSE In marketing research, the universe is the total population to be studied, whether by census or by sampling.

UNPLANNED BUSINESS DISTRICT A group of retail establishments which have grown up together without benefit of formal planning. Central business districts, i.e., downtowns, are examples of unplanned business districts.

UNPROTECTED CONSUMERS Those groups of consumers relatively unable to defend their rights in the marketplace and for whom sufficient protective legislation has not been written. Children, the elderly, the poor, and the infirm are regarded as unprotected consumers. See also *consumer laws* and *consumer advocate*.

UNSELLING See *countermarketing*

UNSOUGHT GOODS Merchandise which the customer: 1) does not know about, 2) feels is not a good value, or 3) does not believe he needs.

UNSTRUCTURED QUESTIONNAIRE A questionnaire in which the number of questions is limited and in which the interviewer is allowed to vary the wording and sequence of the questions. The interviewer is also allowed some latitude in probing the subject for additional information. See also *structured questionnaire* and *questionnaire*.

UPPER CLASS See *social class*

UPPER LOWER CLASS See *social class*

UPPER MIDDLE CLASS See *social class*

UPPER UPPER CLASS See *social class*

UPWARD-FLOW THEORY See *fashion adoption process*

USAGE RATE SEGMENTATION A method of market segmentation based on the rate at which consumers buy and use products. Typically, usage rate segmentation divides the market into heavy, light, and non-users. Data is gathered by research firms (such as W.R. Simmons Associates in their annual *Study of Media and Markets*), usually through the use of a selected group of consumers who records daily purchases in a diary. The data is then analyzed by product category and the terms "heavy, light, and non-users" defined for that category. See also *market segmentation.*

USAGE RATE SEGMENTATION FACTORS See *usage rate segmentation*

USELESS QUALITY A level of quality built into a product in excess of that required by the consumer

USP See *unique selling proposition*

UTILITY The characteristics of a product or service which make it capable of satisfying a need or want on the part of a customer. Utility may be regarded as value. See also *form utility, information utility, ownership utility* and *time utility.*

V

VALIDITY In marketing research and other quantitative inquiries, validity is the test of whether or not the research actually measures the phenomena it is intended to measure. The researcher must take into account whether or not the data was obtained from an informed source and whether the problem under study has been answered with the collected data.

VALUE Value is that inherent worth which is possessed by a product or service. It is generally expressed in terms of its price, i.e., in money terms, or as credit, or as other goods and services. See also *price* and *cost*.

VALUE ADDED BY MARKETING The increase in the worth of a product as a result of the activities it passes through in the distribution chain. It may be computed as the value of sales, less the cost of goods sold, less the cost of supplies, energy, and all other activities involved in the marketing of the product.

VALUE ANALYSIS An effort made by the purchasers of products, parts, and materials to examine the quality level of their acquisitions and to reduce costs to the lowest possible level.

VALUES In terms useful to the marketer, values are those broad standards and ideals shared by the members of a society or a subgroup of that society which reflect the society's moral order. Values, which strongly affect consumer behavior and lifestyle, are factors which the marketer must consider.

VARIABLE COST Costs which vary directly with output levels, sales volume, or other factors such as transportation cost. See also *fixed cost, overhead, direct cost,* and *indirect cost.*

VARIABLE LEADER PRICING
Leader pricing is a strategy in which certain items are offered for sale at prices so low that they yield little or no profit. Variable leader pricing is a strategy commonly found in the supermarket industry in which the leader items are frequently changed, often on a weekly basis.

VARIABLE PRICE POLICY A policy most commonly found at retail in which prices are not fixed, i.e., one in which the seller may alter price to make a deal or in which the buyer may try to negotiate more favorable terms. Variable prices are used primarily where the customer realizes that list prices are merely the starting point in reaching a final price as in the automobile industry.

VARIABLE PRICING See *variable price policy*

VARIETY See *product line*

VARIETY PRONE See *brand switcher*

VARIETY-SEEKING BUYING BEHAVIOR See *brand switcher*

VARIETY STORE The original "five & ten" or "dime store," variety stores now stock a wide range of product classifications, but in a limited number of assortments and at relatively low prices.

VEBLEN GOODS The reference is to Thorstein Veblen (American economist, 1857–1929) best known for his work *The Theory of the Leisure Class* in which he theorizes that certain consumers at the upper reaches of the economic order purchase some goods simply for purposes of display, i.e., they are, in Veblen's terms, engaging in conspicuous consumption. Thus, Veblen goods are those for which the buyer has no intrinsic need.
The demand for these goods, contrary to what is commonly the rule, often increases as the price increases as purchasers tend to identify high price with quality.

VENDING MACHINE RETAILING
See *automatic vending*

VENDOR An individual or business (manufacturer, importer, jobber, agent, wholesaler, etc.) who sells goods to other businesses. Commonly known as a supplier and, in the retail trade, as a resource.

VENDOR ANALYSIS An examination of how well a particular supplier performs. Included in the analysis are matters of price (are they competitive, are terms reasonable), matters of reliability (is merchandise of high quality, are deliveries on time), and resale considerations (how much can merchandise be marked up, what percentage will have to be marked down).

VENDOR PAID MARKDOWN See *price guarantee*

VENTURE TEAM A group of specialists within a firm brought together for the specific purpose of planning, developing, and introducing into the marketplace a new product. Venture teams are usually disbanded when their assignment has been completed. See also *product planning committee.*

VERTICAL ADVERTISING See *cooperative advertising*

VERTICAL CHANNEL CONFLICT
See *channel conflict*

VERTICAL CHANNEL INTEGRATION See *vertical integration*

VERTICAL CONFLICT See *channel conflict*

VERTICAL COOPERATIVE ADVERTISING See *cooperative advertising*

253

VERTICAL INDUSTRIAL MARKET
A narrow market for industrial goods but one in which nearly every organization is a potential customer.

VERTICAL INTEGRATION The ownership, achieved by merger or internal expansion, of the marketing channel intermediaries connecting the manufacturer/producer with the consumer. Vertical integration may be accomplished through forward integration (the manufacturer may own his own distribution network and retail outlets) or through backward integration (in which the retailer controls his sources of supply). Sometimes referred to as a corporate distribution system. See also *dual distribution.*

VERTICAL MARKETING SYSTEM (VMS) Large, centrally managed industrial organizations in which two or more levels of the market (manufacturing, wholesaling, retailing) are controlled by a dominant member of the channel. The system may be organized in one of three ways: 1) administered vertical marketing system, 2) corporate vertical marketing system, and 3) contractual vertical marketing system. Vertical marketing systems have as their objective the achievement of operating economies resulting from greater size, increased efficiency achieved through closer control, economies achieved through the elimination of duplicated activities, and increased bargaining power resulting from large-scale operations.

VERTICAL PRICE FIXING See *resale price maintenance*

VERTICALLY INTEGRATED CHANNEL See *vertical integration*

VIDALE, M.L. See *advertising sales-response and decay model*

VISUAL MERCHANDISING A strategy frequently used in retailing for the in-store presentation of merchandise so that it would be shown to its greatest advantage. Visual merchandising, which includes traditional display techniques, increasingly involves planning store layout, decor, and activities which appeal to other senses, such as music. The object of these efforts is to increase the sale of merchandise. See also *display.*

VMS See *vertical marketing system (VMS)*

VOLUNTARY CHAIN A wholesaler-sponsored voluntary association of independent retailers. The member stores buy all or most of their merchandise from the sponsoring wholesaler who, in turn, provides certain management services such as accounting systems, display direction, standardized merchandise packages, central data processing, etc. Members of voluntary chains often display common identifying names or logos. Also known as a voluntary cooperative or a voluntary wholesale group. See also *retail cooperative* and *consumer cooperative.*

WAGE-PRICE SPIRAL See *inflation*

WAGON DISTRIBUTOR See *truck wholesaler*

WAM See *Women in Advertising and Marketing (WAM)*

WANTS In the study of consumer behavior, wants are needs which have been learned during the consumer's lifetime. For example, everyone experiences thirst, a need, but some consumers have learned to want a particular brand of soft drink.

WAREHOUSE A commercial establishment in which large quantities of goods may be stored. See also *public warehouse, contract warehouse,* and *private warehouse.*

WAREHOUSE RETAILING A form of high-volume, low-overhead mass merchandising characterized by facilities lacking traditional amenities, few customer services, and isolated low rent buildings. Merchandise (especially food, appliances, and furniture) is sold at prices below regular retail in these facilities reminiscent of warehouses.

WAREHOUSE STORE See *warehouse retailing*

WARRANTY An assurance given by the manufacturer of a product as to the quality and performance of the product and a statement relating the conditions under which the product will be replaced or repaired should it prove to be defective. A warranty may be expressed, i.e., it may be represented verbally or in writing, or it may be implied, i.e., that there is a general understanding that the product is safe and in proper operating condition. See also *guarantee.*

WAS-IS PRICING See *psychological discounting*

WASTE CIRCULATION In advertising, waste circulation is the number

255

of persons reached by an ad campaign who are not potential customers for the product or service. Several factors may cause waste circulation, such as the unavailability of the product or service in the reached area.

WDRG See *Women's Direct Response Group (WDRG)*

WEAKEST LINK THEORY The weakest link is that part of a product which wears out first. Thus, the theory holds, other parts should not be so durable as to greatly outlast the part which wears out fastest as the product will generally be discarded.

WEBER, ERNST See *just noticeable difference*

WEBER'S LAW See *just noticeable difference*

WHEEL OF RETAILING THEORY A theory of retail institutional change propounded by Malcom P. McNair (Harvard Business School) in which retail innovators are seen as beginning the growth cycle as low status, low margin, low price operators. A period follows during which facilities become more elaborate, costs increase, and higher margins are required to survive. As the innovative retail institution thus matures, the cycle begins again with the next low margin innovator. The complete cycle is one turn of the wheel.

WHEELER-LEA AMENDMENT (1938) An amendment to the Federal Trade Commission Act (1914) which provides the FTC with the authority to protect consumers from unfair trade practices (particularly those involving deceptive advertising) in cases where it is not possible to prove that competition is being injured.

WHOLE MARKET METHOD A marketing approach which is geared to the entire range of potential customers and which neither recognizes nor attempts to appeal to the differences between various segments. See also *mass marketing* and *market segmentation.*

WHOLESALE See *wholesaling*

WHOLESALE CLUB See *closed-door discount house*

WHOLESALE MERCHANT See *wholesaler* and *full-service wholesaler*

WHOLESALE TRANSACTION A nonretail sale including sales by manufacturers to middlemen and retailers, sales by manufacturers to other manufacturers, sales from farmers to processors, government sales, etc.

WHOLESALER A term applied to a category of wholesaling middleman primarily engaged in buying merchandise from a producer and selling it to an industrial user, institutional user, or retailer, but seldom to the ultimate consumer. The wholesaler ordinarily takes title to and possession of the goods he sells. Wholesalers fall into two broad categories: 1) the full-service or full-function wholesaler who performs a number of functions including assembly, warehousing, breaking bulk, selling, delivery, credit extension, etc. 2) the limited service or limited-function wholesaler who performs fewer service functions than his full-service counterpart. Wholesalers are sometimes called merchant wholesalers, jobbers, and distributors.

WHOLESALER MERCHANT See *wholesaler* and *full-service wholesaler*

WHOLESALER'S SALESPERSON A sales representative of a wholesale firm who calls on retail (and sometimes manufacturer) customers.

WHOLESALING Those marketing transactions which involve the sale of

256

goods to retailers, other wholesalers, and to business, institutional, and industrial users for the purpose of 1) resale, 2) use in performing the organization's basic function, or 3) incorporation into another product. Wholesaling's most important function is breaking bulk, i.e., providing buyers with manageable lots of the merchandise the wholesaler has bought in large quantities.

WHOLESALING MIDDLEMAN A term generally applied to a number of marketing intermediaries which includes wholesaler, agent, broker, manufacturer's branch and sales office, and certain cooperative organizations. Wholesaling middlemen are also known as marketing middlemen and merchant middlemen.

WHOLESOME MEAT ACT (1967) Federal legislation enacted to protect the consumer by strengthening the standards of slaughterhouse and red meat inspection.

WHOLLY-OWNED SUBSIDIARY A separate firm, owned and completely controlled by a parent company.

WIDTH See *product width*

WILDCAT See *problem child*

WITH-PACK PREMIUM A free gift or other item packed inside or outside another product. See also *in-pack premium* and *on-pack premium*.

WOLFE, M.B. See *advertising sales-response and decay model*

WOM COMMUNICATION See *word-of-mouth communication*

WOMEN IN ADVERTISING AND MARKETING (WAM) An association of women in advertising and marketing. WAM serves as a network by promoting professional contact between its members. It publishes a quarterly *Membership Directory,* as

well as a quarterly *Newsletter.* WAM also maintains a Job Bank and a Speakers Bureau. The association's headquarters are in Washington, D.C.

WOMEN'S DIRECT RESPONSE GROUP (WDRG) An association of women professionally involved in direct marketing. The association serves as a network and information center for its membership. WDRG also maintains a career talent bank and sponsors summer internship programs. It publishes a quarterly *Newsletter* and an annual *Membership Roster.* The association's headquarters are located in New York City.

WORD-OF-MOUTH COMMUNICATION Communication via the spoken word on a person-to-person basis. Although not strictly speaking a form of advertising it can be crucially important in the success or failure of certain business endeavors, as, for example, the success of a motion picture.

WORD-OF-MOUTH INFLUENCE See *social channel*

WORKING HYPOTHESIS See *hypothesis*

WORLD BUSINESS See *multinational corporation (MNC)*

WORLD CORPORATION ORGANIZATION A form of decentralized organizational structure applicable to certain multinational firms. In a world corporation organization the world is viewed as the firm's area of operations and no single national market draws greater attention than that merited by its size. Markets, techniques, ideas, personnel, processes, and products are drawn from the entire area of operations. Divisions for each of the national territories operate side by side as equals, rather than as part of a hierarchical scheme.

YANKEE PEDDLER An itinerant merchant popular in the early United States up to the post-Civil War era. The original Yankee peddlers were based in New England and are considered the forerunner of the modern day traveling salesperson.

YOUTH MARKET The segment of the population aged 14–24.

YOUTH RESEARCH INSTITUTE OF NEW YORK (YRINY) A New York based organization which surveys the teenage, college, and young adult market.

YRINY See *Youth Research Institute of New York (YRINY)*

ZERO-LEVEL CHANNEL See *direct selling*

ZONE PRICING A strategy in which a manufacturer charges all customers in the same geographic zone a uniform delivered price without regard to individual transportation charges. Also called zone-delivered pricing.

ZONE PRICING

About the Authors

RONA OSTROW, Associate Professor and Librarian at Baruch College, C.U.N.Y. in the Library Instruction Division. B.A., City College, C.U.N.Y.; M.S. in Library Science, Columbia University School of Library Service; M.A., Hunter College, C.U.N.Y. Currently teaches an undergraduate course: Information Research in Business, and is Associate Director of the Graduate Business Resource and Study Center at Baruch. She is also research consultant to graduate students in the School of Business and author of *Information Research in Business* (a workbook). Ms. Ostrow was assistant business reference librarian at the Fashion Institute of Technology Library from 1978-1980. She also had a long association with the New York Public Library System as reference librarian in the Branch Library System (1970-1973) and research librarian in the General Research and Humanities Division, The Research Libraries (1973-1978).

SWEETMAN R. SMITH, Assistant Professor/Business Reference Librarian, Fashion Institute of Technology/State University of New York. B.A., A.M.L.S., University of Michigan. During his 18 years as a member of the F.I.T. faculty Mr. Smith has developed an extensive information file system to support the college's program in Fashion Buying and Merchandising.